# SELF, SOCIETY, AND PERSONAL CHOICE

DIANA T. MEYERS

# Self, Society, and Personal Choice

COLUMBIA UNIVERSITY PRESS
NEW YORK

*Columbia University Press*
New York      Oxford
Copyright © 1989 Columbia University Press
All rights reserved
*Library of Congress Cataloging-in-Publication Data*

Meyers, Diana T.
  Self, society and personal choice / Diana T. Meyers.
    p.    cm.
  Bibliography: p.
  Includes index.
  ISBN   0-231-06418-7
  1. Autonomy (Philosophy)    I. Title.
B808.67.M49   1989                                                89-30198
128--dc19                                                         CIP

Casebound editions of Columbia University Press books are Smyth-sewn
and printed on permanent and durable acid-free paper

Printed in the United States of America

5-N-91

*For R. and E. Tietjens*

# Contents

# Acknowledgments

AT DIFFERENT stages in my work, Jonathan Adler, Eva Kittay, Lewis Meyers, and George Sher read and gave me detailed comments on this manuscript. Their objections, suggestions, and encouragement have been invaluable to me, and I am deeply grateful to each of them. Many other people have contributed to more discrete parts of this project. I would especially like to thank Kathryn Addelson, Jeffrey Blustein, Norman Bowie, Marilyn Friedman, Virginia Held, and Mary Katzenstein for their helpful comments. Also, I am indebted to the American Council of Learned Societies for the generous support of an ACLS/Ford Fellowship, which freed me to work on this book.

An earlier version of some of the views presented in part 4, secs. 2–3 were first developed in "The Politics of Self-Respect: A Feminist Perspective." I thank *Hypatia* for permission to use this material.

# Preface

THE ORIGINAL impetus for this book came out of my experience teaching a seminar called "The Theory and Politics of Liberal Feminism" with Mary Katzenstein at Cornell University. Both in preparatory discussions with Professor Katzenstein and in class, a conundrum emerged and persistently recurred. If women's professed desires are products of their inferior position, should we give credence to these desires? If so, we seem to be capitulating to institutionalized injustice by gratifying warped desires. If not, we seem to be perpetrating injustice by showing disrespect for these individuals. Frustrated in my attempts to resolve this vexing paradox, I concluded that I needed to understand why some human desires are to be taken more seriously than others. Although no desires are negligible, I conjectured that autonomous desires stand apart and command special consideration. Thus, I was led to the question of personal autonomy, the question of what it is to know what one really wants—to discern the desires of one's authentic self—and to act in accordance with those desires.

Lying at the foundation of moral and political theory, and implicated in such crucial practical issues as the nature of informed consent, the problem of autonomy has generated an extensive literature. While I have drawn on this literature, one purpose of this book is to provide a corrective for the flaws I perceive in previous accounts of personal autonomy. I am convinced that a failure to appreciate precisely how childhood socialization enhances or limits people's ability to make autonomous choices has undermined these accounts. For this reason, I have sought to enrich philosophical analysis and argument with the insights of social psychologists who study the processes of character formation and skills learning. The result of these inquiries is an account of the authentic self as a self profoundly shaped by social experience yet endowed with capacities for independent, sometimes creative, thought and a corresponding view of personal autonomy as a dynamic process and as a phenomenon that admits of degrees.

Despite the centrality of autonomy to the dual question of women's status and justice to women, no feminist theorist has given autonomy a sustained book-length treatment. Another purpose of this project, then, is to fill a gap in the feminist literature. Specifically, I have undertaken to evaluate the oft-repeated claim that women are typically less autonomous than men and that this deficiency contributes to the continued subordination of women. Although I argue that social scientific research corroborates the claim that many women are less autonomous than most men, I stress that few women altogether lack autonomy and that few men are as autonomous as they could be. Nevertheless, feminists have reason to regard institutions and practices that undermine autonomy as especially detrimental to women.

Finally, many moral and political theorists have celebrated personal autonomy, yet many others have condemned it. My contention is that the theory of autonomy I propose is not only philosophically sound and true to psychological reality, but also that it is defensible against charges that valuing and pursuing autonomy merely disguises the perpetuation of wrongful forms of social and economic domination. Properly understood, personal autonomy does not serve as a convenient excuse for untrammeled egoism or for superficial emotional ties. Rather, by placing interpersonal and social bonds on an egalitarian and reciprocal basis, it deepens these bonds while securing the dignity of the people involved along with their self-realization.

It is my hope that the abstract account of personal autonomy offered here will find application in general moral and political theory, in the quandaries that service professionals face, and, most importantly, in people's everyday lives.

# SELF, SOCIETY, AND PERSONAL CHOICE

# PART I

# Personal Autonomy and Related Concepts

## EXHIBIT

In *The Portrait of a Lady* (Henry James), Isabel Archer, a young woman with no income and no social position, refuses to marry either Lord Warburton, a respected and wealthy peer, or Caspar Goodwood, a solid American. She gives as her reason her love of liberty, her desire to know life, and her determination to form her own views.

## EXHIBIT

In *Jules et Jim* (François Truffaut), Catherine (Jeanne Moreau) disguises herself as a man with wide trousers and a patchy little moustache. She goes parading through the streets of Paris courting detection, but she is never found out.

## EXHIBIT

Simone de Beauvoir and Jean-Paul Sartre refused to marry or even to live together and freed one another to have affairs. Yet, they pledged their love and, after their fashion, their fidelity to each other.

## EXHIBIT

In *Pat and Mike* (George Cukor), Pat (Katharine Hepburn), a natural athlete, loses tournament after tournament because the calculatedly mild enthusiasm of her patronizing fiancé, Collier, flusters her and ruins her concentration. After one of these defeats, the golf pro at her club asks her what her handicap is. Forlorn, Pat can only reply, "My fella." When Mike (Spencer Tracy), a hard-nosed sports promoter, discovers her and offers her the chance to escape from this corrosive influence, Pat is able to fulfill her potential, at least when Collier is not around. With Mike, nothing is more important than Pat's winning, and their relationship is on a strictly equal basis. As he likes to put it, "You and me, we're partners—five-oh/five-oh" [fifty/fifty]. Finally, Pat triumphs over her insecurities by winning the Women's National Pro Golf Tournament despite the unexpected appearance of her fiancé.

## EXHIBIT

Gertrude Stein studied psychology with William James at Harvard and then went on to medical school at Johns Hopkins. Close to completing her M.D., Gertrude Stein quit medical school, moved to Paris, and became one of the most influential writers and art collectors of the twentieth century. While still a student, she had been prodded by a close friend to remember the cause of women and to serve this cause through her work and stature as a physician. Gertrude Stein replied, "You do not know what it is to be bored."

## EXHIBIT

*Lost Horizons* (Frank Capra) opens with a display of Robert Conway's (Ronald Colman) heroics in the teeth of a local rebellion in China. We learn that a naval cruiser has arrived in Shanghai to take Conway back to England where an illustrious career as Foreign Secretary awaits him. But he is hardly elated about the prospect. After voicing his privately held pacifist sentiments, and shocking his brother, he dejectedly recants, "I'll be the best little Foreign Secretary England ever had, just because I haven't the nerve to be anything else. I'll be a good boy." Unbeknownst to him, his plane has been hijacked, and he is at that very moment being taken to Shangri-La, a community isolated by the Himalayas, where greed and struggle are unknown.

His companions are an assortment of English and American types. Upon arrival, they begin to suspect the motives of their serene host, Chang, and the uncanny tranquility of Shangri-La gets on their nerves. Conway feels at peace, however, and experiences intimations that he has been to this place before. Eventually, his brother shakes Conway's trust in Chang's honor and prevails on Conway's sense of duty to induce him to leave Shangri-La. But Conway soon realizes his mistake, and, after many perils and travails, he returns to the place where he knows he belongs.


## EXHIBIT

Elizabeth Bennet, the heroine of *Pride and Prejudice* (Jane Austin), accepts the conventions of early nineteenth-century England. Like her sisters and all her friends, she wants to marry well and spend her life managing her home. But, unlike most of the women around her, Elizabeth is not willing to marry a man she does not respect. She receives two proposals—one from a dull-witted and obsequious but respectably situated cousin, Mr. Collins, and the other from an imperious, well-connected, and wealthy scion of a distinguished family, Mr. Darcy. Despite her modest dowry and her lack of other prospects, Elizabeth unhesitatingly refuses Collins, though her close friend, Charlotte, rushes to accept his subsequent proposal to her. Believing Darcy to have been instrumental in dashing her sister's fond hopes of marrying his friend, Mr. Bingley, as well as in helping to ruin an amiable officer, Mr. Wickham, and offended by his contempt for her ill-bred, unpropertied family, Elizabeth also refuses Darcy and forthrightly informs him of her reasons for doing so. Her pronouncements stir Darcy to explain his conduct vis-à-vis her sister and Mr. Wickham and to mend his haughty manners. Gradually, Elizabeth realizes that she has misjudged Darcy's character, and she appreciates the transformation of his social demeanor. When Darcy eventually repeats his offer of marriage, she accepts.

EXHIBIT

Antoine Roquentin, the protagonist of *Nausea* (Jean-Paul Sartre), is trapped in a narrative approach to life. Not only is he researching a biography of a shadowy eighteenth-century figure whose obscure activities have left only fragmentary documentary traces, but also he animates his own life by recalling his adventures—episodes in which events infused with an air of excitement seem to proceed in a necessitous progression. Yet, Roquentin recognizes that both of these modes falsify life. For lack of evidence, the biography of the Marquis de Rollebon is largely a fabrication. And Roquentin has taken solace, but experienced just as little reality, by invoking his own adventures. At the end of the novel, having eschewed the impulse to transform life into stories but bereft of any new direction, Roquentin hears a jazz recording of a tune called "Some of These Days." As he listens to the music, he is transfixed by the orderliness and completeness of the melody, and he imagines the composer working on the song and the singer performing it. His vision of these people's redemption through their art spawns Roquentin's plan of action. He resolves to write fiction—to stop distorting his life by pretending that it has the qualities of art; instead, he will create art.

EXHIBIT

In *A Portrait of the Artist as a Young Man* (James Joyce), the boys at Stephen Dedalus' Catholic school are obliged to participate in a religious retreat. During this period, they are subjected to daily harangues conjuring up the torments of hell and entreating them to repent before it is too late. Terrified that the sins his adolescent sexuality has led him to commit could plunge him into eternal damnation at any moment, Stephen becomes a model communicant. In fact, he becomes so pious that, after observing him for several years, the director of the school asks him to consider becoming a priest. Though Stephen considers the suggestion, he soon realizes that "his soul was not there to greet it . . . that the exhortation he had listened to had already fallen into an idle formal tale. . . . He was destined to learn his own wisdom apart from others or to learn the wisdom of others wandering among the snares of the world" (p. 162).

## EXHIBIT

Torvald Helmer's misogynous condenscension brings *A Doll's House* (Henrik Ibsen) to its climax:

HELMER: . . . Try to calm yourself and collect your thoughts again, my frightened little songbird. You can rest easy now; I've got wide wings to shelter you with. . . . Don't be afraid of anything, Nora; just open your heart to me, and I'll be conscience and will to you both. . . .

NORA: . . . . Our home's been nothing but a playpen. I've been your doll-wife here, just as at home I was Papa's doll-child. And in turn the children have been my dolls. I thought it was fun when you played with me, just as they thought it was fun when I played with them. That's been our marriage, Thorvald.

HELMER: There's some truth in what you're saying—under all the raving exaggeration. But it'll all be different after this. Playtime's over; now for the schooling.

NORA: Whose schooling—mine or the children's?

HELMER: Both yours and the children's, dearest. . . .

NORA: Tomorrow I'm going home—I mean home where I came from. . . .

HELMER: Abandon your home, your husband, your children! And you're not even thinking what people will say.

NORA: I can't be concerned with that. I only know how essential this is . . . now I'll begin to learn for myself. I'll try to discover who's right, the world or I . . .

HELMER: May I write you?

NORA: No—never. You're not to do that.

HELMER: Oh, but let me send you—

NORA: Nothing. Nothing.

HELMER: Or help if you need it.

NORA:  No. I accept nothing from strangers. . . . (She goes
   out down the hall.)
HELMER:  (sinks down on a chair by the door, face buried in
   his hands): Nora! Nora! (Looking about and rising.)
   Empty. She's gone . . .
(From below, the sound of a door slamming shut.)


## EXHIBIT

In *Una Vita Difficile* (Dino Risi), the protagonist (Alberto Sordi)
appears first as a resistance fighter and, after the war, as a communist whose livelihood and freedom are constantly threatened
and frequently enough lost as a result of his unswerving dedication to principle. Refusing all compromise with the class enemy, he gradually alienates his wife. In a last-ditch attempt to
win her back, he embarks upon a career as toady to the indus-
trialist whose propositions he had earlier spurned. He does his
best to endure the humiliations of his position but finally cannot
stop himself from reasserting his dignity. During an elegant
cocktail party at his boss's luxurious home, before a church dig-
nitary and other assembled guests, the tragicomic hero slaps his
boss in the face and knocks him into the swimming pool.

*       *       *

EACH OF these exhibits presents either a climactic moment or an ongoing practice of liberation, and, for that reason, many people find
them exhilarating. Each represents the possibility of vibrant, engaged
life. Not trouble-free life, but compelling. In each, a momentous decision and its subsequent course of action spring from the depths of
the individual's being. One may not care to follow suit, but one does
not think the person acting is making a mistake since each does what
makes sense in terms of his or her own identity. The figures in these
exhibits are hardly oblivious to other people, much less narcissisti-
cally self-absorbed; yet they are not so influenced by others that their
choices seem a committee product. Acting out of their own imperatives, their integrity is not that of mundane honesty and probity;
rather, it is the unity and completeness of the unduplicatable agent-

self. For this reason, their conduct excites our admiration, though it may not arouse our envy or move us to emulation.

Arguably, it is the presence of personal autonomy in each of these exhibits that elicits this response. However, I do not wish to fuel controversy about the works of art or the biographies to which I have alluded. Any ostensible case of autonomy could be debated. Was the crucial choice exactly the right one to make, or not? Was the agent really in control of his or her life, or not? I mean only to call to mind a sufficiently diverse series of exhibits to guide readers' reflections on their own preferred examples of this dauntingly elusive phenomenon.

Now, my illustrations of autonomy may be questioned by some who assume that no one can ever exert the control that personal autonomy promises. I would ask that these skeptics—readers who have considered all of my exhibits and found them wanting and who doubt that any better ones can be found—suspend disbelief for a while. Perhaps, doing so will prove less onerous than they would think. For I am not setting anyone the task of convincing himself or herself that free will transcends the deterministic net of ineluctable causes and effects, nor am I asking anyone to picture a person immune to social influences. I propose merely that the reader imagine someone who lives—at least part of the time—by his or her own lights. For the sake of wide familiarity, I have used literary, cinematic, and historical figures, but an unsung friend would do just as well. The example need not pick out an exceptional individual; it need not endow that person with an unerring sense of direction; it need not depict a dramatic course of action. It need only feature someone who in some respect has a sure sense of personal identity and who sometimes manages to act accordingly. Anyone who has ever been acquainted with someone like this, I submit, has encountered personal autonomy.

The arts and humanities, together with social experience, help to fix intuitions about the concept of personal autonomy by making it palpable. However, this concept belongs to a family of closely allied concepts—moral autonomy, legal autonomy, economic autonomy, and political autonomy—from which it must be gently extricated. I say "gently" advisedly, since sharp boundaries cannot be drawn between personal autonomy and these other concepts. Yet, personal autonomy has a core that can be identified and explored quite apart from these related matters.

To begin, then, political autonomy is the most distant from personal autonomy. In common parlance, political autonomy is attributed to nation states, and nation states are obligated to respect one another's political autonomy. Roughly, political autonomy is the right of a people to govern itself according to its own traditions without outside interference. Neatly delimiting what constitutes prohibited intervention in the internal affairs of a nation state has proved insuperably difficult, for nation states engage in trade which creates international dependencies, and they form alliances which create additional ties. However, the fundamental constituents of political autonomy are respect for the territorial integrity of other nation states along with respect for their government institutions. We shall find these themes of independence and self-governance threaded through all of the conceptions of autonomy to be considered in this discussion.

Advocates of democracy sometimes argue that the conception of political autonomy as justice between nations is secondary to a domestic conception. According to this view, no nation state that is not legitimate is autonomous, and legitimacy can only be derived from the consent of the citizens. Since these individuals can only grant their consent through fair elections, political autonomy requires that mechanisms for popular sovereignty be instituted. On this view, then, political autonomy presupposes recognition of and respect for democratic rights of participation—the right to vote in contested elections, the right to run for public office, the rights to freedom of assembly and speech, and so forth. Here political autonomy touches upon personal autonomy. Insofar as these political rights secure means of expressing one's views and means of pursuing one's goals, they can be seen as supports for personal autonomy. For instance, in *Una Vita Difficile,* the postwar Italian government's repression of dissent often thwarts the activism of the movie's protagonist. However, people who are not stirred by politics and whose projects are not adversely affected by government policy—Gertrude Stein and Stephen Dedalus belong in this apolitical category—can attain personal autonomy without the benefit of these participatory rights.

Legal autonomy overlaps this democratic conception of political autonomy but incorporates a larger set of rights. Legal autonomy guarantees the individual's equality before the law—in the phraseology of the United States Constitution, the due process of law and the equal protection of the laws—but it also defines a private sphere in which individuals are free to pursue their own projects in their own way. Equal opportunity and the right to own property are two ineliminable components of legal autonomy. Liberal thinkers from John Locke to John Rawls are unanimous in viewing property rights—personal property, if not ownership of the means of production—as supports for personal independence and as insurance against government intrusion in private concerns. Likewise, equal opportunity, in protecting the individual from unjust discrimination, frees each person to develop his or her talents and to use them as he or she sees fit. Thus, equal opportunity, too, promotes independence and forms a barrier against government intervention in people's lives. But legal autonomy is an elastic concept that some see compassing sundry welfare rights, such as the rights to education, decently remunerated employment, medical care, and housing. Inasmuch as these goods have become necessary to effective functioning in modern societies, these rights plausibly adapt the idea of a robust private sphere to contemporary realities.

As with political autonomy, legal autonomy is not strictly necessary to personal autonomy. In the most repressive societies, some people contrive to live in harmony with their convictions and inclinations. Many such individuals occupy privileged positions which afford them unusual latitude—for example, Isabel Archer's unchaperoned European travels after she inherits a fortune from her uncle. But some are rebels who are intent on righting the wrongs that rankle them—for example, the Alberto Sordi character in *Una Vita Difficile*—while others are conventional folk who find congenial callings within the constraints their societies impose—for example, Elizabeth Bennet in *Pride and Prejudice*.

Nor is legal autonomy sufficient for personal autonomy. People can be legally entitled to engage in certain activities, yet stifling child-rearing practices or societal norms can prevent people from availing themselves of these official options. In *Pat and Mike*, there is no law prohibiting Pat from playing golf; her problem is that custom bars women from outstripping men in sports. Still, it is evident that legal restrictions can curtail personal autonomy. Pat's difficulties would be redoubled if it were illegal for women to play golf. Thus, legal autonomy puts at everyone's disposal an array of instruments that can be used to pursue diverse personal visions, but individuals can enjoy legal autonomy without achieving personal autonomy.

While conceding that personal autonomy is not equivalent to legal autonomy, it might be supposed that legal autonomy defines the proper ambit of personal autonomy—in other words, that all choices that the law neither requires nor forbids, and only these, are personal choices that can be made autonomously. However, this would confuse matters in several respects. First, the concept of legal autonomy can be associated with empirical conditions. Used in this way, the extent of people's legal autonomy is demarcated by the laws under which they actually live. Since these laws can be unjustly restrictive, they can wrongly deprive people of opportunities to act autonomously. Second, legal prohibitions are not always effective. For example, people who have grievances against their governments commonly disobey the law in protest. Though such actions are not necessarily autonomous, they can be. Thus, legal autonomy can be narrower than personal autonomy, and claims of personal autonomy can be asserted as justifications for legal reform. Finally, and conversely, legal autonomy is broader than personal autonomy. The law does not require people to do everything that is morally obligatory. All sorts of lying and cheating are legally permissible but morally forbidden. Thus, legal autonomy affords scope for moral autonomy as well as personal autonomy, and, since morality should constrain personal choice, the proper ambit of personal autonomy includes fewer prerogatives than legal autonomy sanctions.

The central idea of economic autonomy is that of financial self-sufficiency. In the strongest version of this concept, people are economically autonomous only when they need not depend on any other individual to supply their needs and desires. The farmer who is able to secure his or her own subsistence and the successful entrepreneur epitomize this conception of economic autonomy. But since it is obvious that relatively few people can own farms or other businesses, and yet that many people are not unduly constrained by their economic position, the concept of economic autonomy is usually widened to include anyone who has a secure job that pays enough to sustain a satisfactory existence.

Whereas legal autonomy aims mainly to shield people from unwarranted government interference, economic autonomy extends the idea of individual independence to interpersonal relations. People seek economic self-sufficiency to rule out the possibility that others might gain power over them through their needs. If one can take care of oneself, one is beholden to no one—neither to the state nor to any other individual. Thus, one is at liberty to live as one chooses. In view of the traditional marital division of labor in which the wife performs unpaid domestic work while the husband earns a living outside the home, Simone de Beauvoir and others concerned with injustice to women have underscored the dangers of economic dependency with respect to self-determination. In keeping with this view, Simone de Beauvoir and Jean-Paul Sartre were by and large self-supporting and maintained separate households throughout their long relationship.

All of the conceptions of autonomy I have discussed so far are negative conceptions. They specify conditions—constraints on government or supplies of material resources—that free people to act as they please. But they say nothing about how people should live. Two forms of autonomy address the question of what kind of life is desirable: moral autonomy and personal autonomy.

Moral autonomy, in its traditional Kantian form, consists of following rules that one chooses for oneself. But, of course, not just any rule a person might subscribe to qualifies as a moral rule. The rules of baseball and etiquette are not moral rules. Moreover, people can embrace morally defective rules, such as "Torture enemy prisoners until they talk." Moral rules are those which people embrace as rational beings. In Kantian phraseology, they are universalizable rules—ones that hold for everyone in relevantly similar circumstances; ones that are impartial. The morally autonomous individual elects his or her own principles, but these principles turn out to be ones that everyone else has reason to adopt. As rational beings, people are all alike; hence, they will not differ over what morality requires unless their judgment is clouded.

Still, morally autonomous people are self-governing. Not only are they charged with responsibility for establishing their own moral convictions, but also they possess a criterion which they can use to test popular moral beliefs. As rational agents, therefore, they need not bow to any putative moral authority. They are free inasmuch as they are not subservient to any other person, yet they are constrained inasmuch as they have undertaken to abide by a set of rationally certified, absolutely binding rules.

Now, it is possible to take issue with Kant's conception of moral autonomy in a number of ways. Many commentators have questioned the viability of the universalizability criterion as well as the tenability of Kant's absolutism. (For a non-Kantian account of moral autonomy, see Meyers 1987b:148–152.) However, his view allows us to extract two features that any account of moral autonomy must share. First, morally autonomous people are self-regulating. The grounds of morality are within them, and they are capable of discovering for themselves what morality requires. Second, however they go about arriving at moral solutions, morally autonomous people regard their conclusions as obligations. Thus, moral autonomy sets the boundaries of permissible conduct—some actions are mandatory; the remainder are left to personal discretion.

Against this view, Susan Wolf has maintained that morality is not an "ever-present filter through which other values must pass" (1982:438). It is somewhat difficult to assess the force of Wolf's claim, for she advances it in the context of a critique of moral perfection. If what she means is that it makes no sense for all-consuming, extremely demanding moral ideals to grant people permission to be moral delinquents, she is plainly right. But if what she means is that acceptable personal choices can routinely violate a morality that imposes a set of basic requirements regulating interpersonal relations and that classifies unrelenting dedication to others' interests as supererogatory (this is the type of moral theory Wolf advocates, and I concur with her view [Meyers 1985:76–81]), her position underrates the constraints of morality. Though there may be situations in which urgent personal considerations can override relatively minor moral dicta, in general, when one's personal inclinations come into conflict with morality, the former must give way to the latter.

Consider, first, decisions about overall life plans. Suppose that Sandra places a very high value on courage and presence of mind in the face of danger, and, in keeping with this view, she is contemplating becoming either an assassin for hire or a mountaineer. Basic moral requirements rule out opting for a career as a mercenary assassin, but, unless Sandra has assumed moral responsibilities that curtail her right to indulge her enthusiasm for danger, nothing prevents her from attempting to scale the most formidable peaks. Thus, morality places outer bounds on personal choice.

Still, Wolf might counter that in particular situations morally admissible nonmoral values may come into conflict with basic moral requirements. In this regard, Bernard Williams has affirmed that such personal attachments as love for one's spouse can compete with and prevail over impartial morality (1976:215). Using the case of a man who must decide whether to save his drowning wife or a simultaneously drowning stranger, Williams doubts that impartial morality would authorize saving his wife simply because she is his wife

(1976:213—214). However, considering the matter from a Rawlsian standpoint, there is little reason to think that persons behind a veil of ignorance would not make provision for some forms of favoritism toward their loved ones (Sher 1987:186—187). If such provisions were not made, life would be emotionally barren or fraught with tension, and everyone would be worse off.

Nevertheless, Williams continues, even if impartial morality would allow the husband to save his wife, the thought that doing so is morally permissible is "one thought too many" (1976:214—215). I readily grant that a wife should have grave doubts about her husband's love if, in the clutch of events, he would dwell on the moral permissibility of saving her. Moreover, I would add that, if the husband believed that he had a moral duty to save her, the thought that he should save her because it is morally compulsory to do so would betoken a sadly bloodless marriage. Yet, I fail to see anything disturbing about subjecting one's emotional ties to moral scrutiny in a cool moment. After all, some expressions of love for one's family—nepotism, for instance—are morally wrong and ineligible as personal choices.

The category of morally permissible actions, then, constitutes the orbit of what I shall call personal autonomy. Living well presupposes that people fulfill their moral obligations. But, assuming that morality does not decide every issue that people face, how are people to go about making the rest of their decisions? How are people to decide whether to go to college or to trade school, which institution to attend, whether to pursue this career or that, whether to accept *this* job offer, whether to marry, whether to accept *this* proposal, whether to have children, how many children to have, whether to get a divorce? The list is endless.

Since many of these questions are morally tinctured, the category of personal decisions cannot be neatly distinguished from the category of moral decisions. If one's actions have allowed someone to believe that a proposal of marriage would be welcomed, refusing it takes on a moral cast. Yet, doing so is clearly within one's rights. No type of decision, however, invariably falls within the range of purely personal prerogative. One's choice of a spouse is ordinarily a personal matter. But, if one has actively encouraged a suitor to think that his or her love is returned and that a proposal of marriage would be accepted, it may be immoral to refuse, or, at any rate, refusing may require a moral justification showing that one's rights outweigh one's voluntarily assumed duties to one's suitor. Nor is it possible to state precisely (and noncontroversially) what kinds of effects on others constitute moral issues or how serious these effects must be to call morality into play. Trifling with people's feelings is immoral, but there is no formula specifying the difference between exploring the possibilities of relationships and trifling with others' feelings. These determinations must, therefore, ultimately rest on judgment which takes into account the peculiarities of individual cases, and reasonable people will sometimes disagree as to whether a decision should be classified as moral or not. Nevertheless, that the distinction between the moral and the personal cannot be rigorously drawn does not entail that there is no distinction to be made. We condemn some actions as foolish, others as wrong. People admire one another more or less for their personal decisions. But people do not hold one another morally responsible for all of their decisions, and the decisions that people do not hold one another morally responsible for are personal.

Still, philosophers working in the Aristotelian tradition might urge that no decisions are nonmoral, inasmuch as all decisions either contribute to or detract from a good life, and inasmuch as virtues or vices shape all decisions. In declaring that "the good life for man is the life spent seeking for the good life for man" and in defining virtues as acquired qualities that enable people to achieve this end together with more specific goods, Alasdair MacIntyre appears to find this view congenial (1984:219, 191). Yet, MacIntyre does not hold that all decisions are of the same moral magnitude. He maintains that a theory of the virtues must be complemented by a theory of moral law, that is, a theory of morally mandatory precepts (1984:151, 200). Furthermore, he recognizes that different people occupy different social positions which give their lives their "moral particularity" (1984:220). It seems obvious as well that, since people have different capabilities and concerns, they will justifiably rank values in different ways and will realize the virtues in different ways (Kraut 1979:180, 194). As a result, they will conduct their lives differently, though blamelessly and, perhaps, equally commendably. MacIntyre's suggestion that the search for the good life is the ground of the virtues intimates his acknowledgment of this variation, for, according to MacIntyre, there is no recipe for the good life and the good life can never be found apart from the journey (1984:219).

In view of the individuality that is inextricable from the project of seeking the good life, it is not perspicuous to collapse all of the decisions involved in pursuing the goal of the good life into morality. As Susan Wolf puts it, "Even if responsible people could reach agreement as to what constituted good taste or a healthy degree of well-roundedness, for example, it seems wrong to insist that everyone try to achieve these things or to blame someone who fails or refuses to conform" (1982:434).

Yet, there are additional moral grounds on which personal autonomy could be questioned. From what has been said so far, it might seem that moral autonomy is to be identified with altruism, whereas the province of personal autonomy is selfishness. If this is so, a theory of personal autonomy is a prescription for self-absorption and indifference to others; as such, it jeopardizes morality. However, this objection rests on an over-simplification of morality, as well as on a misunderstanding of personal autonomy. Moral deliberation takes into account one's own needs and desires as well as those of others— morality is not synonymous with self-sacrificial attendance upon others. Moreover, personal deliberation can turn on social ideals or on one's identification with other people—personal autonomy does not rule out joining the Peace Corps. There is nothing disgraceful, then, about personal autonomy.

No doubt, people can reasonably differ over the reach of morality—some confine it to a narrow set of questions, while others exclude little from its purview. Still, if the claim that a decision is a moral decision is to have any more substance than the claim that a decision is a human decision, morality must be conceived as an arbiter of acceptable and unacceptable conduct. Given such a pointed account of morality, it seems clear that morality should not be seen as dictating everything we do. The interstices of morality leave room for personal values and judgment—Antoine Roquentin's abandoning his biography of Rollebon to take up writing fiction (*Nausea*) and Robert Conway's repudiating worldly ambition for the tranquility of Shangri-La (*Lost Horizons*), if not Catherine's sexually ambiguous high jinks (*Jules et Jim*). For the purposes of this study, it does not matter how extensive a domain the reader assigns to morality. All that need be acknowledged is that moral deliberation cannot dispose of all of life's questions and that some of the remaining questions are important.

The way in which people answer these questions is often of great moment to them. For this reason, viewing personal autonomy simply as a right to make certain decisions without undue interference from family, friends, employers, and the state fails to capture a vital dimension of this concept. To be sure, this comprehensive liberty establishes a social context conducive to personal autonomy. But people may avail themselves of their liberty—they may make a broad range of decisions for themselves—yet lack personal autonomy. What could be missing?

People's intense concern with their personal decisions, the complexity of the processes whereby they ponder their options, and the ways in which they sometimes criticize the choices they have made would be inexplicable if personal autonomy were reducible to uncoerced choice. If that were all there was to it, from the standpoint of autonomy any decision would be as good as any other as long as the individual made it freely. Though people would want to make the most advantageous decisions they could, and to that end they would weigh the relative strengths of their desires and seek plans that would harmonize their desires, only being subjected to force could render their conduct nonautonomous. However disappointed or distraught they may feel when they realize that they could have chosen more wisely, however troubled they may be by inner conflict, however empty they may judge their lives to be, their autonomy would not be called into question unless these responses could be traced to others' coercive stratagems.

But responses of this kind are rarely attributable to impingements on people's negative freedom. Typically, they reveal a deeper dimension of personal autonomy. The wisdom people yearn for is not merely the ingenuity needed to maximize desire satisfaction; rather, people want to want genuinely good things. Moreover, mere advantage-seeking seems insufficient to account for the emotional density and the subtlety of people's deliberations; rather, these latter phenomena evidence the extent to which choices can tap personal identity. Similarly, people do not confine their self-criticism to success as measured against a preordained scale; rather, they sometimes ask whether their lives and their selves are not out of kilter.

Robert Conway's predicament illustrates the difference between uncoerced choice and autonomous choice. An educated and well-connected product of a liberal society, Conway is hardly the victim of overpowering force. Moreover, in terms of the appurtenances of self-interest as it is ordinarily understood, Conway lacks nothing. A man who enjoys as much individual freedom as anyone could hope for, who has a wide acquaintanceship along with a number of intimate friends and warm family ties, who performs worthwhile work that secures both wealth and prestige, Conway still suffers from doubts about the value of his life and ambivalence about the course he has taken. However fortunate and free he may be, Conway's self and his overall life plan are in tension. His propensity for contemplation and his longing for a sense of unity with other people can find no outlet in his diplomatic career. In his case, as in others, the self-governance constitutive of personal autonomy cannot be reduced to negative liberty or, for that matter, to negative liberty coupled with a socially sanctioned form of success. It requires living in harmony with one's self.

In doing what *they* really want to do within the sphere of moral permissibility, personally autonomous agents control their own lives. They are not other individuals' or their society's playthings. Ibsen's Nora needs to break out of her husband's stifling emotional grip and also out of her society's hold on her apprehension of her proper role. Nor are autonomous people the victims of imperious forces within themselves. Fears of eternal damnation temporarily snare Joyce's Stephen Dedalus, and Zelda Fitzgerald's neurosis drove her to fling herself into one project after another but prevented her from ever bringing any of them to a successful conclusion. There is, then, a quartet of threats to personal autonomy: social pressure, externally applied coercion, internalized cultural imperatives, and individual pathology. The first pair of threats confirm that autonomous agents must live in harmony with their selves. They cannot allow outside forces to displace their own desires and thereby to assume control over their lives. But the second pair, in raising the possibility of alien forces operating within the self, suggests that autonomous agents must live in harmony not merely with their selves but with their "true" selves. To be in control of one's life is, then, to live in harmony with one's true—one's authentic—self. Just as moral autonomy would be unintelligible without criteria of correct judgment, personal autonomy requires a touchstone. That touchstone is the unique authentic self.

But it is by no means evident what the authentic self is or whether people can locate and understand their authentic selves. The social sciences have toppled the belief that individuals are discrete atoms endowed with sui generis properties and are sufficient unto themselves. To mention only two well-known dimensions of the problem, Marx argued that economic status has a marked impact on the trajectory of people's lives, and Freud defended an account of unconscious forces collaborating with social circumstances to mold people's personalities. Briefly, if people are products of socialization, they have no true selves, and they cannot control their own lives. It seems to follow that personal autonomy is an anachronistic myth.

Personal autonomy is vulnerable to socialization at three points: *self-discovery, self-definition,* and *self-direction.* To achieve personal autonomy, one must know what one is like, one must be able to establish one's own standards and to modify one's qualities to meet them, and one must express one's personality in action. Without self-discovery and self-definition, what appears to be self-direction could turn out to be disguised heteronomy, that is, others' internalized direction. But self-discovery and self-definition can also be influenced socially. Introspection may find a thoroughly conditioned self. Likewise, a decision to change may reflect socially instilled values and preferences, and a meta-decision confirming that decision may again reflect socially instilled values and preferences. In sum, self-administered checks on the autonomy of the individual may themselves be products of socialization, and any review of these reviews may be socially tainted, as well.

The search for the authentic self thus appears to set in motion an infinite regress. Accordingly, to explicate personal autonomy in the context of socialization, it is necessary to consider how this regress can be halted or neutralized. That is the overarching objective of parts 2 and 3 of this book—part 2 addressing this problem primarily from the standpoint of the philosophy of mind, and part 3 considering it primarily from the standpoint of social psychology. I shall argue that previous treatments of personal autonomy have faltered because they regard the problem of personal autonomy as subsidiary to the problem of free will. As a remedy for the deficiencies of these views, I shall suggest that we can profitably circumvent the issue of free will by focusing on the thought that personal autonomy is a way of living in harmony with one's true self. Conceived as the exercise of a competency comprising diverse self-reading and self-actualizing skills, I shall urge, personal autonomy is not only compatible with the civilizing influences of socialization, but it depends on socialization to cultivate the requisite skills. While the fact that people are shaped by social interaction is largely responsible for rendering the concept of the authentic self suspect, it does not render this concept otiose.

The social scientific critique of the true self notwithstanding, the idea of personal autonomy has hardly been drummed out of our thinking. In psychotherapy and through other more exotic disciplines, people quest after personal insight and liberation. Likewise, conscientious physicians and researchers worry about whether their patients and subjects have genuinely consented to their ministrations, and social workers and other counselors wonder how they can help pregnant teens and battered women to gain control over their lives. Furthermore, contemporary moral and political philosophers—John Rawls is the most prominent of them—continue to found compelling and influential theories on the assumption that individual self-governance is an indisputable good. Despite the paucity of progress in reconciling the social scientific view of humanity with the ideal of personal fulfillment so many of us implicitly endorse, the currency of appeals to personal autonomy has not diminished. In part 4, I shall turn to normative issues and consider how personal autonomy is implicated in the concepts of the good life and social justice.

(Hereafter, to avoid needless repetition, I shall use the term "autonomy" to refer to personal autonomy, and I shall specify other types of autonomy by using qualifying adjectives when I refer to them.)

# PART II

# A Procedural Account of Personal Autonomy

I am not in my first youth—I can do what I choose—I belong quite to the independent class. I have neither father nor mother; I am poor; I am of a serious disposition, and not pretty. I therefore am not bound to be timid and conventional; indeed I can't afford such luxuries. Besides, I try to judge things for myself; to judge wrong, I think, is more honorable than not to judge at all. I don't wish to be a mere sheep in the flock; I wish to choose my fate and know something of human affairs beyond what other people think it compatible with propriety to tell me. . . . Let me say this to you, Mr. Goodwood. You are so kind as to speak of being afraid of my marrying. If you should hear a rumour that I am on the point of doing so—girls are liable to have such things said about them—remember what I have told you about my love of liberty, and venture to doubt it.

Isabel Archer in *The Portrait of a Lady* by Henry James

# SECTION 1

# Recent Accounts of Autonomy

IN AN era of ascendance for the social sciences, we have seen, it has become exceedingly easy to call into question the cogency of the concept of autonomy (part 1). To acknowledge the profound impact of socialization continuing from infancy into adulthood is to raise the question of whether people have any traits, beliefs, or capabilities that can be called their own and, therefore, whether the direction of their lives is not merely an outcropping of acculturation. Consider a person—call her Janice—who desperately wants to be famous. How can Janice ever hope to disentangle her own reasons for hankering after such renown from the influence that pervasive media coverage of glamorous celebrities may have had? How can Janice be sure that the lure of fame does not reduce to the fact that public adulation would compensate for her father's withholding love when she was a child? Whatever grounds for seeking fame Janice discovers—the excitement of the chase, the stimulating experiences and opportunities available to the famous, and so forth—it always seems reasonable to suggest that she is attracted to these goods as a result of prior socialization. No one's grounds for avowing certain values, goals, interpersonal ties, and the like ever seem altogether extricable from his or her background.

Autonomous people are in control of their own lives inasmuch as they do what they really want to do (part 1). But, if people are products of their environments, it seems fatuous to maintain that the agency of individuals has any special importance, for personal choice dissolves into social influence. Moreover, it seems vacuous to maintain that there is a significant distinction between what a person wants and what that person really wants, for people have no desires apart from those that socialization has molded, if not implanted in them. The chief task of a theory of autonomy, then, is to reclaim the distinction between real and apparent desires.

Of course, people can miscalculate and as a result fail to achieve some of their goals. In this sense, they can be said not to have done what they really wanted, but this is a superficial conception of "really wanting." It presumes that all of a person's desires are equally candidates for satisfaction and thus that autonomy is nothing more than maximizing desire satisfaction. When we talk about really wanting this rather than that, however, we often mean to draw a qualitative distinction between our desires. We are not merely saying that one desire is stronger than another. We are saying that one desire is more integral to our identity than another or that one of the desires is altogether alien to our identity. People suffering from physical addiction or illness sometimes regard desires springing from these conditions as external to them. Still, this disowning of desires is not limited to such blatant disruptions of people's integrity as agents. Perfectly normal desires can seem alien.

Suspicion then falls on socialization—the subtle, indeed, hardly noticeable processes whereby people become recognizable members of communities. When traumatic social experience leads to neurosis, it is clear that socialization contributes to the emergence of alien desires. But perhaps the phenomenon is more general. Perhaps social experience invariably insinuates a great many alien traits, beliefs, values, aspirations, and the like into our personalities, and desires stemming from these characteristics are the ones that we do not really want·to satisfy. The authentic self, on this hypothesis, is a self liberated from the grip of the socialization processes that instilled these alien desires—a free will, as it were. In this section, I shall consider three theories of autonomy that grant that socialization can rob people of control over their lives, but that seek to explain how people can separate their authentic selves from what social experience has made them.

Philosophers have defended three main ways of rescuing autonomy from socialization: examining the socialization process in which one has been reared (Emmet 1966:120–121; Young 1979:370; J. Richards 1980:86); testing the phenomenal self for coherence (Benn 1975:126–128; Frankfurt 1976:250); and identifying with traits, appetites, emotions, values, objectives, and the like that one finds in oneself (Frankfurt 1971:15–17, 1976:249–251; G. Dworkin 1976:24–25; Young 1979:373; Watson 1982:109). These methods are not mutually exclusive. Indeed, they can supplement one another, and many theories of autonomy interweave them. However, none is necessarily dependent on any other, and, for the sake of clarity, I shall treat them in somewhat artificial isolation.

Initially, it might be supposed that the point of seeking to understand the socialization process one has undergone is to separate innate characteristics from implanted ones. But a requirement that autonomous people express only their innate characteristics would be too stringent, for it would freeze these individuals in limited and, in some cases, undesirable forms of conduct. Innate characteristics are apt to be primitive response patterns which, taken alone, would comprise a personality so elemental that it would not be recognizably human. Moreover, learned characteristics may displace innate ones and become integral to the self. A baby's gradual substitution of speech for bawling to announce its discomfort illustrates such a shift. Plainly, there is no reason to believe that people should expunge all of their implanted characteristics, nor that they should retain whatever innate characteristics they can find in themselves.

Accordingly, some advocates of this route to autonomy maintain that the object of probing one's upbringing is not to penetrate to a primordial personality layer but rather to liberate oneself from stultifying aspects of one's socialization (Young 1980:573; J. Richards 1980:83–86). Granting that socialization may well shape all parts of the human personality, these students of autonomy contend that the knowledge obtained through autobiographical reflection brings personal freedom. When people ascertain how they came to have certain characteristics, they may also realize that they do not want to be products of *that* sort of social process, and they may find that the very knowledge of the sources of their respective characteristics suffices to quash the power these previously unexamined forces had over their lives (Young 1979:370). Or conversely, people may willingly accept previously obscured parts of their selves as a result of this retrospective reflection but gain control over them through consciousness of their workings (Young 1980:573–574). In bare outline, these are the premises of the psychoanalytic method Freud pioneered. However, it is worth recalling that Freud saw the process of gaining control over earlier traumas as one that could be obstructed through "intellectualization" and as one that required "working through." Thus, Freud would not have agreed that consciousness alone could secure autonomy.

Regardless of how complex the process of assimilating the revelations of these autobiographical inquiries is acknowledged to be, a difficulty remains. It is possible that prior socialization determines the outcome of one's self-examination and that this socialization operates unconsciously (Young 1980:575). For example, by molding people's values, unconscious forces can lead people to choose to reinforce or to suppress this characteristic or that, and socialization may have instilled these unconscious forces. To the extent that people fail to bring to consciousness the explanation of their decisions to change or to accept themselves, they remain heteronomous, according to this view of autonomy. But once one concedes that unconscious forces are at work in human psychology, it seems that no one can ever be satisfied that he or she has remembered all pertinent events, has grasped the intricacies of the gradual process of personality formation, and has assimilated his or her past emotionally. For it is in the nature of unconscious forces that they are inaccessible and may be unsuspectedly influencing the individual.

Robert Young claims to dispatch this problem, first by asserting that only unconscious forces manipulate and coerce people, and then by pointing out that the foregoing line of objection improperly collapses the distinction between socialization and coercion (1979:374, 1980:576). According to Young, since socialization ceases to be coercive once it has been brought to consciousness, it thereby ceases to impair autonomy. Unfortunately, this reply assumes that the unconscious or, at least, that part of the unconscious that is implicated in a particular desire or trait can be made transparent, but this is precisely what the objection disputes.

Although Young admits that his account of autonomy implies that "fewer people are free for less of the time than we are inclined in our unreflective moments to believe" (1979:376), I would urge that it is not clear that on Young's account anyone is ever free. Unless it can be shown that someone has plumbed the murky depths of unconsciousness in regard to the genesis of at least one component of his or her personality and has acted in the light of this awareness, Young's acount will not certify anyone's autonomy.

Seeking to forestall this conclusion, Young shifts the discussion from the question of whether unconscious forces have shaped the beliefs one deploys to assess oneself to the question of whether socialization has shaped one's introspective faculties—that is, the techniques one uses to examine oneself. Young baldly states that some people's retrospective self-scrutiny just does not seem to be prey to unconscious socialization but rather seems to depend solely on these individuals' reflective powers (1980:576). But surely such impressions cannot circumvent the need to distinguish autonomous from heteronomous reflection. At this point, Young must specify the sorts of circumstances under which a person is justified in believing the origins of his or her reflective powers to be fully disclosed, and the same doubts as to whether the unconscious can ever be made transparent arise again, but this time in connection with the evolution of the person's reflective powers. The only alternative would be to demarcate autonomous retrospective self-scrutiny by adverting to innate reflective powers. But, innate reflective powers undoubtedly would prove too crude for the purposes of autonomy. As portrayals of children who have grown up without the benefit of socialization reveal (Francois Truffaut's *The Wild Child* is a well-known example), a great deal of nurturance is required for the most rudimentary self-understanding.

While it seems undeniable that coming to terms with one's socialization somehow contributes to autonomy, it is evident that we cannot rely on the concept of a mastered social background or, in other words, the concept of a pellucid self to provide a tenable account of autonomy. For this kind of self-knowledge is vulnerable to allegations that it, too, is a product of socialization. Robert Young recognizes this limitation and does not rest his account of autonomy entirely on the idea of informing oneself about one's past. However, it is important to note that one cannot avoid being drawn into an epistemological regress if one insists on analyzing autonomy as a state of having overcome socialization through self-consciousness.

Stanley Benn's treatment of autonomy as a form of coherence seeks to bypass this quagmire by linking autonomy to a desideratum that cannot be dismissed as another culture-bound manifestation. On Benn's view, autonomous people actively render their personalities coherent (1975:126–128). Though Benn contends that autonomous people must apply their critical faculties to received beliefs in order to accept or reject these beliefs—a member of a monolithic culture that imbues people with a coherent belief system but does not provide them with the critical resources needed to assess this belief system cannot be autonomous—he denies that people ever transcend socialization, whether in virtue of the faculties they exercise or in virtue of the beliefs they come to hold (1975:126). Their faculties are developed in a social context, and the ideas they use to question their traditions are taken from their intellectual environment. What distinguishes autonomous people is that they have disavowed those beliefs that do not square with the rest of their system of thought, and they have reconciled those beliefs that they incorporate into their system of thought.

Benn's conception of autonomy contrasts with Young's since Benn does not try to discern a form of reflection or a distinctive relation to one's beliefs that altogether defies socialization. However, it seems to me that Benn, like Young, is drawn to the thought that autonomous people must somehow move beyond socialization. Why else would he insist that autonomous people not only must have coherent belief systems, but also must have constructed such belief systems through the exercise of their critical faculties? Furthermore, I would suggest that the allure of this idea leads Benn to adopt an excessively abstract criterion of autonomy.

In associating autonomy with coherence, Benn provides a basis for silencing questions about the unconscious underpinnings of an individual's beliefs and faculties. For Benn, it does not matter whether critical reflection penetrates every recess of past socialization and confronts every current pressure to conform, for coherence provides a standard of autonomy that is independent of the process of meeting it and that thus provides a resting point for inquiry. Though Benn maintains that people must test their beliefs in order to be autonomous, he does not specify how profoundly these beliefs must be probed to be considered critically assessed (1975:127–128). A person who has constructed a coherent belief system is autonomous.

Much of the plausibility of coherence as a criterion for autonomy stems from the fact that the desirability of coherence is not tied to any particular historical culture. Belief in the desirability of coherence may not emerge without socialization, but it may be that every viable socialization process inculcates this belief. Thus, without any pretense that the standard of coherence transcends socialization as such, it can nevertheless be argued that this standard transcends each particular mode of socialization. Moreover, should anthropological evidence show that some socialization processes eschew coherence, it can be urged that its acceptance is rationally required. On Benn's account, however much a product of socialization autonomous people may be, these individuals instantiate a pan-social value that sets them apart from the peculiar features of their respective upbringings.

Still, that people have coherent belief systems and are thus united with a pan-social value is not sufficient to render them autonomous. An insane person who happened to have consistent, though delusory beliefs would not qualify as autonomous, for such a person would not have control over his or her beliefs. It is necessary to ask, then, how a rationally constructed, coherent belief system is related to autonomy.

I do not wish to take issue with the claim that a coherent belief system is good. Rather, I propose to question the feasibility of understanding autonomy in terms of this standard. An initial question concerns the relationship between a coherent belief system and a coherent personality. In his discussion of autonomy, Benn focuses on beliefs—especially a person's judgments about social roles and principles of action. Given this narrow context, the criterion of rationally constructed coherence is plainly germane. However, autonomy is not confined to the state of the individual's intellect. It also concerns people's emotional responses and commitments, their involvement in immediate projects, and their hearkening to long-run goals. In this expanded context, it is difficult to assess Benn's position since he gives little indication what a coherent personality is.

Perhaps, Benn would say that a rationally constructed, coherent personality is one in which the individual has amalgamated all of his or her traits, feelings, inclinations, desires, values, beliefs about the world, and the like into a practicable life plan. But this proposal seems too stringent as an account of a rationally constructed, coherent personality. Consider the case of Max's unrequited, yet enduring love for Alice. Max loves Alice despite knowing that Alice does not return his affection. Moreover, Max realizes that he can never express his feelings as he would like to express them. In this predicament, Max can choose to sustain his love and worship Alice from afar, or he can choose to look for someone else to love. Neither of these options blends all of Max's beliefs and feelings into a practicable life plan. But whereas the former option does not rule out Max's having a rationally constructed, coherent personality, it does rule out his being autonomous.

Choosing to cherish and nurture an unreciprocated love seems compatible with a rationally constructed, coherent personality. That Max holds a factual belief—namely, that Alice does not and never will love him—that would lead most people, but not Max, to modify their goals does not entail that his personality is irrational and incoherent. A personality that harbored such competing constituents as loving Alice and wanting to make her miserable would seem irrational and incoherent. Likewise, if Max felt perfectly ridiculous nursing this hopeless amour but persisted just the same, his person- ality would seem irrational and incoherent. But Max's personality can compass feelings that are pragmatically irreconcilable with one of his true contingent beliefs without succumbing to irrationality and incoherence. People can have—indeed, they can rationally choose to have—coherent personalities which they know they must suppress.

In contrast, it is doubtful that an autonomous person would pine away nurturing an unreciprocated love. Unlike coherence, autonomy requires self-direction—that is, expressing oneself in ways that one deems fitting and worthy of oneself. (For discussion of the possibility of autonomously cultivating attributes that cannot be expressed through socially available channels and instead expressing them in idiosyncratic ways, see part 2, sec. 5.) Accordingly, if one can have a rationally self-chosen and coherent personality that is doomed to dormancy, this pair of criteria is insufficient to account for auton- omy.[1] Coherence places constraints on the relations between the con- stituents of a personality, but it leaves open the question of whether these constituents can be put into practice.

Undeniably, coherence has a role to play in regard to autonomy. People cannot live in harmony with themselves unless the discovery of incompatible beliefs precipitates critical scrutiny of these beliefs aimed at resolving the conflict. More generally, it is evident that the autonomous person's discovery of tensions within his or her personality must elicit efforts to understand and to relieve these disturbances. Still, having a rationally constructed, coherent personality is compatible with being unable to do what one really wants to do, for the rationality and coherence of one's personality does not ensure the realizability of one's plans. Accordingly, a tenable account of autonomy must link the abstract desideratum of coherence to practicability.

The two accounts of autonomy I have so far discussed stress methods of self-discovery. One version of the requirement that autonomous people examine the socialization to which they have been subjected holds that this inquiry gives people control over their futures by giving them control over their pasts. Similarly, the coherence requirement is best interpreted as defining an indicator of conflicts within the self which call for personal change, rather than as an end-state to be achieved. But people often know what their problems are and even why they have them, yet they fail to see workable solutions. Self-knowledge is necessary but not sufficient for autonomy. The third criterion I listed at the beginning of this section—identification with one's appetites, emotions, traits, values, objectives, and the like—is meant to supply this lack. Not only do autonomous people know themselves, but also they identify with and thus control those parts of themselves that give rise to action.

An influential version of the identification criterion is founded on the claim that people have first-order desires for particular goods or to do particular acts and, in addition, they can have second-order desires regarding their first-order desires. In Harry Frankfurt's parlance, autonomous and, in general, non-wanton people have second-order volitions that one or another of their first-order desires be effective (1971:8–11). By desiring that a certain desire be acted on, people withdraw their selves from other desires that are being experienced and identify their selves with the desire selected for satisfaction. As Gerald Dworkin observes, this identification must occur under conditions of procedural independence—that is, the agent's reflection on his or her first-order desires must be free of interference (1976:26–28). Nevertheless, the individual's identification with a desire that issues in action is pivotal. A person's conduct may diverge from his or her second-order volitions, but, when it does, the person is driven by an alien force (Frankfurt 1971:13). Though such people are not wantons, neither are they autonomous.

A major difficulty with this account of autonomy is specifying what is involved in identification. Advocates of this view have given two main accounts of this crucial relation. Frankfurt maintains that a decision to count a first-order desire as a candidate for satisfaction and to deny another desire (or other desires) this status constitutes identification (Frankfurt 1976:250). Dworkin formulates the question in terms of attitudes: an approving attitude which leads a person to affirm some first-order desire (or desires) while repudiating others constitutes identification (G. Dworkin 1976:25). Each of these suggestions poses problems. For example, Frankfurt's position does not rule out arbitrary decision making at the meta-level, and Dworkin's position disallows the possibility of self-acceptance that stops short of positive approval. However, I shall concentrate on three problems that these accounts share: the problem of the persistence of identification, the problem of implicit identification, and the problem of finalizing identification.

Preliminary to addressing the problem of the persistence of identification and that of implicit identification, it is necessary to consider the relation between autonomy and regret. One of the strongest indications that a person lacks the harmony of self and action that underlies autonomy is the recurrence of nagging regrets in regard to the individual's activities and projects. As a form of self-criticism, regret of this kind is symptomatic intrapersonal dissonance. Although autonomous people may occasionally find fault with their values, emotional ties, personal goals, and the like, they could hardly be said to control their own lives if they were not able to reconsider and adjust these commitments to bring them into accord with their selves. In addition, although autonomous people may experience disappointment as a result of circumstances beyond their control, they have no reason to regret their conduct if they handled the situation as well as could be expected. Similarly, although autonomous people may occasionally be dissatisfied with their choices, particularly spontaneous ones made in situations that preclude careful deliberation, they must be able to take whatever measures are necessary to prevent repeated divagations from their abiding values, emotional ties, personal goals, and the like. In short, autonomous people are able to control their lives in ways that generally obviate regret.

Against this view, Bernard Williams has argued that regret can be an appropriate response even when a person is not responsible for what happened and that a regret-free life would be a terribly superficial one (Williams 1981:28–29). Williams points out that people who have accidentally injured others properly regret what they have done and act accordingly (Williams 1981:28). While I would grant that a person who did not respond in this way would be callous, I doubt that the same response usually befits misfortunes one has inflicted on oneself. The assymmetry between these cases stems in part from the fact that the harm to another person would be immoral if it had been inflicted deliberately, whereas the harm to oneself would not be immoral—it would be merely imprudent unless it interfered with one's moral responsibilities. (For further treatment of the distinction between the moral and the personal, see part 1.) Thus, in the interpersonal case, there is a residual sense of wronging another person that has no place in the intrapersonal case. Furthermore, corresponding to the sense of having wronged someone in the interpersonal case is a desire to make amends to that person which would be odd from the intrapersonal perspective. Although people sometimes decide to pamper themselves after a grave disappointment—one might decide to take an extravagant vacation to assuage the pain of a nasty divorce—such self-indulgent gestures are best understood as providing surcease as opposed to compensation.

Nevertheless, I do not wish to maintain that regret is never warranted in intrapersonal life, nor that regret is altogether foreign to autonomous living. Thus, I concur with Williams' denial that rationality could require the absence of regret (Williams 1981:29). What I wish to stress is that recurrent regrets signal failed autonomy. Autonomous people take occasional regrets as opportunities to learn and to adjust their conduct and their plans. But when people are chronically regretful—whether because ongoing circumstances are hostile to their plans or because they repeatedly act in a self-defeating manner—their regret evidences their inability to control their own lives. Non-autonomous people are unable to use regret constructively. Accordingly, an adequate account of autonomy must explain not only why the autonomous individual is not immune to regret, but also why the autonomous individual does not suffer from recurrent regrets. This requirement raises what I call the problem of the persistence of identification.

If identification with one's traits is to constitute autonomy, it must persist. It is not enough that the autonomous person identifies with his or her desires as they are being acted on, for, in order to be capable of learning from regret, this person must continue to identify with these desires whether or not action taken to satisfy them has proved successful. Autonomous people do not cope with failure by automatically switching goals; they have settled (though, of course, not static) identities. Also, it is not enough that the autonomous person identifies with his or her desires as they are being acted on, for, in order subsequently to gain satisfaction from the action, the agent must continue to identify with the desire that gave rise to it. If one desire is supplanted by another as soon as action motivated by the first desire is taken, the agent may even regret conduct that succeeded in satisfying the first desire because it precluded or postponed satisfying the second. Autonomous people do not defeat themselves by spurning goals as soon as they have accomplished them; again, they have settled (though, of course, not static) identities. Yet, from the standpoint of Frankfurt's and Dworkin's treatments of the identification relation, it is reasonable to assume that identification would often prove transitory.

It is well-known that today's decisive commitments may be reversed tomorrow, and today's enthusiastic attitudes may vanish tomorrow. Notoriously, after being sternly warned about the dangers of a sedentary life, people leave their doctors' offices wanting to rid themselves of flab and resolving to exercise regularly, but these emphatic decisions commonly do not go any further. Often the reason for this delinquency is countervailing pressures at work or at home—there is no time to add another activity to busy schedules. In such cases, people may never reject their desire to start an exercise program, and identification is not transitory though it is not effective. Still, the explanation could be quite otherwise. It may be that the person's earlier self-image—say, as a reclusive, contemplative sort—reasserts itself once the burst of anxiety induced by the physician's recitation has subsided. If the person believes that no form of exercise is compatible with this self-concept—the possibility of meditating or reading while riding a stationary bicycle is overlooked—the desire to institute an exercise program goes out the window. In this kind of case, identification with the desire to cut a lean, vigorous figure occurs but does not last. Such an individual cannot regret lapsing back into sedentary habits and cannot benefit from the warning regret would sound, for this individual has ceased to identify with the desire that motivated the resolution to exercise.

People commonly vacillate in identifying with their desires. But if autonomy requires that people be capable of experiencing regret but that they not be plagued by chronic regret, and if the persistence of people's identification with their desires is necessary to account for these relations between autonomy and regret, a convincing account of autonomy must guarantee the stability of the autonomous individual's identification with his or her desires. Although Frankfurt attempts to address this problem by affirming that the decisions he is talking about are "resounding" commitments (Frankfurt 1971:16), there is nothing to distinguish a decision or an approving attitude that will issue in long-lived identification from one that will not.[2] Sincerity is no guarantee. And certainly, the mere fact that the decision or approving attitude is a second-order one does not ensure that it will be at all stable. Since no restraints on the basis for identification are built into either of these conceptions, they establish no presumption that identification will persist.

Now, it might be thought that Gary Watson's version of the identification criterion provides a solution to this problem. Watson urges that rational evaluation of desires or of possible courses of action separates those that are worthy of being satisfied or pursued from those that are unworthy, and he maintains that no one can be dissociated from these valuations without losing his or her identity (Watson 1982:105–106).[3] If identification consists of rational evaluation, identification will persist. Once a desire has been rationally found to be worthy, it cannot promptly degenerate into baseness. The trouble with Watson's account is not that it allows for too much volatility, as Frankfurt's and Dworkin's do, but rather that it does not allow for enough individuality.

Watson's Platonic view of identification privileges the rational ratification and disqualification of desires. Autonomous people act on good desires while suppressing or expunging bad ones. Though this approach seems well suited to the problem of moral autonomy, it is inadequate to the problem of personal autonomy. (For an account of the distinction between moral and personal autonomy, see part 1.) The trouble is that, in Watson's view, no sense can be given to the claim that each person's valuations express a distinctive self. Quite the contrary, all rational valuations should converge. According to Watson, autonomous people would lead different lives because of differences in their circumstances and abilities. In view of their differing backgrounds and talents, Mikhail Baryshnikov and Nelson Mandela are bound to follow different paths. However, this variation is not attributable to these agents' true selves, which qua rational evaluators are uniform. Both men should agree that *Giselle* is a great ballet and that Apartheid is evil. In sum, Watson's account secures the persistence of identification at the sacrifice of the unique autonomous individual. Though there are no autonomous chameleons, there equally are no autonomous clones. An adequate treatment of autonomy must accommodate a stable, but distinctive personality.

A second difficulty with the identification criterion arises because people usually do not reflect on their desires unless those desires have somehow been called into question. As long as a desire does not create problems, one is unlikely to ponder whether to identify with it or not. If anything, people identify with such untroublesome desires implicitly. But it is hard to see how Frankfurt's schema could accommodate implicit identification.

For Frankfurt, implicit identification would have to come about as a result of favorable tacit decisions. But, if such tacit decisions are introduced, it will become necessary to distinguish tacit deciders from those individuals who refrain from deciding at all, namely, wantons. People can be protected from chronic regret in virtue of their control over their lives—their autonomy—or in virtue of their lack of commitment to guiding values and goals—their wantonness. Accordingly, if tacit deciders are simply people who do not frequently regret their conduct, they are indistinguishable from wantons. Still, a tacit decider could be someone who would decide to identify with a desire if doubt were ever cast upon it. However, this solution implies that a tacit decider is no different from a wanton vis-à-vis a particular desire until an explicit decision is made. If that is true, either people are only autonomous with respect to those parts of their lives in which they have overcome perceived deficiencies, resolved conflicts, or faced difficult choices, or people only manage to live autonomous lives by becoming obsessively self-conscious. Neither of these conclusions is acceptable. If autonomy is not to be a sporadic or undesirable phenomenon, implicit autonomy must be possible. But, on Frankfurt's theory, implicit identification is not possible.[4]

The third defect of the identification criterion echoes one I remarked in regard to the mastery of socialization criterion. Just as agents engaged in retrospective reflection can never be sure that their insights are not themselves products of socialization, agents engaged in identification can never be sure that their self-appropriations are emanating from their true selves (Friedman 1986:25–26; Shatz 1986:458, 478 note). Consider again Janice, who hungers for fame, and suppose that she identifies with her desire for fame and shuns a contrary desire for anonymity. What authenticates this identification? It is not obvious that Janice's second-order desires are more authentic than her first-order desires. Moreover, as Frankfurt acknowledges, people can have third-order desires, fourth-order desires, fifth-order desires, and so on, indefinitely. Why should Janice's identification with the first-order desire for fame suffice for autonomy? Why is it not necessary that she identify with the second-order desire to desire fame? With the third-order desire to desire to desire fame? The identification criterion generates an infinite regress in the absence of an independent basis for terminating the multiplication of identifications.

As one reaches for higher and higher levels of identification, the distinctions between one level and the next become blurred as the content of higher order desires becomes increasingly thin. Thus, the project degenerates into an exercise in futility. Moreover, the outer limit of repeated identifications is paralytic pathology. But autonomy surely does not require that people consume their time and imperil their sanity by flirting with this limit. To avoid these absurd results, Frankfurt introduces the idea of a decisive commitment or, elsewhere, simply a decision (1971:16, 1976:250–251). He maintains that, unlike attitudes, decisions cannot be viewed as external to the self and therefore can be invoked to terminate the regress of desires before it reaches intolerable proportions. Although Frankfurt remarks that his "conception of freedom of the will appears to be neutral with regard to the problem of determinism," it is not clear that his treatment of identification escapes the charge that it seeks but fails to explain how socialization can be overcome (1971:20).

The work that decisions are supposed to do according to Frankfurt is the same that the achievement of a coherent personality is supposed to do according to Benn. Decisions place a limit on worries about the influence of socialization. Once a decision to identify with a certain desire has been made, a person is entitled to dismiss queries about whether the desire is lodged in his or her authentic self. The decision guarantees that it is. But, if, as Frankfurt holds, an attitudinal account of identification is unsatisfactory because attitudes can be products of socialization, Frankfurt's reliance on decisions is unsatisfactory for the same reason (Frankfurt 1976:247). People have grounds for their decisions, and these grounds may be products of socialization. If so, no decision can finalize identification, for none can be shown to free the individual from the tyranny of socialization.

Though each of the criteria I have explored—mastery of socialization, coherence, and identification—raises its characteristic problems, a single defect underlying all of these criteria can be diagnosed. All of them reduce personal autonomy to a special case of free will. (For further discussion of the failings of reducing autonomy to free will, see part 2, sec. 2.) Instead of addressing the question of how a person can live in harmony with his or her authentic self, these theories are fundamentally concerned with explaining how people can elude socialization, that is, how the authentic self can transcend the impact of social causes. Young maintains that knowledge sets us free; Benn maintains that coherence sets us free; Frankfurt maintains that deciding sets us free. Only incidentally do they consider the characteristic unity and vigor of the autonomous life.

Whatever faculty—retrospective reflection, critical reason, or volition—or state of the personality—transparency or coherence—they advert to in order to account for transcendence of socialization, these theories neglect the complexity of the phenomenon of autonomy. As a result, they provide incomplete accounts. Still, the deficiency of these accounts cannot be remedied by combining them into a comprehensive theory, for these criteria also suffer from undue rigidity. One requires that people learn more about their life histories than anyone ever can know; one requires that people fit themselves into an abstract pattern that few can ever attain and that no vital personality could invariably maintain; one requires that autonomous people execute an indefinite series of reflexive maneuvers. In their dedication to showing people how to overcome their social environment, these theories, not surprisingly, impose unmeetable demands on autonomous agents.

One way to mitigate this problem would be to contend that socialization is not all-pervasive. Joel Feinberg enunciates this qualified view of socialization:

> Right from the beginning the newborn infant has a kind of rudimentary character consisting of temperamental proclivities and a genetically fixed potential for the acquisition of various talents and skills. The standard sort of loving upbringing and a human environment in the earliest years will be like water added to dehydrated food, filling it out and actualizing its stored-in tendencies. (Feinberg 1980a:149)[5]

Feinberg recognizes that the child's social environment, through its language, institutions, and systemic values, inevitably leaves a pronounced imprint. However, he correctly cautions that human malleability has unbreachable limits, and he humanely advocates structuring socialization to suit the individual child. A salutary consequence of Feinberg's view is that it reorients speculation about personal autonomy. Instead of asking how the prefabricated adult can gain control over a manufacturing process run wild, Feinberg's insight encourages us to ask how the socialization process can be adjusted to promote the harmonious development of the individual. Of course, the determinist can parry that Feinberg's formulation does not loose the individual from the bonds of his or her genetic complement. And I would add that Feinberg exaggerates the importance of an original endowment of innate characteristics. Nevertheless, the import of Feinberg's line of thought should not be dismissed.

It is a fact that people sometimes feel satisfied that they have done what they really wanted (although they may only notice this satisfaction when their self-direction has somehow gone awry). Likewise, people sometimes feel distraught at the mismatch between their conduct and their selves—"if only I had said (done) . . . " is all too familiar a refrain. It is a further fact that people can critically examine states of personal harmony and dissonance and can strive with varying degrees of success toward integration. Moreover, innovative ways of life are sometimes born of this process. While it is an interesting philosophical puzzle whether these phenomena are possible because people are capable of defying socialization or because socialization is not all-pervasive, it is a mistake to think that we cannot make important philosophical progress in regard to the problem of personal autonomy without solving this conundrum. We have already seen that attempts to solve the problem of personal autonomy by devising a mode of socialization-transcendence have failed. Still, personal integration and life-plan innovation are phenomena which demand philosophical treatment, and these are the phenomena upon which I propose to concentrate attention.

# An Alternative Account of Autonomy

IN THE preceding section, I argued that three major accounts of personal autonomy prove sterile because they construe autonomy as a special case of free will. Construing autonomy as a form of free will implies that the problem of autonomy is primarily an ontological question that raises subsidiary procedural questions. On this understanding, autonomy will be unintelligible unless a free agent can be found. With respect to personal autonomy, a free agent must be one untainted by socialization. Since these theories take the true self of the autonomous individual to be a socialization-transcending agent, the procedures they commend for achieving autonomy are designed to cleanse the individual of the stain of socialization. Either these procedures are schemes to trick socialization into exposing itself so that its captive can escape and perhaps get the upper hand, or they are techniques whereby the cunning prisoner of socialization can break its stanglehold through sheer disdain for its power. We have seen that neither type of procedure can convincingly claim to produce a free agent of the requisite sort.

The disappointing results of interpreting autonomy as a kind of free will provide an initial impetus to reinterpret the problem. A more direct reason for doing so is that successfully exhibiting a true self conceived in this way would not explain autonomy. Let us suppose that within each person there is a collocation of traits or a capability with which the forces of socialization have not tampered or from which the unwanted effects of socialization can be purged. Further, let us suppose that we have discovered a method which anyone can easily use to locate this free self or to distill a free self from the socialized admixture. How would we have advanced our understanding of autonomy?

It might be pointed out that, since autonomous people live in harmony with their authentic selves, we must be able to find the authentic self before we can explain the relation obtaining between this self and the autonomous person's outward life. Autonomy is not merely doing what one wants but doing what one really wants. The difference between the two is that wants of the latter kind originate in the true self, whereas wants of the former kind may originate elsewhere. If not a self purified of social taint, it may be asked, what could the authentic self be?

This salvo is daunting, to be sure. Yet, the argument seems much less persuasive once a major omission is highlighted. This conception of autonomy has two components: self-discovery and self-direction. Autonomous people are acquainted with their true selves, and they act in accordance with their true selves. They do not, so far as this conception is concerned, conceive and institute changes in their true selves. Self-definition has been left out, and, I shall urge, there is no plausible way in which this conception can accommodate this third form of self-mastery. As a result, the free will account of autonomy proves to be dispiritingly fatalistic, as well as incomplete.

Self-definition is a necessary component of the concept of autonomy, and a concept of self-definition that involves no more than cleaning out the detritus of socialization is insufficient for the purpose of explicating autonomy. Only if every socialization-free self is naturally a unified, admirable self is autonomy possible without self-definition. On realistic assumptions, however, it seems probable that many unmanipulated, socialization-free selves would contain traits that vie with one another. But people who cannot adjudicate such intrapersonal conflicts cannot act in accordance with their true selves because their true selves give incompatible directions. Their ongoing ambivalence would subvert autonomy. Constantly torn by opposed beliefs and feelings, such people could not assert control over their lives. In addition, it is reasonable to suppose that many unmanipulated, socialization-free selves would contain juvenile, if not contemptible, traits. But people who cannot modify qualities which they judge to be undesirable are victims of their true selves and can hardly be said to control their own lives.

Though it is reasonable to suppose that socialization poses a threat to autonomy and therefore that people cannot be autonomous unless they exert some sort of control over their socialization, the stronger claim that people are autonomous once they have rid themselves of social influences is not reasonable. Not only is it doubtful that people can accomplish this goal, but also privileging a self purged of social influence places the individual at the mercy of that self, regardless of what it turns out to be like. Without self-definition, people afflicted with unlucky endowments would be doomed to heteronomy. Thus, for at least some people and probably for most people, the self-regulation that self-definition affords is indispensable to autonomy.

At this point, someone might counter that free agency can comprise self-definition. Several advocates of this conception of the authentic self defend a conception of purification through appropriation. (For my recounting of these criteria, see part 2, sec. 1.) On this view, the self shapes itself by embracing some of its traits and repudiating others. In this way, the authentic self surfaces.

But what, it must be wondered, is free about a self-selected self? How does the activity of self-selection rid the self of extraneous socialization? Unless we suppose that the selecting self is already a free agent deploying standards independent of socialization in making its choices, this mode of self-definition will not escape the self's immersion in the social world. (For related discussion of the radically contingent, appropriating self, see Sandel 1982, 162–164.)

But self-definition becomes superfluous, if not impossible, once we grant the suppositon that the selecting self is a free agent. Implicit in this assumption is the contention that each self has a pre-social or possibly a trans-social core. This core could take either the form of a set of attributes or that of a pure will capable of choosing ends.

This sector of the self would constitute the true self. However, if the true self is a set of attributes, the appropriation process is just part of the complicated, sometimes arduous, process of uncovering that self and ensuring that conduct accords with it. To be accurate, this latter process is self-discovery coupled with self-direction; it is not self-definition. Yet, if the true self is a pure will unencumbered by values or emotional bonds, it may capriciously opt for incompatible traits and projects, thus rendering a life in accordance with these choices impossible. But more importantly, such a self could associate itself with an array of traits and projects, but it could not incorporate those traits and projects into itself (Sandel 1982:58–59, 62). In other words, it could create a persona though it could not define itself. Self-definition is a dynamic process, but both of these conceptions of the authentic self are inescapably static.

Ultimately, the free-agency conception of autonomy must resort to innate attributes to explain what a self purged of socialization is. But, as I have argued, innate attributes are not necessarily conducive to autonomy. Unless desirable innate attributes (if there are any such) are reinforced and undesirable ones are altered, unless desirable socially fostered attributes are cultivated and undesirable ones are stifled, and unless all of these attributes are orchestrated into a unified personality, autonomy will falter. Granted the need for self-discovery and self-direction to be coordinated with self-definition, as this series of imperatives implies, the primarily ontological view of the authentic self is eclipsed by a primarily procedural view.

Each of the accounts of autonomy discussed in the preceding section recommends a procedure through which autonomy can be gained, but each of them resists the conclusion that the authentic self is nothing more than the product of these procedures. Once autonomy is cast as a form of free will, that is, as a form of obeisance to a self untainted by socialization, this conclusion is inadmissible. On this view, the true self is like a sunken treasure—a pre-existing, hidden entity. Though there are diving procedures fortune-hunters can follow to locate it and float it, there is no guarantee that any given expedition will succeed in retrieving the treasure. The true self may elude a well-equipped seeker of autonomy, yet it remains intact awaiting the day when its secrets will be brought to light. But, since this conception cannot yield an adequate treatment of autonomy— it cannot supply an account of self-definition—I can see no compelling reason to be bound by it.

In doing what they really want to do, autonomous people control their own lives. Of course, no one can control all of the circumstances that might help or hinder one's projects. Strictly speaking, then, no one can dictate his or her own fate. But, inasmuch as autonomous people are able to match their conduct to their selves within the constraints of the opportunities that circumstances afford and are sometimes able to enlarge their opportunities to suit their selves, they exercise as much power over their destinies as anyone can. How do they do this?

Consider the cases of Sharon and Martin. Martin, the son of a physician, has always been groomed to follow in his father's footsteps. Also, his parents have taught him to feel deeply guilty whenever he disappoints their expectations. Upon entering college, Martin enrolls in the pre-med program. Throughout his undergraduate years, Martin excels in his science courses, but he minimizes his efforts in general education requirements and selects reputed "gut" courses in order to fulfill a college requirement that he take electives outside his major. Nevertheless, his superb record in his pre-med courses gains him admission to his father's medical school. Though Martin finds medical training grueling and often feels he is engaged in running one needlessly difficult gauntlet after another, it never occurs to him to probe these feelings, let alone reconsider his career choice. By the age of forty, Martin has become a respected and wealthy surgeon.

Sharon's biography proceeds a bit less smoothly. Sharon is the only daughter of a widowed high school tennis coach who dotes on her. While supporting his daughter's forays into diverse activities as she is growing up, he hopes to bequeath his love of sport to her. Aware of the dangers of parental domination, he exercises restraint in pursuing this objective. Nonetheless, he takes advantage of every opportunity to cultivate Sharon's considerable aptitude for tennis, and her record on her high school tennis team is spectacular enough to earn her an athletic scholarship. Yet, Sharon enters college without definite career plans, and she looks forward to exploring her options with eager anticipation. Despite the demanding training and tournament schedule to which her athletic scholarship commits her, Sharon takes her studies seriously and experiments with courses in various fields. Each semester, she asks herself which of the many course offerings is most attractive to her and even whether she should try something that does not immediately strike her fancy or that might prove too difficult for her. As her education progresses, she begins to find the strident rivalry amongst her teammates oppressive, and she begins to resent the single-minded dedication to winning that her coaches expect of her. Simultaneously, her satisfaction from her studies grows. After weighing the financial advantages of going on to play professional tennis against her other interests and values, and after consulting with the financial aid office about alternative methods of paying for her education, Sharon finally decides that she does not want to go pro and quits the tennis team. Instead, she concludes, her talents and inclinations suit her to become a physical therapist, and her continuing fondness for sports can be best expressed through a specialty in sports medicine. Sharon's coaches do not take their star player's defection lying down, and periodically they attempt to lure her back to tennis. Confident that she has made the right decision, Sharon thereafter dismisses such solicitations automatically and concentrates on the goal she has set herself.

The contrast between Martin and Sharon is instructive. Despite his outward success, there is nothing in Martin's story to indicate that he is autonomous. On the contrary, the relentlessly unidimensional socialization to which he has been subjected and his unwillingness and, very likely, his inability to reshape his plans argue for his lack of autonomy. In view of Martin's insensitivity to his own responses to his experience, it is doubtful that he knows his own mind, and, in view of his blindered approach to life, it is clear that he does not engage in self-definition. He may be doing what he wants, but there is no reason to suppose that he is doing what he really wants.

In contrast, assuming that Sharon's self-assessments have been realistic and that, despite her father's early efforts to steer her in the direction of tennis, her decisions have been made without undue pressure from her father or her peers, Sharon's conduct is recognizably autonomous. Sharon meets life's possibilities head-on. She does not pretend that she knows what she wants without testing herself, and she is prepared to live by her own lights. Unlike Martin's, Sharon's self-direction reflects both her active engagement in shaping her self and her intimate knowledge of her evolving self. Sharon's commitment to sports was not there from the start, and it may eventually disappear—she might move to a geriatric specialty. If it does, however, Sharon seems the sort of person who will see this change as affording expanded possibilities for experience and who will seize the opportunity for personal development. Sharon demands much of life.

She expects fulfillment, not merely success as it is conventionally understood. What distinguishes Sharon from Martin and what leads us to attribute autonomy to Sharon is the spirit in which she lives and the way in which she makes her decisions.

My brief biography of Sharon illustrates a central feature of autonomous living. People direct their lives *episodically* and *programmatically*. Autonomous episodic self-direction occurs when a person confronts a situation, asks what he or she can do with respect to it— the options may include withdrawing from it as well as participating in it in various ways—and what he or she really wants to do with respect to it, and then executes the decision this deliberation yields. Autonomous programmatic self-direction has a broad sweep. Instead of posing the question "What do I really want to do now?" this form of autonomy addresses a question like "How do I really want to live my life?" To answer this latter question, people must consider what qualities they want to have, what sorts of interpersonal relations they want to be involved in, what talents they want to develop, what interests they want to pursue, what goals they want to achieve, and so forth. Their decisions about these matters together with their ideas about how to effect these results add up to a life plan.[1]

Sharon's semester-to-semester decisions to enroll in a variety of courses are instances of episodic self-direction. Each is a thoroughly considered decision made with Sharon's full appreciation of the advantages of this experimentation and the costs of declining to specialize early. Also, Sharon does not randomly register for these courses; she makes her choices methodically, based on her understanding of her needs and interests as well as her limitations. There is every reason, then, to believe that Sharon's course selections are autonomous and that her college program readies her to make an autonomous career choice. Though Sharon follows in her father's footsteps insofar as she chooses an occupation associated with sports, there is no reason to believe that she is not doing what she really wants to do.

From the standpoint of autonomy, what is wrong with Martin's semesterly decisions to avoid humanities and social science courses when possible and to neglect those that he must take is that these decisions are dictated by an overarching plan which Martin has adopted under the lifelong influence of his parents and without ever seriously looking into any other options. Indeed, the course of study Martin embarks upon is, if anything, designed to foreclose reconsideration of Martin's professional aspirations. Not only is Martin's college program heteronomous, but also this program reinforces the heteronomy of his career choice. Never having prepared himself to make an informed and thoughtful decision to undertake professional education, Martin does not take the occasion of applying to professional school to think over his objective.

It would be impracticable, however, for anyone to live autonomously if autonomy required that every action be cleared through self-aware deliberation. Sharon does not waste time reexamining her rejection of a professional tennis career each time an opportunity to rejoin the college team arises; she declines these offers without further ado. Thus, an adequate account of autonomy must explain how autonomous spontaneous conduct is possible, and, I shall urge, autonomous programmatic self-direction certifies the autonomy of many spontaneous actions. (For further discussion of the relation between autonomous life plans and the autonomy of particular acts, see part 3, sec. 3.)

Programmatically autonomous people have autonomous life plans. A life plan is a comprehensive projection of intent, a conception of what a person wants to do in life. Any life plan must include at least one activity that the agent consciously wants to pursue or a value that the agent consciously wants to advance or an emotional bond that the agent consciously wants to sustain. But most people want to enjoy a variety of goods, and their life plans must distribute their energy and time so as to satisfy these diverse desires. Typically, a life plan couples an ordering of assorted concerns and objectives with some notion of how to initiate progress toward fulfilling some of them and detailed schemes for ensuring the successful realization of others. Thus, different parts of a life plan are more or less fine-grained. Nevertheless, life plans are usually loose enough to allow for the inception and satisfaction of unanticipated desires.

People rightly regard their life plans as unfolding programs that are always subject to revision. Under closer scrutiny, an aim may be jettisoned; or, as the time to carry out a sub-plan approaches, it may be filled in with a more precise sequence of steps; and so forth. Life plans are dynamic. Yet, by introducing some degree of order into people's lives, life plans enable people to want more and to satisfy a greater number of their desires than random satisfaction-seeking possibly could.

As I have emphasized, the core of the concept of personal autonomy is the concept of an individual living in harmony with his or her authentic self. Life plans can be alien—they can be imposed by others, or they can manifest automatic conformity to popular conventions. However, life plans can also articulate the desires, both enduring and occasional, of the true self. Formulating a life plan affords individuals the opportunity to ask themselves what they really want and to puzzle out an answer. When they manage to answer correctly, their life plans mirror their authentic selves. (For treatment of this notion of a correct answer, see part 2, secs. 3–6.) Consequently, adhering to well-wrought life plans while attending to intermittent needs to adjust them ensures that these individuals' conduct will be congruent with their authentic selves. As a result, individuals who have carefully worked out life plans are less likely to suffer the psychic dissonance of persistent and irremediable regrets. (For further discussion of the relation between autonomy and regret, see part 2, sec. 1.) In both of these ways, life plans facilitate the harmony autonomy requires. Yet, since life plans can undergo frequent revision, they also support the vitality and openness to life's possibilities that are characteristic of autonomy.

Returning to Sharon and Martin, it is because Martin is relatively ignorant of and incurious about other options he might reasonably pursue, oblivious to the import of his negative feelings, and only concerned with others' expectations for him that his becoming a doctor is not autonomous. While this lack of autonomy with respect to his career choice does not entail that Martin is in no way autonomous— for example, he might make episodically autonomous medical decisions or take episodically autonomous stands within his profession—it is clear that a major component of his plan has not been checked against his self. (For the relation between episodic autonomy and nonautonomous life plans, see part 3, sec. 3.) In contrast, Sharon's approach to life plans is intensely personal and open-minded. On the basis of her appraisal of her dissatisfaction with her athletic experience and her knowledge of other occupations available to her, Sharon sensibly decides to seek employment elsewhere. While cognizant that her father will be disappointed to learn of her defection from tennis, she has not been made to feel that he will be devastated by her decision nor that she would be betraying him in going her own way. Though her decision covers the overall direction of her life, the way in which Sharon makes it and the context in which she makes it strongly suggest that it is an autonomous decision. When people formulate life plans paying attention to their own capabilities, inclinations, and feelings, and when they elect these plans unencumbered by coercive external pressures, their life plans are autonomous. Now, it might seem that the emphasis I have placed on life plans reserves autonomy for a self-aware, verbally sophisticated, intellectual elite. However, this is a misapprehension. Life plans should not be pictured as complicated, highly detailed flow charts spanning a lifetime. Rather, a life plan is a largely schematic, partially articulated vision of a worthwhile life that is suitable for a particular individual. Life plans provide some specific directions and a great deal of general guidance. Agents amplify and refine them as they feel the need to do so. In fact, I think that almost no sane person—with the possible exception of those who regularly lack basic necessities—is without a life plan.

From the standpoint of autonomy, however, the issue is not whether most people have life plans but whether anyone can be autonomous without one. In view of the profound influence of socialization, people can hardly assume that their first impulses reflect their true selves. Thus, the alternative to having a life plan is to consult one's self at length with regard to each and every personal decision, that is, to have no preaffirmed dispositions and no preestablished policies. But it is doubtful that anyone's life could meet this requirement. Not only would such a practice involve investing an inordinate amount of time in decision-making as opposed to acting, but also it is not clear what consulting one's self would involve if none of one's disparate decisions were ever consolidated into a life plan of any sort.

People's self-concepts stand in a reciprocal relation to their life plans. Life plans flesh out people's self-concepts in projected courses of conduct. Thus, people's growing insight into themselves as captured in their evolving self-concepts often ratifies but sometimes forces modifications in the life plans they embrace, and, contrariwise, carrying out their life plans often reinforces but sometimes calls for adjustments in people's self-concepts. Without life plans, then, the self-concepts against which people would check their decisions would be untested and, for that reason, tenuous. Compare, for example, the predicament of a pregnant teenager who is determined to become an Olympic sprinter and who believes that abortion is morally permissible, and the predicament of a pregnant teenager who has no firm goals or moral views. The former would have a clear reason to have an abortion and have it early, whereas the latter would have to rely completely on her feelings, intuitions, and arguments of the moment.

Since one's immediate responses to circumstances are likely to be strongly colored by one's upbringing, along with the peculiar features of those circumstances, there is little reason to suppose that those responses accurately represent one's authentic self. Though creating life plans is a piecemeal process and no one's life plans could possibly cover every contingency, life plans seem to be indispensable to autonomy.

Still, it is necessary to consider how life plans set the parameters of autonomous spontaneous conduct. Subsequent to her decision against a professional tennis career, Sharon spontaneously refuses all invitations to rejoin her college team; however, the facts that these refusals are congruent with her programmatic career choice and that this overall plan has not been called into question render these actions autonomous, too. Provided that Sharon remains alert to possible shifts in her inclinations—she would recognize and deal with feelings of boredom or other signs of dissatisfaction—there is no reason to doubt that her spontaneous actions represent her true self. Like Sharon, Martin has a life plan guiding his decisions, but the trouble with Martin's life plan is that it was not selected autonomously and is never reconsidered despite Martin's sense of subjection to arbitrary demands. Since Martin's life plan was adopted in deference to his parents, and since he does not attend to signs of dissatisfaction with it, the fact that he acts in accordance with this plan implies nothing about the autonomy of his conduct. When a person's spontaneous conduct accords with his or her current life plan and this plan has been chosen and remains in force autonomously, there is good reason to count this conduct as autonomous. For it is as much an expression of the agent's authentic self as episodically self-directed conduct is.

If the ontological conception of autonomy is mistaken, and if the conception of autonomy implicit in the contrast between Sharon's and Martin's stories is correct, it is clear that the main problem for a theory of autonomy is to explain how autonomous decisions are made. Whether episodic or programmatic, what makes the difference between autonomous and heteronomous decisions is the way in which people arrive at them—the procedures they follow or fail to follow. Autonomous people must be disposed to consult their selves, and they must be equipped to do so. More specifically, they must be able to pose and answer the question "What do I really want, need, care about, value, etcetera?"; they must be able to act on the answer; and they must be able to correct themselves when they get the answer wrong. The skills that enable people to make this inquiry and to carry out their decisions constitute what I shall call *autonomy competency*.[2]

This competency and its relation to the authentic self are explicated in detail in the remaining sections of this part; however, it is worth noting at this point that the procedures advocates of the free will conception of autonomy have proposed—autobiographical retrospection, detection and reconciliation of conflicts within the self, and identification with preferred components of the self—are among the skills needed for this competency. Yet, to be personally autonomous a person need not have a personality composed of original or immutable characteristics. Whether or not a person is autonomous depends on whether or not the person possesses and successfully uses the skills comprised by the competency of autonomy. An authentic self is a self that has autonomy competency and that emerges through the exercise of this competency.

Now, it might be pointed out that no one's life plan, however comprehensive it may be, can possibly provide for all contingencies. People are bound to encounter situations in regard to which their life plans are silent. Unless they are ridiculously cautious and slow to act, they will sometimes act in ways that neither accord with nor conflict with their life plans. Moreover, people may sometimes act spontaneously in ways that do conflict with their current life plans but that they do not regret. Thus, it seems doubtful that prior programmatic self-direction is the only way people can avoid heteronomous spontaneity.

Although programmatic self-direction provides a kind of insurance policy protecting people against their own worst impulses, it makes no sense to say that spontaneous action must have the imprimatur of a life plan in order to express the agent's true self. The true self is not merely a creation of a person's life plan, but neither is it a static core that life plans merely articulate. A reciprocal and dynamic relation holds between the true self and life plans.

Let us examine the case of Nancy, an adult who conceived a strong leadership propensity at an early age.[3] Let us suppose that Nancy does not question her ability to persuade others to follow her and that she has happily built a career and a network of friendships around her inclination to take charge. In short, she takes her leadership ability to be part of her authentic self, and she has incorporated it into her way of life by adopting such practices as joining community organizations where her skills will be appreciated and avoiding situations in which she would be likely to find herself in abrasive competition with other strong personalities. One day, despite a debilitating head cold, Nancy attends an organizational meeting for her church's Building Fund Committee. Feeling too tired to propound her own views and to impress her leadership qualities upon her associates, Nancy finds herself listening to others and being assigned an ancillary role in the group. Yet she does not resign, and at subsequent meetings she makes no attempt to secure her more accustomed position for herself. Is it possible that Nancy has acted autonomously?

Nancy has violated her life plan, but she has not necessarily acted heteronomously. On the one hand, if Nancy's response to her experience of rank and file participation is disgust or dismay, she may well have betrayed, however inadvertently, her true self. Yet, on the other hand, if Nancy finds herself relishing the intimacy and camaraderie of behind-the-scenes committee work, and if she interprets this unpremeditated outcome as a first step toward moderating a tendency to domineer over others that she now realizes she would gladly quell, it would make no sense to declare her action heteronomous. Since her true self seems to be in transition, a better characterization would be that her action is an autonomous expression of this evolving self. This view of the incident acknowledges the possibility of self-direction without advance deliberation, but it establishes a check on spontaneous autonomy. That check is provided by Nancy's ability to reflect on her conduct and determine whether or not she really wants to act that way.

Like the stories of Martin and Sharon, Nancy's story argues for regarding autonomy as the exercise of a competency. We have seen how anticipatory decision-making—both immediate and long-range—can be autonomous if it meets certain conditions. However, it would be odd to suppose that people are not doing what they really want to do unless they have previously confirmed that their conduct is expressive of their true selves. Such a supposition would amount to a presumption in favor of heteronomy which would require of autonomous people a degree of self-absorption and intellectuality incompatible with vital responsiveness to actual life situations. What Nancy's story shows is that autonomy can be the retrospective exercise of a competency.

Nancy is sufficiently attuned to herself to recognize signs of discord within herself—the evidence of this discord could have taken the form of disturbing feelings instead of unexpected behavior. Moreover, since Nancy is ready to act in accordance with a revised understanding of herself, she is capable of discovering that her self is changing, and she is capable of following this lead. Thus, she can retrospectively realize that her spontaneous conduct was an expression of her authentic self. In other words, she can retrospectively certify conduct as autonomous. The capacity to make such determinations is only intelligible if autonomy is the exercise of a competency.

Still, there remains a question about the individual who is basically self-satisfied, though not smug. Such people receive no warning signals from their selves, but, as long as they have the competency of autonomy, their conduct can be presumed to be autonomous though it is not the upshot of prolonged retrospective or prospective deliberation. Obviously, it is difficult to assess whether or not people like this have autonomy competency. They may be indifferent to their selves, rather than satisfied with them. (For further discussion of this problem, see part 2, sec. 4 and part 3, sec. 4.) They may be complacent about their conduct, rather than satisfied with it. Nevertheless, it must be possible for such people to have the requisite competency, for it is evident that those people who exercise this competency most skillfully will be satisfied with themselves and will seldom regret their conduct. (For further discussion of autonomy and regret, see part 2, sec. 1.) Thus, exercise of autonomy competency can be largely a background phenomenon—an ongoing sensitivity to one's self and a willingness coupled with an ability to deal with symptoms of discord within one's self.

Viewing autonomy as a competency allows us to evade the traps set by the primarily ontological account of the self without unhinging conduct from all standards of faithfulness to the self. (For criteria of autonomy competency, see part 2, sec. 4.) The difference between autonomous people and nonautonomous ones depends on the capabilities people have at their disposal and the way in which people go about fashioning their lives. Autonomous people are not vouchsafed a glimpse of their inner selves that other people are denied. Rather, they possess and exercise skills that maintain a fluid interaction between their traits, their feelings, their beliefs, their values, their extended plans, their current possibilities for realizing these plans, and their conduct. Nevertheless, it might be objected that autonomy is quite different from standard competencies, and I shall take the rest of this section to argue that autonomy does belong in this category.

\*       \*       \*

THERE ARE various kinds of competencies, which range from the wholly natural to the wholly conventional. In the biological realm, competency is the capacity of living tissue to react, and, in the legal realm, competency is the possession of the requisite qualifications to perform a designated act. But, in its more common usage, competency concerns a person's ability to perform an activity or to fill a social role. In this context, dubbing an individual competent can be disparaging—the appelation indicates only that the person is not noticeably unmeritorious—or it can be neutral—the appelation indicates sufficient ability without ruling out high praise. The latter of these senses adumbrates a conception of competency that is particularly illuminating in regard to autonomy.

Many activities do not draw on competencies that make it intelligible to compliment people admiringly for their performance. Biological processes and natural activities do not allow for such expressions of enthusiastic regard. Thus, for example, people are not said to be competent breathers or walkers. Furthermore, this exclusion extends to predominantly physical activities which make virtually no demands on the intelligence of their practitioners. Infantry soldiers, dishwashers, or assembly-line workers are not deemed competent except as a way of saying that they do a task satisfactorily. However, this way of speaking is meant to signal only that the individual being evaluated is willing to follow simple directions and perform a job that almost anyone could fill. It does not imply that the individual possesses a special competency needed for a particular line of work.

In contrast, when affirmation of someone's competence does not preclude high esteem, the affirmation presupposes that the activity makes special demands on the individual which can only be met by someone who possesses distinct capabilities. Thus, calling someone a competent cook, carpenter, pilot, chess player, musician, writer, or manager is compatible with calling someone an excellent cook, carpenter, pilot, chess player, musician, writer, or manager. All of these activities are complex, inasmuch as they can be carried out in a variety of ways which pose choices for the agent.[4] Moreover, none of them can be performed unless the agent possesses a repertoire of coordinated skills geared to the particular activity. Accordingly, I shall take a competency to be a repertoire of coordinated skills that enables a person to engage in a complex activity.

At this point, it might be suggested that there are upper limits, as well as lower limits, on the sophistication of the activities that will sustain a judgment of competence that does not rule out extravagant praise. For example, it might be urged that calling an aspiring painter competent can only mean that this individual is not sufficiently creative to merit the honorific "artist." Thus, it seems that, just as the most elementary activities do not presuppose competencies, neither do the most subtle and intricate activities.

While I would concede that art criticism has no use for the idea of competence apart from its condemnatory functions, I do not think that the practices of this unusually hyperbolic linguistic community are dispositive. Consider the case of singing. While it is clear that untrained vocalizing involves no special competency and that dubbing an opera star's performance competent is dismissive, there are many people who make a hobby of singing and who have acquired special skills, such as a knowledge of musical notation, in the pursuit of this avocation. Though the accomplishments of gifted artists go far beyond what is captured in the concept of a competency, the arts allow for competent but worthy participation. In view of this more modest yet by no means negligible level of attainment, it would be unduly restrictive to deny that the most subtle and intricate activities draw on competencies. Thus, the extraordinary complexity of autonomy is no bar to its being the exercise of a competency.

The examples of competencies I have cited suggest a number of features that competencies share. First, they presuppose native potentialities, but it is not possible to acquire the repertory of coordinated skills that makes up a competency outside a social setting. Individuals may have more or less aptitude with respect to a given complex activity—some people are born musicians while others are tone-deaf—and this potential for accomplishment may be more or less fully realized through instruction and practice—Mozart might not have blossomed into a child prodigy if his father had been an illiterate field-hand instead of a court composer. Thus, competencies are neither purely natural nor purely social. From this point of view, it is plausible to suppose that autonomy is a competency. It has been observed that some people display a remarkable facility for self-governance, whereas others must struggle to gain a modicum of control over their lives (Frankfurt 1971:17). Moreover, people who are endowed with considerable natural potential for autonomy sometimes confront repressive social environments that block its full development (Thalberg 1979:33–34). Accordingly, I shall assume that virtually all people have the inborn potential necessary for autonomy, but that they learn how to consult their selves through social experience.

A second feature characteristic of the competencies under consideration is that each has an overarching function. In the case of carpentry, it is the construction of wooden objects or buildings; in that of cooking, it is the preparation of nourishing and tasty dishes or meals. To the extent that the function requires it, a competency is rule-governed. Yet, competencies are open-ended inasmuch as they permit improvisation and some bending of the rules. Sound management practice may ordain that employees keep regular hours, but the phenomenon of the two-income family with young children may warrant instituting flextime work schedules. Still, competent performance has faults and excellences and admits of degrees of success. A chess game can be conducted hesitantly and cumbersomely, or it can be conducted fluently and incisively. Sometimes authors barely communicate their thoughts; other times they convey their thoughts vividly and forcefully. For each competency, the standards of achievement derive from the function the competency serves. Since each competency has its standards, a person who has the competency can err in exercising it. Nevertheless, communities of competent individuals (often there are competent experts who are not competent practitioners—for example, opera critics who cannot sing) are the ultimate arbiters of the adequacy and the merits of their performance. In this sense, competence depends on others' expectations and is conventional. Finally, it is interesting to note that the idea of a competency only seems to be applied to desirable activities. We do not talk about competent poisoners or competent tyrants, though we do talk about competent pharmacists and competent governors.

I shall reserve exploration of the relations between individual aptitude and autonomy and between autonomy and society for part 3, and I shall not take up the question of the goodness of autonomy until part 4. In what remains of part 2, I shall defend the claim that autonomy is the exercise of a competency by showing that an overarching purpose orders autonomous activity (sec. 3), that a repertory of skills is necessary for autonomy (secs. 4–6), and that there are standards which determine adequate exercise of this competency (sec. 4). In the process, I shall explicate autonomy competency.

# Self-Direction and Personal Integration

LIKE OTHER competencies, autonomy competency has an overarching function that determines what skills people must have at their disposal and how they must use these skills in order to exercise the competency successfully (part 2, sec. 2). That function, of course, is self-governance—controlling one's life by ascertaining what one really wants to do and by acting accordingly. But, since the nature of self-governance is itself mysterious, this characterization of the function of autonomy competency is unedifying, and the question immediately arises as to what more definite aim this competency could have that could be shown to support self-governance. I shall urge that the overarching function of the competency of autonomy is to secure an integrated personality. To have control over their lives and to be able to act spontaneously without compromising this control, people must have integrated personalities. Because the concept of an integrated personality requires an ordering of the personality without dictating the traits the personality must compass, integration provides for stability while respecting the uniqueness of individuals. Thus, it is singularly suited to account for unpremeditated yet autonomous conduct.

Programmatic self-direction and the life plans in which it is articulated should not be understood in an overly mechanical way. A life plan is not merely a list of projects, a schedule for undertaking them, and a set of strategies for carrying them out. Implicit in this agglomeration of projects is a conception of a desirable personality, and this conception may be more or less conducive to autonomy.

Completing a part of one's life plan does not simply add an item to a person's roster of accomplishments; fulfilling a particular plan insinuates itself into the individual's personality by weakening or reinforcing some of the individual's traits, by modifying the relations among them, or by engendering new ones. For example, a person—call him James—can inadvertently strengthen a tendency toward superficiality by overloading his agenda. Although people cannot anticipate all of the ways their projects will ramify in their personalities, it is evident that autonomous programmatic self-direction cannot ignore this dimension of life plans. Not only does the personality formed by an individual's activities affect that individual's ability to do other things, but also this self-defined personality becomes the individual's authentic self—that is, the measure of the autonomy of subsequent conduct.

This relation between conduct and personality formation does not entail that autonomous people are obliged to endorse any personality that happens to emerge from their activities. Life plans commonly include explicit personal ideals—conceptions of the traits and the relations obtaining among these traits that one thinks a good person embodies. Nevertheless, the personality forged by a person's activities may fail to coincide with this individual's personal ideal. Contemptuous of shallowness, overly busy James might be alarmed by his growing superficiality and deplore the self he sees developing.

Still, from the close tie between conduct and personality formation, it does follow that autonomous people—people who command the skills of autonomy competency—cannot disclaim responsibility for their selves. Assuming that he has autonomy competency, James could counteract his drift toward superficiality by arranging to concentrate on a few important concerns. However, if James is aware of his shallowness and is not dissatisfied with it—he may value variety over depth—or if he is mildly dissatisfied with it but does not care to check it, this trait will gradually be incorporated into his true self. Autonomy competency ensures that people are sufficiently reflective to have personal standards, sufficiently attuned to themselves to make it unlikely that they will overlook gross failings, and sufficiently ingenious to devise effective ways of correcting deficiencies. (For a detailed explication of the skills constitutive of autonomy competency, see part 2, sec. 4.) Though they are not infallible, their skills are well enough honed so that one can presume that, if they are not undertaking change, they are as they really want to be, at least for the nonce. Though disliked traits can be tenacious without gaining admission to the authentic self, liked and tacitly accepted traits make up the authentic self of a person who has autonomy competency.

An important advantage of the competency view of autonomy is that it recognizes that the authentic self is dynamic and explains how individuals can gain control over their selves, along with their conduct. Armed with a repertory of skills that enables them to comprehend and critically assess their own proclivities and that enables them to take steps to act in ways that reflect their own conclusions about how they should act, autonomous people indirectly shape their selves. But, since they can hardly be expected to pinpoint how particular acts or courses of action will affect their enduring traits, situational choice alone—even when the agent has autonomy competency— cannot account for the autonomous person's control over his or her self. The personal ideal component of life plans fills this gap. Not only does it provide general guidelines that find application in a broad range of circumstances, thus counterbalancing the pull of immediate circumstances; but also it provides individualized criteria of success, thus superseding merely cultural norms. The self of the person who exercises autonomy competency, then, is an authentic self—a self-chosen identity rooted in the individual's most abiding feelings and firmest convictions, yet subject to the critical perspective autonomy competency affords.

Self-direction is inextricable from self-definition (For additional consideration of this relation, see part 2, sec. 2.) To live in harmony with one's authentic self, one's current life plan must be consonant with one's contemporaneous authentic self, and one's evolving self must not persistently violate the personal ideal included in one's current life plan. Since measuring up to an ideal tailored to one's own dispositions, capabilities, and values is central to autonomy, it is necessary to ask whether there are any restrictions on the form or content of personal ideals. I shall argue that there are such restrictions and that autonomy is possible in part because of the structure of the autonomous personality.

That the spontaneous activity of autonomous people accords with their authentic selves implies that autonomy involves a state of mind akin to Benn's conception of coherence (part 2, sec. 1). This related state, I shall maintain, is personal integration. I have said that autonomous programmatic self-direction—the autonomous formulation and execution of life plans—certifies many spontaneous actions as autonomous (part 2, sec. 2). But if a person's life plans call for a welter of conflicting traits or goals, the individual will often be paralyzed by confusion and ambivalence. Moreover, such a person will rarely be able to act with confidence that the action satisfactorily represents his or her true self. It is my view, then, that both spontaneous and deliberate self-direction will be at odds with an individual's personality unless self-definition creates and sustains an integrated personality.[1]

This claim that the successful exercise of autonomy competency brings about an integrated personality could be challenged by arguing either that our intuitions about autonomy can be captured by a less exacting conception of the overarching aim of autonomy competency or that these intuitions necessitate a more exacting conception of this aim. It could be objected that integration is too strong an objective—in this view, mere sanity would suffice for autonomy—or that integration is too weak an objective—nothing less than happiness, in one view, or eccentricity, in another view, would suffice for autonomy. I shall argue that our understanding of autonomy is best advanced by placing minimal strictures on the ordering of the autonomous personality but that sanity alone is not sufficient to support autonomy.

Suppose that the maintenance of a non-psychotic personality were taken to be the overarching function of autonomy competency. In that case, an autonomous individual's personality could be severely fractured provided that it did not disintegrate into multiple personalities, hallucinations, or some other type of derangement. Consider, for example, Stanley, who has embarked upon a career in social work and who, in exactly similar circumstances, sometimes approaches his work with fiery ambition and dedication and sometimes approaches his work in a self-effacing and lackadaisical fashion. These periodic reversals are not produced by the ebbing and flowing of Stanley's vitality, nor are they induced by any feature of his social surroundings. They are simply products of attitude swings. Though no doubt neurotic, Stanley is sane. Assuming that Stanley regards these attitudinal changes as an acceptable aspect of a rich and varied personality and is not upset by them, it might be maintained that he is autonomous.

As I have set up this hypothetical, Stanley is not deluded about either his feelings or his behavior in regard to his vocation. Stanley knows that his attitudes run to extremes. Thus, it seems that he engages in self-definition and self-direction based on self-knowledge. Recognizing his attitudes for what they are, he accepts them and acts accordingly. A straightforward instance of autonomy, it would seem.

I believe, however, that this inference will not survive scrutiny. Concerning his work, Stanley lacks sustained attitudes that would give unity to his personality and regularity to his conduct. Yet, his attitudes are not compartmentalized. He does not confine one set of attitudes to one kind of situation and then, forgetting all about this first set of attitudes, exhibit the second set in a different kind of situation. He knowingly expresses opposite attitudes in identical situations. What can it mean to affirm that Stanley accepts his contradictory personality? Here, I would suggest, self-acceptance can only be a form of self-referential toleration, if it is not finally self-referential indifference.

Stanley could rationally think it ill-advised to attempt to stabilize his attitudinal swings. Perhaps he realizes that these swings provide a needed release for pent-up anxiety. Such a personality is compatible with a degree of autonomy, but it also is indicative of the extent to which autonomy has not yet been achieved. People can reasonably decide to tolerate such fragmentation temporarily in order not to block the psychological safety valve it provides. But, meanwhile, people striving for autonomy must be trying to ascertain their real attitudes and must be contemplating measures designed to remove the cause of the disturbance that the attitude swings subdue. Otherwise, there would be no reason to believe they were expressing their authentic attitudes, and there would be good reason to doubt that they were in control of their lives.

Stanley cannot autonomously endorse opposite attitudes as equally expressive of his authentic self. Suppose that Stanley's ambitious moments correspond to his goal of achieving prominence in his profession, while his self-effacing moments correspond to his goal of getting along with his co-workers. Assuming that Stanley correctly believes that his ambition annoys his associates and that his self-effacingness limits his chances of rising to the top of his profession, two conclusions are possible. Either Stanley has incompatible goals, or he has yet to discover an approach to his work that will enable him to secure both. If Stanley's goals are incompatible, he is not autonomous since he cannot avoid frustrating one of his desires. If Stanley's goals are simultaneously realizable but not by the means he is using, he is not autonomous, for he is failing to satisfy his authentic desires. Accordingly, a fragmented personality like Stanley's can be tolerated conditionally, but it cannot be accepted as one's authentic self.

Now, it might be countered that Richard Wollheim has convincingly defended self-toleration as the linchpin of the ideal personality. Wollheim starts from the contention that rational people must take a very different view of their beliefs, on the one hand, and their desires, on the other. As Wollheim puts it, "We require our beliefs to fit the world, but we require the world to fit our desires." (1984:53) Hence, rational people strive to secure a consistent set of beliefs. Otherwise, their beliefs could not match a possible world, and, insofar as their achieving their aims depends on their having true beliefs, they would be frustrated (Wollheim 1984:173). But, Wollheim maintains, rational people merely seek to render their desires coexistent (1984:175). Coexistent desires are ones that do not conflict in ways that the individual cannot tolerate, and an individual's level of tolerance depends on the point at which anxiety sets in (Wollheim 1984:184). Thus, toleration is geared to affective cues, and the capacity to tolerate intrapersonal conflict varies from person to person. But people are so attached to their desires that rationality counsels cultivating toleration for conflicting desires, rather than relinquishing desires in order to iron out conflicts among them.

Before considering the merits of Wollheim's position, it is important to distinguish his project from mine. Although Wollheim is interested in such questions as how people can be dominated by their pasts and how they can liberate themselves from such domination, Wollheim seems more concerned with the concept of a healthy life— what is neurosis? and how can persons free themselves from it?— than with that of an autonomous life. Since he never uses the language of autonomy and heteronomy, and since mental health and autonomy are plainly not identical, there is no reason to suppose that he is offering self-tolerance as an ideal for the autonomous personality.

Still, I do not wish to deny toleration a role in the autonomous life. It is clear that a person can have abiding desires that cannot be fully satisfied together and that it would be an impoverished conception of autonomy that required that one be expunged. However, there are some conflicts that are incompatible with autonomy even if they do not induce anxiety. When the fulfillment of opposed desires cannot be assigned to separate spheres or alternating occasions or when competing desires cannot be satisfied to an acceptable degree, the person who has them cannot ever do all that he or she really wants. Whether or not anyone can attain serene equanimity in regard to such vying impulses, people who have them have authentic selves that can never be adequately expressed. As a result, these people cannot be autonomous. (For the relation between desire-fulfillment and the dominance principle, see part 2, sec. 5)

At this juncture, it might seem that my line of argument pits autonomy against health. Apparently, the healthy person learns to tolerate conflicting desires, whereas the autonomous person opts for one or the other. However, this impression stems from Wollheim's oversimplification of the relation between beliefs and desires.

Wollheim overrates our attachment to our desires and therefore exaggerates the desirability of self-tolerance because he neglects the ways in which beliefs and desires interact. In its simplest form, this interaction involves factual beliefs and related desires. As a result of noticing that circumstances will not permit two desires to be satisfied and that circumstances are more conducive to the satisfaction of one of the desires, a person may find that the more viable desire is strengthened while the other is weakened and eventually disappears. The basic pattern can be varied in many ways. Although Jon Elster has disparagingly labeled this type of adjustment "adaptive preference formation" and there is no question that it can be pernicious, it is necessary to recognize that autonomy is one form of the art of the possible (Elster 1983:25). Elster's reservations notwithstanding, people who cannot adapt themselves to circumstances which are acceptable to them lose out on autonomy for no good reason. Thus, it is critical for autonomous people to be able to distinguish acceptable from unacceptable circumstantial constraints and to be able to distinguish unacceptable circumstantial constraints that they can change from ones that are fixed. This brings us to a second link between beliefs and desires.

A more complicated way in which beliefs and desires interact highlights Wollheim's excessively narrow conception of beliefs. When two of a person's desires conflict and one of the desires also conflicts with one or more of the individual's values, the desire that offends the person's values may be eroded and finally disappear. In regard to the issue of acceptable and unacceptable circumstantial constraints, beliefs about values enable people to discern which constraints should be resisted because they frustrate desires that are central to their authentic selves and which constraints pose no threat to their authentic selves. (For further discussion of the role of critical reason in autonomy, see part 2, sec. 4 and part 3, sec. 4.) Because Wollheim treats beliefs as if all beliefs concerned facts, he overlooks the profound and sometimes liberating effects that beliefs about values can have on people's desires. Assuming that there is no conflict between psychological health and commitment to personal values, toleration need not be viewed as the sole guarantor of health or, for that matter, as the chief one.

Still, it must be admitted that Stanley's attitude swings need not be outcroppings of anxiety or symptoms of competing desires. Let us suppose, instead, that Stanley accepts erraticism or, at least, unpredictable spontaneity as a constituent of his life plan. Perhaps, Stanley believes there are advantages in keeping his associates guessing or simply wants to avoid settling into stodgy middle age. In either case, wildly fluctuating attitudes will be one of the traits, if not the dominant trait, uniting Stanley's personality.

Although I think that freely chosen volatility is rare—most of the time erratic people just do not know what they really want—such a personality is in principle possible. However, it is important to notice that this type of personality would supply an exception to my claim that programmatic autonomy makes episodic, spontaneous autonomy possible. Accordingly, I shall urge, this type of personality could afford, at best, a truncated form of autonomy.

Most life plans presume the desirability of order and are then organized around a group of values, goals, emotional ties, and the like. What is distinctive about Stanley's self-chosen volatility is that his personality is organized around a blanket rejection of the orderly pursuit of satisfaction. Accordingly, Stanley endorses erraticism, but from this it does not follow that he endorses any of the actions he takes or any of the results he produces. Since no action or result is incompatible with the value of erraticism, it is vacuous to say that autonomously fulfilling the latter value transmits autonomy to the particular actions and results. The particulars of Stanley's life—his proximate desires and whatever springs from them—are merely tolerated in the name of the encompassing value of erraticism. Thus, Stanley has control over the general shape of his life but, curiously, not over his everyday activities. For this reason, he can hardly be said to be autonomous.

Sane but promiscuous self-acceptance is not a tenable basis for autonomy. Still, the advocate of a weak guiding aim for autonomy competency could argue that personal integration exacts more continuity than is necessary for autonomy. Many people's personalities are compartmentalized, at least in part. Such people present altogether distinct personae in different arenas though they have little or no awareness of these precipitous discontinuities. For example, an attorney, Jennifer, might be known to her colleagues as an aggressive, demanding, unforgiving overlord and to her family as an attentive, patient, tender parent, yet she might be completely oblivious to this radical cleavage. Though Jennifer's personality is compartmentalized, she is sane, and it might be urged that nothing bars her from being autonomous.

In keeping with this conclusion, it might be thought that a compartmentalized personality can be autonomous provided that a part of the self assumes command and directs the transformations from one persona to the next. In that case, the supreme self would be the individual's authentic self, and the individual would be living in harmony with this self.

Unfortunately, an overseer self of the kind envisaged violates one of the definitive features of compartmentalization. All people modulate their self-expressions according to circumstances—the openness appropriate among intimates is bizarre among strangers. However, the discrete sets of desires constitutive of compartmentalized personalities are incommensurable.[2] Whether because the aims characteristic of the respective compartments are incompatible yet compelling—Jennifer loves both her husband and her work, but her husband hates her working—or because the divisions erected between the compartments bar inter-compartmental comparison—at work, Jennifer cannot imagine her home-life clearly, and, at home, her work-life fades from view—people with compartmentalized personalities cannot gain an overview that would enable them to assess the relative merits of their discrepant sets of desires. A common symptom of compartmentalization is dismay and despair over the three-ring circus one's life has become. Compartmentalized people may profess a desire to change, but they lack a foundation from which to begin to unify their lives. Another common symptom of the incommensurability of compartmentalized desires is that compartmentalized people often defend themselves against this state of affairs by repressing awareness of the extent of the transformations they execute in moving from context to context. Thus, the perspective of a supreme self deliberately orchestrating a compartmentalized personality is not one that is available to such people.

If compartmentalization is to support autonomy, compartmentalized personalities must have as many authentic selves as they have compartments, and each of these authentic selves must find its outlet through a distinct persona in a distinct sphere of activity.[3] It is doubtful, however, that the compartmentalized personality is a manifestation of multiple authentic selves. People do not usually become compartmentalized by entering different situations and figuring out how to express themselves in a socially viable manner. More likely, such people's collocations of traits and the divisions between them are formed reactively. Someone who feels compelled to blend into disparate social milieus accomplishes this assimilation by imitating models and conforming to accepted norms. Jennifer's insecurity about matching the hard-hitting practices that prevail among male attorneys might prompt her to sharply divide her behavior at the law office from her behavior at home. Rather than striking a balance between her own style and the conventions of her profession, Jennifer overcompensates and mimics (indeed, she outdoes) her successful colleagues. But, since she cannot transfer her legal persona to the context of family life, compartmentalization sets in. Absorption of social imperatives, not projection of the self, typically brings about compartmentalization. Thus, compartmentalization obscures the authentic self and prevents people from living in harmony with their authentic selves.

Finally, it is worth noting that, contrary to what might be expected, compartmentalization undercuts people's control over their lives. Compartmentalization might be seen as a way of coping with the extremely different contexts into which people choose to enter or are thrust willy-nilly. By assuming a guise suitable for each context, the individual can function more effectively in each. While it is undeniable that people can lose control over their lives by trying to inject a rigid personality into unyielding situations, compartmentalization is not a satisfactory solution from the standpoint of autonomy.

Flexible adaptation need not collapse into compartmentalization. People need neither ignore their selves nor repress their awareness of the adjustments they are making. If they do, the resulting fragmentation of their personalities blinds them to the ways in which their conduct in one sphere can affect their activity in others. The compartments into which compartmentalized personalities partition both themselves and their worlds are seldom impermeable. But for the most part compartmentalized personalities perceive only one box at a time and act as if each were airtight. This problem is the reverse of the one we found in the case of the deliberately erratic person. Whereas deliberate erraticism sacrifices episodic autonomy for the sake of an overarching value, compartmentalization jeopardizes global control for the sake of narrow situation-specific control. Lacking self-knowledge and letting circumstances define their traits, compartmentalized personalities are, at best, marginally self-directing.

While it is undeniable that sanity is necessary for autonomy, some of the minor disorders that sanity countenances are inimical to autonomy. The erratic person's and the compartmentalized person's limited ability to achieve autonomy can be traced to their lack of reasons for their attitudes, feelings, and conduct. In neither case does the individual recognize the continuum of circumstances from one situation to another or from one time to another. Thus, neither responds in similar ways to the similar circumstances threaded through their lives. Stanley randomly reacts to his professional undertaking; Jennifer systematically ignores, for example, the emotional needs of her subordinates while caring deeply for those of her family members. Although people do change—sometimes dramatically—what is a reason for a person at one moment rarely ceases to be a reason for that person an instant later. In any event, reasons for a person do not sporadically burst back and forth in and out of existence. Self-directing people are not simply driven to behave one way or another. They act in accordance with their own reasons. Fractured personalities are incapable of autonomy to the extent that they are incapable of sustaining reasons, and they are incapable of sustaining reasons to the extent that they are fractured.

In contrast, integrated personalities are complex and evolving, yet unified. Saints and monsters apart, integrated personalities exhibit apparently incompatible qualities which surface in different ways suitable to different situations. People with integrated personalities need not behave the same way at fractious political meetings and in bed with their lovers. They are not saddled with packages of static, preblended properties. Still, since an integrated personality cannot be an overtly conflictual or a compartmentalized one, integrated personalities support autonomy in ways that merely sane personalities do not.

When asked what a person is like, we mention a distinctive set of dominant qualities—a set of what I shall call characterological strands. These strands can be stylistic qualities (vivacity or melancholy), virtues (patience), vices (arrogance), or foibles (excitability); they can be ways of processing experience (careful sifting of accumulated evidence or quick intuition); they can be ardently held principles ("the environment must be saved from the ravages of toxic waste"); they can be commitments to a role (community leader), to a career (film director), or to other people (one's children). In an integrated personality, the same characterological strands are not in evidence at all times—that is one difference between an integrated and an obsessive personality. Moreover, a characterological strand is not invariably associated with the same evanescent traits. Excitability, for instance, might be conjoined with enthusiasm about a new play or with determination to win an election. Nevertheless, in an integrated personality, as opposed to a compartmentalized or otherwise disjointed one, characterological strands unite the disparate elements of the true self. These characterological strands ground the reasons that govern the autonomous individual's conduct.

An integrated personality displays both constancy and variability. What, then, is the difference between the diverse manifestations of an integrated personality and those of a fragmented one? In other words, how is an integrated personality constant? We can begin to answer these queries by ruling out two modes of constancy.

Since the circumstances in which people must act vary enormously, integration cannot require that there be at least one characterological strand that the person's conduct expresses in all situations. Of course, we could say that all integrated personalities must exhibit responsiveness to changing circumstances. But this quality would not account for integration; it equally typifies certain fractured personalities. Furthermore, it would be counterproductive to insist that integrated personalities must unfailingly express some more definite trait—such as volubility or reserve—since this requirement would render integrated personalities maladapted in some of the situations they are likely to encounter. No characterological strand that could plausibly be said to unify a personality can be expressed appropriately in all circumstances (Mischel 1973:258).

Furthermore, since the circumstances in which people must act sometimes change tremendously from moment to moment, requiring that succeeding characterological strands overlap would also impose an excessively strong conception of unification. The idea would be to ensure continuity by requiring that a person's conduct in successive situations blend gradually into conduct befitting each new one. While it is undeniable that the characterological strands an integrated personality has been projecting in one situation often carry over into a new situation, it seems possible for a personality to be integrated without always meeting this requirement. Especially when a person must move rapidly between extremely different circumstances, this criterion may not be met. The somber sympathy befitting a morning funeral might rapidly give way to the gay jubilation befitting a wedding scheduled for that afternoon. Surely, occasional radical transformations would not condemn a personality to fragmentation.

A more plausible conception of integration would hold that, in similar circumstances, similar characterological strands are expressed, and, when circumstances beyond the individual's control do not powerfully militate against it, expression of some characterological strands extends from one situation to the next. In an integrated personality, characterological strands normally wax and wane rather than bursting in and out, and some characterological strands may be virtual constants in the individual's conduct. Nevertheless, to allow for the fact that integrated personalities can sometimes fail to exhibit such interweaving, it is necessary to consider what other relations obtain among an integrated personality's characterological strands.

From this standpoint, what is striking about integrated personalities is that their constituent characterological strands can be grouped and regrouped in indefinitely many ways. For the most part, their characterological strands do not clash, nor are these strands clustered in discrete collocations. This fluidity makes the overlapping of the integrated personality's characterological strands possible. Moreover, it explains why the integrated personality is unified even when a person who has an integrated personality acts in discontinuous ways.

To illustrate, consider the case of Julia, one of whose characterological strands is an even temper. Julia's unflappability allows her both to enjoy the company of people with whom she firmly disagrees without abandoning her own convictions and also to ease interpersonal conflicts without belying her assessment of where justice lies. Nevertheless, she sometimes gets angry, but, when she does, she usually feels that a calm response would have been too mild in view of the magnitude of the offense that provoked her anger.

Two points are notable here. First, Julia's even temper is adapted to a wide range of circumstances. It is a characterological strand that can be combined with many others, including sociability and judiciousness. But, second, her even temper does not prevent Julia from expressing warranted outrage. It is a dominant, but not an invariant feature of Julia's personality. Since irritation is a departure from Julia's usual balance, the latter trait links her conduct in various situations though it may temporarily be in abeyance. Thus, the characterological strands of an integrated personality are amenable to and are exhibited in numerous combinations. Unifying without fossilizing the integrated personality, these characterological strands establish the groundwork for the autonomous person's distinctive identity, and they enable the autonomous person to project this identity while responding appropriately to diverse situations.[4]

Complementing and completing this ordering of the integrated personality's characterological strands is a self-referential component. An integrated personality is not self-condemnatory; that is, such persons do not detect traits in themselves which they abhor but which they cannot expunge, and they are not dejected by the ways in which their traits are expressed in action. (For further discussion of the relation between autonomy and regret, see part 2, sec. 1.) In sketching Julia's case above, I emphasized that she does not regard her anger as alien and disruptive pique. Rather, she is satisfied that it is only aroused in proportion to serious threats to her integrity—or, at any rate, that it never gets so far out of hand that it leads her to mistreat other people or to engage in self-defeating conduct. If this were not so, Julia could not have an integrated personality, for she would be in conflict with herself. In sum, integration requires that one's characterological strands match one's personal ideal.

To meet this criterion, people need not introspect often—the willingness to recognize and inquire into the reasons for personal dissonance suffices. Moreover, they need not altogether refrain from self-criticism—autonomy entails neither perfect insight into one's self nor splendid choices regarding conduct. Nevertheless, integrated personalities must generally be content with themselves. Unlike people with sane, but fragmented personalities, people with integrated personalities are able to act spontaneously without incurring persistent regrets.

In sum, to achieve an integrated personality through the exercise of autonomy competency is to have a personality marked by characterological strands that are amenable to combination and recombination both amongst themselves and also with various evanescent traits. On the one hand, the characterological strand requirement ensures that autonomous individuals have distinct identities—that these individuals do not simply adapt to variable circumstances. People with integrated personalities have reasons for acting as they do. On the other hand, the mixability requirement ensures that autonomous individuals' identities allow them to act appropriately in a wide range of circumstances without betraying themselves—that is, to control their lives by projecting their own beliefs, desires, values, and so forth in suitable ways. The reasons stemming from an integrated personality's characterological strands regularly find expression in that individual's life. In addition, to have an integrated personality is to be satisfied—whether explicitly or implicitly—with one's traits and the ways in which these traits find expression in action. This self-approval requirement ensures that, when deciding how to act, autonomous individuals will not seek to suppress constituents of their identities and also that, when acting spontaneously, autonomous individuals will still do as they really want. In other words, self-approval arising from the exercise of autonomy competency indicates that one does not regard one's self as alien and thus that the self that one expresses is one's authentic self. When integrated personalities are achieved through autonomy competency, people have reasons of their own.

Characterological strands must unify the autonomous personality, and indiscriminate self-acceptance cannot adequately unify it. Thus, integration is necessary for autonomy. Still, it might seem that integration is too paltry an aim to subsume autonomy competency. Beyond this, it might be urged, autonomy should bring sufficient satisfaction to make autonomous people happy.

One reason to think that happiness is the guiding aim of autonomy competency is that the autonomous individual's existence is harmonious. Since, as I have acknowledged, autonomy may involve adjustment to outward circumstances, it seems to follow that autonomous people will establish an equilibrium between their selves and their environment which will secure their happiness. Of course, I do not deny that autonomous people can be happy; however, it is a mistake to hold that autonomous people must be happy.

Take the case of a pair of artists at the beginning of the twentieth century. Both are experimenting with bright pigments which they apply to their canvases in bold swathes, and both exhibit their work in the Salon des Independants. The day after the opening the reviews appear, and every critic mocks their entries. One critic contemptuously dismisses them as "Les Fauves"—the wild beasts. This ridicule affects these two artists very differently. Maxine is humiliated by it; Henri delightedly adopts the label and takes it as a confirmation of the revolutionary force of his work. These artists' fundamental values prevent them from retreating from their common course. Despite her dejection over the critics' unanimous condemnation, Maxine cannot abandon her style in order to gain popular approval without surrendering her artistic integrity. Yet, this artist is not so grandly indifferent to public humiliation that she is not stung by it. Plainly, autonomy will not ensure Maxine's happiness, at least not for the foreseeable future. In contrast, Henri is shielded from the critics' onslaught and can at once uphold his artistic values and be happy.

Unhappiness can arise from various sources, two of which are particularly germane to the issue of autonomy. People can be unhappy with themselves, or they can be unhappy with their position in the world (or both). Unhappiness with one's self is incompatible with autonomy. For such unhappiness stems either from one's failure to become the sort of person one wants to be (failure with respect to self-definition) or from one's failure to act in accordance with one's authentic self (failure with respect to self-direction). But since autonomous people do not suffer from chronic regret, this type of unhappiness is ruled out. (For the relation between autonomy and regret, see part 2, sec. 1.) But unhappiness with one's position in the world is compatible with autonomy. For, rightly or wrongly, the world may be inhospitable to one's true self, and one may lack the power to win it over. Autonomous people may be unable to arrange for a sufficiently receptive environment to guarantee their own happiness, and autonomy may forbid the very compromises with conventionality that would secure contentment. Thus, happiness is too comprehensive an aim for autonomy competency to serve.

At this juncture, someone might concur that happiness and autonomy can conflict but insist that this is because happiness is too banal an objective to govern autonomy. Furthermore, in this view, personal integration is to be equally despised for being too mundane an objective. To be autonomous, according to this position, a person must be eccentric. Unless people distinguish themselves from the masses as well as from their immediate surroundings, they have no way of knowing that they are not common conformists. The attraction of this view is that it establishes a stark contrast between autonomy and heteronomy and provides a litmus test for autonomy. It is not enough to be a beatnik in Greenwich Village; one must be a beatnik in Greenwich, Connecticut, to qualify as autonomous.

To glorify eccentricity in this way is to assume that every true self is startlingly different from every other true self or that autonomy is reserved for an elite who possess extraordinary true selves. Although there is good reason to believe that true selves are more varied than appearances suggest, there is no reason to believe that true selves bear hardly any resemblance to one another. After all, these selves belong to a single species. Furthermore, requiring autonomous people to be eccentric would establish society as the ultimate arbiter of autonomy since no one could be autonomous without rebelling against social conventions. Thus, autonomy would inflict an inverted brand of social bondage on the individual. Finally, there is no reason to espouse an elitist theory of autonomy since the requirement that autonomous people be eccentric is at bottom beholden to the free will construal of autonomy that I have sought to discredit (part 2, sec. 2). Eccentricity proves that the individual has transcended socialization, if not that the individual has succumbed to lunacy. But a mark of such transcendence is beside the point, once autonomy is recognized as the exercise of a competency.

People can be autonomous without being happy, and they can be autonomous without being abnormal. Yet, autonomy is conducive to felicity, and it honors the uniqueness of individuals, for an integrated personality is both harmonious and distinctive. While it is undeniable that a person can occasionally act autonomously without having achieved an integrated personality, an autonomous life requires an integrated personality. People can consistently control their lives and express their authentic selves only when they sustain integrated personalities by exercising autonomy competency.

# SECTION 4

# Autonomy Competency

I HAVE argued that the problem of the authentic self is best interpreted procedurally (part 2, sec. 2). Autonomous people must be able to pose and answer the question "What do I really want, need, care about, believe, value, etcetera?"; they must be able to act on the answer; and they must be able to correct themselves when they get the answer wrong. To perform these tasks, people must have autonomy competency—the repertory of coordinated skills that makes self-discovery, self-definition, and self-direction possible. The authentic self is the evolving collocation of traits that emerges when someone exercises autonomy competency. To be autonomous, then, a person must possess and successfully use the skills constituting autonomy competency.

Although Rawls does not label it as such, his discussion of rational choice in regard to life plans provides a partial account of this competency (1971:410–423). According to Rawls, rational choice in regard to life plans concerns the good of individuals. By making choices in accordance with a set of principles of rational choice and with deliberative rationality and by carrying out decisions made in this way, people ensure their own happiness (Rawls 1971:123). For many people, this view of rationality seems to be correct; through some such process, people often succeed in promoting their own welfare. But, since many people are happy quite coincidentally, rationality in regard to life plans is not necessary for happiness. Moreover, since many people who scrupulously deliberate about their decisions seem to be inveterately miserable, this form of rationality does not seem to be sufficient for happiness. (For further discussion of the tenuous link between autonomy and happiness, see part 2, sec. 3.) As Kant observed, reason can be inimical to happiness, and instinct could have secured this good much more efficiently (1959:11).

Ironically, it seems to have been Kant's influence on Rawls that led Rawls to associate rational choice in regard to life plans with happiness. As is well known, the only form of individual autonomy Kant recognizes is moral autonomy—the autonomy of a rational will giving universal laws to itself. Any choice involving emotions, goals, or other quotidian concerns is heteronomous, on Kant's view. In short, there is no room in Kant's lexicon for "personal autonomy." Duly impressed by Kant's insights into the relation between reason and morality, Rawls applies the term "autonomy" to the moral realm. People are autonomous insofar as they adhere to principles that would be chosen in the original position—these are the principles of free and equal, rational beings (Rawls 1971:252–253). However, unduly impressed with Kant's contempt for instrumental reason, Rawls reserves the term "autonomy" for the moral realm and is blinded to the possibility of autonomy in personal matters. (For a similar view of Rawls' position, see Sandel 1982:164.) He is thus obliged to locate the good of rationality in regard to life plans elsewhere.

Free of the Kantian lexicon and taking a cue from conventional usage, we can entertain the idea of personal autonomy, and, as a result, we can better situate Rawls' treatment of rational choice in regard to life plans. If personal autonomy requires the exercise of a competency that enables people to answer the questions "What do I really want, need, care about, believe, value, etcetera?" and "How can I act on my understanding of myself?" it is obvious that we cannot understand this competency without an account of rational choice in the personal sphere. Rawls proffers just such an account.

Rawls enumerates several principles which aid in the selection of life plans. These principles enjoin people to opt for the plan that is an effective means to a settled end, for the plan that makes it possible to achieve more ends than other available plans, and for the plan that is more likely than other available plans to succeed (Rawls 1971:411–412; see also D. Richards 1971:28–29). In addition, Rawls commends postponing decisions until pertinent information becomes available (1971:410, 420). In a more intuitive vein, he suggests keeping in mind the ways in which decisions interact and shape one's life, trying to give one's life plan a "certain unity, a dominant theme," and avoiding a roller coaster ride of exaltation and misery (1971:411, 420–421). Rawls sums up these recommendations as follows:

> a person's plan of life is rational if, and only if, (1) it is one of the plans consistent with the principles of rational choice when these are applied to all the relevant features of his situation, and (2) it is that plan among those meeting this condition which would be chosen by him with full deliberative rationality, that is, with full awareness of the relevant facts and after a careful consideration of the consequences. (1971:408)

Rawls' view is that, through a sensitive but rigorous and informed sifting of their options, individuals can discover what is good for them. Each can elect that course of conduct which best suits his or her self.

Rawls' account of rationality in regard to life plans has two components—the principles of rational choice and deliberative rationality. The principles of rational choice guide decisions once a number of conditions have been met. Deliberators must know what sorts of things are important to them, must estimate the relative intensity of their desires, must order their preferences consistently, and must envisage alternative plans of action (Rawls 1971:418–419; see also D. Richards 1971:30–31). Until these tasks have been completed, the principles of rational choice cannot be deployed. The job of sufficiently organizing and articulating the deliberator's viewpoint to provide material for the principles of rational choice to work on is assigned to deliberative rationality.

Evidently, the power of the principles of rational choice is severely limited. I suspect that most people would say that, once their desires, values, aims, and so forth are clear enough for the principles of rational choice to be applied, it is usually obvious what they should do. At this point, applying the principles is either superfluous or merely serves as a check on especially important decisions. Thus, it seems that Rawls packs the main problems of autonomy into the comforting phrase "deliberative rationality." The most complicated, indeed, the downright mystifying, phenomena of self-knowledge and self-definition are all covered by this expression. Although Rawls offers a few hints about how to achieve deliberative rationality—for example, seek a dominant theme, and avoid extreme ups and downs—his account is radically incomplete.

When formal decision rules are inapplicable, people are obliged to advert to their inclinations and feelings. They must rely on affective cues—such as frustration or gratification and shame or pride—to guide their judgments. For example, a person who is feeling frustrated must determine whether this trouble stems from a particular condition which could be avoided without major alterations in the individual's life plans or whether it is symptomatic of a need for a radical change in life directions. Reading feelings of this kind enables people gradually to identify integral sentiments, propensities, values, and goals.

Plainly, this process of self-reading involves a number of faculties and draws on each of these faculties in more than one way. By introspecting, a person notices self-referential responses, tracks the relations between these responses, and probes these responses to figure out their possible sources. But since people are not always able to discern the origins of a vexing self-referential response through simple introspective perception, this inquiry into the possible sources of self-referential responses may bring five additional faculties—memory, imagination, verbal communication, reason, and volition—into the self-reading process. Both memory and imagination may join forces with instrumental reason to generate tentative explanations of the self-referential response under scrutiny. (For an illuminating treatment of the workings of imagination in this process, see Wollheim 1984:79–90.) Often, however, people need the additional stimulation of others' interpretations of their situation in order to notice self-referential responses or in order to find plausible explanations of these responses. When this is so, conversation becomes central to the self-reading process. Once a person has assembled some proposed explanations of a self-referential response, deciding among them may require a sort of informal experimentation. Either by imagining themselves in situations in which a candidate explanation would be operative—this imaginative project is sometimes carried out alone, sometimes in discussion with friends—or by actually placing themselves in such situations, people find out what their self-referential responses will be. They thereby test their hypotheses about themselves and develop a self-portrait.

But an accurate self-portrait is not yet autonomy. People who know what they are like but despise themselves or systematically suppress their own desires, attachments, values, and so forth, lack integrated personalities and are not autonomous. In addition to self-discovery, self-definition and self-direction are necessary for autonomy. Autonomous people can adjust their own characteristics along with their behavior to match their respective conceptions of what kind of people they should be and what kind of life is worthwhile. (For the role of personal ideals in life plans, see part 2, sec. 3.) Autonomous people must be able to envisage life plans, and they must be able to fulfill the standards implicit in these plans.

Obviously, someone's concocting plans that far outstrip that person's abilities contributes nothing to autonomy. The life plans of autonomous people must be relative to the resources of the individuals who adopt them. On the one hand, they must set standards that these individuals could fail to meet, but, on the other hand, these standards must be ones that these individuals can realistically hope to attain. Thus, the process of establishing such plans starts from a person's self-portrait. But it is important to remember that this self-portrait is not static. People who succeed in making changes they believe in must adjust their self-portraits to keep abreast of these developments, and it may become appropriate for them to modify their personal ideals and goals in light of their revised self-concepts. Thus, the enterprises of self-discovery and self-definition are intertwined, and, as we shall see, the enterprises of self-definition and self-direction are inseparable, too.

How are life plans formed? First, memory, imagination, and instrumental reason, usually enhanced through conversation with others, enable people to envisage options—to conceive of combinations of traits they could embody and aims they could pursue. Of course, these concepts vary in scope. They can concern the details of an individual's personality or commitments, or they can concern the broad outlines of an individual's ambitions. However, for present purposes, what is important is the process through which individuals assess the relative merits of these alternatives.

Evaluation of an option (or an array of options) requires the generation of desirability-characterizations (or comparative desirability-characterizations) and the exposition of the circumstances surrounding the option (or options) (Gauthier 1963:43–44; for related discussion of the interplay between introspection and self-interpretation, see Wollheim 1984:167–173). A desirability-characterization is a reason for acting which may point out the fact of someone's wanting to do so or other goods contingent upon so acting. Often it is necessary to divide an option into components or to exhibit the relations between an option and seemingly independent concerns before beginning to evaluate it. David A. J. Richards aptly calls this type of practical analysis "parsing" and observes that it is among the "fundamental features of human rationality" (1971:44). With a parsed option at hand, a person can produce an acceptably subtle, yet perspicuous desirability-characterization of it.

Two basic approaches to this kind of practical evaluation stand out. First, desirability-characterizations can appeal directly to felt self-referential responses. Presented with options, people can ask themselves how they would feel about being this way or that or behaving in this way or that. Their attraction to or aversion from the prospect provides a reason for or against the option, and the strength of their attraction or aversion enables them to rank various options. For example, suppose that Brian feels deeply resentful of his parents but that he is very fond of his brother. While he finds attachment to his parents smothering, his bonds to his sibling bring him a secure sense of belonging. This constellation of responses might provide the basis for Brian's attraction to a practice of taking his brother's side when the latter comes into conflict with their parents. And this attraction supports Brian's pursuing this course.

Yet, complementing this experiential procedure is a second one that emphasizes critical rationality. Desirability-characterizations can invoke values that do not directly depend on the deliberator's feelings or inclinations. Charles Taylor helpfully characterizes them as "articulations" (1976:294–296). Again, in the case of Brian, let us suppose that his preferences regarding filial respect are firmly negative. He might nevertheless become persuaded of the warrant for filial respect (in at least some contexts) once he has appreciated its connection with the broader and, let us assume, undisputed values of forbearance and loyalty. This view of Brian's relations to his parents would raise doubts about his fraternal partisanship and would at least argue for giving his parents' ideas a sympathetic hearing. By identifying the various reasons which support an option—both those deriving from one's felt self-referential responses and those deriving from critical rationality—and assessing these reasons in light of the overall impact that adopting the option is likely to have, people gain insight into the relative merits of the options available to them.

The preceding discussion might strike some readers as too relativistic. Are there not, it might be asked, universal goods that people *should* want to obtain, regardless of whether they do in fact want to attain them? Are there no values that all autonomous lives must share?

In answering these questions, it is important to remember that we are not concerned with moral autonomy, but rather with personal autonomy, and that personal autonomy operates within the realm of the morally permissible. While there may be substantive as well as formal and procedural goods that all morally autonomous lives exhibit, there is little reason to expect that all personally autonomous lives will likewise share a set of substantive goods.

The leading phenomenon of personal autonomy is human diversity. Unless one is impressed by the uniqueness of individuals, and unless one delights in this variegation, one will not suppose that these unique personalities should somehow be manifest in people's lives, and one will never wonder how personal autonomy is possible. Of course, this uniqueness does not entail that people have nothing in common. Still, it does entail that not everyone shares all of the same qualities and that no one's mix of qualities duplicates anyone else's. If this is so, and if self-governance means giving expression to one's own qualities, self-governing people will create a variety of lives incarnating a variety of substantive goods. Talented athletes who lack musical aptitude or aesthetic sensibility need not struggle to master the violin or even to enjoy the fine arts. Likewise, talented musicians who lack athletic ability or enthusiasm for sports need not invest their time in skiing lessons or spectator sports. Arguably, each of these groups is missing something, but it need not be autonomy. For only individuals can be the measure of their own autonomy. Apart from the formal good of an integrated personality (part 2, sec. 3) and the procedural good of autonomy competency, autonomous lives are remarkable more for their differences than for their similarities. To affirm a list of universal personal goods or an account of an objectively good personal life and to maintain that every autonomous life must realize such goods is to deny the uniqueness of individuals. It is to create a mold that autonomous lives must inevitably break.

Now, as presented so far, self-definition may seem a highly, perhaps excessively, abstract exercise. But such criticism overlooks the active side of this process. In an important respect, the process of deciding whether to adopt a personal ideal parallels the process of constructing a self-portrait. It couples trying out options with introspective reflection on and discussion of the results. To some extent, proposals for personal change can be examined imaginatively. But, once straightforwardly unacceptable options have been eliminated in this way, trial runs are often indispensable. If Brian opts to support his brother obdurately regardless of what his parents have to say, he may end up feeling embarassed by his childish adamancy, or he may feel exhilarated by the camaraderie that unequivocal support for his brother has generated. Often people's feelings prove to be an amalgam of favorable and unfavorable responses which need to be sorted out and assessed. Nevertheless, it is ultimately by acting on an option (perhaps, repeated trials or variations will be necessary) that people confirm its advisability or decide they have erred. Furthermore, as Aristotle points out, it is by acting on one option or another that people reinforce or weaken different aspects of their personalities (*Nicomachean Ethics,* 1114a 5). Thus, self-direction is necessary to self-definition.

At this stage, volition assumes the paramount role. Unless people are able to carry out the plans they elect, their inquiries will be nugatory. Two volitional modes are necessary to autonomy—resistance and resolve. To be self-directing, a person must be able to resist unwarranted pressure from other individuals—Brian cannot allow his brother to buy him with the promise of affection; must be able to resist automatic conformity to societal norms—Brian cannot bow to his parents simply because convention requires him to defer to them; and must be able to resist impulses stemming from disapproved traits or discredited beliefs—Brian cannot continue to dismiss his parents once he has been persuaded that he owes them a measure of respect. In virtue of self-knowledge and self-definition, a person is in a position to distinguish the forces that should be resisted from those that should be vented.

Important as resistance is, however, self-direction would be reduced to quiescence without resolve. Resolve is a person's determination to act on his or her own judgments. Though people may change their minds as a result of making an experiment based on their own deliberations, refusing to try out a creditable possibility compromises autonomy. Brian might be reluctant to defy social norms and ally himself with his brother, yet this may be the most authentic projection of his self. What the overly timid person really wants may well be the very thing this person balks at undertaking. Moreover, even if it turns out that this is not what he or she really wants, the failure to make that determination would blur the individual's self-portrait and possibly distort future deliberation. Needless to say, people's resistance and resolve are commonly reinforced by the support of their associates. Nevertheless, since such emotional sustenance is not always forthcoming—others may have all sorts of reasons for not wanting one's authentic self to be expressed—autonomous people need to be capable of standing by their own judgments despite the opposition or faint encouragement of others.

The autonomous individual is engaged in a dynamic process of meshing a self-portrait with a life plan that provides for an integrated personality. Indispensable to autonomy is the exercise of a competency which comprises an ingrained disposition to consult the self, a capacity to discern the import of felt self-referential responses as well as independent beliefs, values, and goals, and a capacity to devise and carry out conduct congruent with the self. Skillful exercise of autonomy competency not only enables people to correct perceived faults, but also it enables them to arrange their lives so as to give fuller expression to accepted qualities. In sum, it makes it possible for people to develop a sure sense of their own identities and to act accordingly—that is, to be self-governing.

At this juncture, three serious objections could be raised against this account of autonomy. First, although autonomy is usually enhanced by discussion with other people, autonomy seems to isolate people emotionally from one another. Autonomous people would be parasitic on others, but not emotionally attached to them. Second, since autonomous deliberation is a complex and difficult process, the pursuit of autonomy would consume so much of people's lives that they would fail to experience other important values. An autonomous life would be an impoverished life. Third, since autonomous deliberation is a looping process in which decisions made through the exercise of autonomy skills remain subject to the test of subsequent beliefs, feelings, desires, and the like, there can be no standards of autonomy. Claims of autonomy would be incorrigible.

Does this conception of autonomy consign autonomous people to a narcissistic vacuum? Would they be so absorbed by the play of their self-referential responses and so preoccupied with arranging for the expression of their selves that they could not tolerate dependency, could not subordinate their interests to those of others, and therefore could not love? Gerald Dworkin dismisses the claim that autonomous people must have substantive independence on the grounds that such independence condones selfishness and rules out compassion and loyalty (1976:26). Since compassion and loyalty are plainly desirable, Dworkin maintains, either autonomy does not require that degree of self-sufficiency which excludes them, or autonomy itself is not desirable.

Understood as I have proposed, autonomy can accommodate substantive independence along with deep emotional commitments, for substantive independence is explicated in terms of autonomy competency rather than in terms of separation from others. In this view, the difference between autonomous lovers and heteronomous ones is that the former have used the repertory of skills constituting autonomy competency to ascertain that they really love the beloved and that their loving behavior expresses values and comports with norms that they really accept. Contrariwise, heteronomous lovers may be sublimating other desires and mindlessly aping dubious practices. Of course, it is undeniable that friends and lovers can make demands on autonomous people that strain their control over their lives. However, it is also clear that no realistic person can expect other people to be unconditionally devoted to him or her. Still, since autonomy competency does not conflate self-interest with a narrow conception of private advantage, it does not bar altruistic conduct (part 2, sec. 5). Nowhere is autonomous affection better illustrated than in Jane Austen's portrayal of Elizabeth Bennet in *Pride and Prejudice*. Devoted to her sometimes trying family, yet blessed with an incisive and independent mind, Elizabeth invariably conducts herself in a manner that reconciles her love for her parents and her sisters with her doubts about their wisdom. Just the reverse of promoting embattled isolation, autonomy competency fosters a form of affection that is compatible with reciprocal dependency and care, as well as with personal dignity.

It might be granted that autonomous people need not keep their emotional attachments to a minimum, while exploiting their associates to promote their autonomy. Still, it might be objected that my conception of autonomy leaves the impression that autonomous people must make autonomy their major preoccupation in life. Plainly, this would be a serious defect in any account of autonomy, for it would entail that autonomous people are primarily concerned with thinking about how to live and only secondarily engaged in living. However, viewing autonomy as the exercise of a competency does not have this consequence unless having control over one's life necessitates constant self-conscious use of this competency.

No one who lacks the skills constitutive of autonomy competency can be autonomous. Since people who never answer the question "What do I really want?" to their own satisfaction and who never carry out such decisions give no evidence of possessing this competency, and, moreover, since facility with respect to this competency requires practice, people who never exercise autonomy competency can be presumed not to have it. Thus, a person may be happy and productive—the individual's life may be going entirely smoothly—and yet that person may not be autonomous. In the context of pervasive and powerful socializing influences, one cannot take autonomy for granted in the absence of proven heteronomy. It is autonomy that must be demonstrated.

Nevertheless, infrequent use of autonomy skills does not condemn people to heteronomy. Autonomy can be usefully compared to common sense in regard to physical health. Among other things, people who are competent to look after their physical well-being must understand basic principles of nutrition, but such people's preventive health care mainly takes the form of establishing good eating habits. It is not necessary to count calories and nutriments every day to protect oneself from obesity or dangerous dietary deficiencies. Similarly, autonomous people must conceive and follow life plans that are consonant with their respective true selves, but, once they set upon these courses, they need not regularly question their suitability.

Still, in addition to healthy eating habits and other everyday routines, competence with respect to one's physical health requires a knowledge of certain emergency procedures. People must be familiar with rudimentary first aid measures and must know when medical assistance should be sought. Likewise, autonomy requires that people attend to dissonance within their selves and minister to it when it occurs. Autonomous people need not be engaged in incessant introspection; however, they must be alert for anomalous self-referential responses which demand investigation (Kuflick 1984:274). Shame, embarrassment, dismay, exasperation, or disgust with oneself are symptomatic of deficient exercise of the competency. In indicating a person's dissatisfaction with his or her self or with the way he or she has projected this self in action, these responses reveal the person's occasional failure to control his or her life. Furthermore, just as everyone expects to get sick once in awhile, so everyone must presume that he or she does not invariably act autonomously. To reject this presumption would be to embrace a form of human infallibility. Thus, the complete absence of discontent with oneself or one's conduct is itself cause for suspicion and reason to actively review one's plans and practices. Though such attentions need not lead to major changes, and though the need to reexamine one's life plans follows no schedule and may arise infrequently, autonomy cannot be sustained without the exercise of autonomy skills, for these skills atrophy with disuse.

Still, my treatment of autonomy competency might be accused of plunging autonomy into the darkest recesses of subjectivity, leaving no place for objective criteria that establish who is autonomous and who is not. Autonomous people, it might be urged, will turn out to be those who are sufficiently arrogant to believe they control their lives, and more modest people will worry that they lack sufficient competence to call themselves autonomous. While it must be conceded that psychological factors such as arrogance and modesty will inevitably influence people's judgments and testimony about their autonomy competence, it does not follow that no standards can be provided to guide these judgments, nor does it follow that people cannot recognize autonomy and heteronomy in others. Autonomy requires a well-developed competency and successful exercise of the competency, and autonomy is amenable to evaluation in both respects.

People who have a well-developed competency are curious about and sensitive to their inner lives; they have a lively recall of their own experiences and of human experience they have learned about through conversation, reading, or the dramatic arts; they easily generate alternative courses of action for consideration; they vividly imagine themselves acting in various ways while anticipating the probable consequences of each; they compare the reasons supporting various options with assurance; they candidly communicate their concerns to others; they listen to and assimilate others' impressions and suggestions openmindedly; they marshall the resolve to carry out their own decisions; they are alert to both their own and others' negative and positive reactions to their conduct. These are skills with which everyone is acquainted and with respect to which each of us knows roughly how proficient he or she is. There may not be any tenable method for assigning numerical ratings to these skills, but that is no reason to conclude that no one has the slightest idea how competent he or she is.

In the passage quoted below from Margaret Drabble's *The Garrick Year*, Emma Evans confesses her own incompetency with respect to autonomy:

> When I got home I could not get to sleep: the enormity of my hope seemed to me the enormity of my failure and disappointment, and I did not wish to feel sorry for myself, I did not wish to have failed. I lay there and wondered what frightful depths of need the chance words of a man whom I did not know and had no reason to like had revealed in me; and I saw then clearly what later became confused, that I was about to be chained, in a fashion so arbitrary it frightened me, to a passion so accidental that it confirmed nothing but my own inadequacy and inability to grow. As a child I used to comfort myself by saying, "I am a child, this will pass." But I was no longer a child, there was no reason why this kind of blind rashness should ever pass. (p. 132)

Though this pronouncement is fictional, Drabble's character is poignant and convincing because her subjection to circumstances and her realization that she lacks the resources to overcome this immersion in the flow of events are familiar. Heteronomous people are not always so staunchly lucid about their limitations, but plainly they can be and often are cognizant of them.

Broadly speaking, chronic obliviousness to self-referential responses, awkwardness or rigidity in envisaging and appraising options, uncommunicativeness about one's needs, desires, values, and so forth, imperviousness to others' feedback, timidity about acting on the basis of one's own deliberations, and obstinate inflexibility in executing a chosen plan indicate poor development of autonomy competency. These limitations signal the individual's inability to fathom his or her authentic self and consequent habitual indifference to this self, or they signal the individual's inability to project his or her identity in action and consequent repression of this identity. Such people may lead lives that conform to customary expectations about what constitutes a worthwhile life—thus they may be mistaken for autonomous people—but a cursory inspection of their decision-making procedures will reveal that they do not control their own lives—thus they are not autonomous.

Undeniably, the situation is complicated by the fact that possession of autonomy skills does not automatically ensure autonomy. A person's competency in the area of autonomy may not be in doubt, yet the person may not always make use of this competency when it would be appropriate to do so or may use it to no avail. The explanation of a competent person's flawed use of the competency can be external or internal. External explanations include someone's deceiving the individual about relevant facts or someone's pressuring the individual for a hasty decision. More broadly, social structures or mores can defeat autonomy skills and produce distorted deliberation by prohibiting and penalizing expression of certain traits, beliefs, or values that an individual holds. (For further discussion of the impact of social norms on autonomy, see part 4, secs. 2D and 3.)

Among the internal explanations are self-deception in regard to one's traits or in regard to relevant circumstances, carelessness in examining one's situation or in reasoning about it, discombobulation over the exposure of a sensitive point, and failure of nerve. (For further discussion of this type of obstacle to autonomy, see part 3, sec. 4.) Recurrent incidents of failed autonomy may be due to a tenacious fault, a persistent blind spot regarding a trait, or the deviation of one's life plans from the dominance principle or from the principle of responsibility to self. (For detailed consideration of the dominance principle and the principle of responsibility to self, see part 2, secs. 5 and 6.) Also, neurosis can prevent people from effectively exercising autonomy skills. Thus, people can go through the motions of autonomous deliberation, but satisfactory answers may elude them. Moreover, people may have some autonomy skills but lack others. For example, some people are good at discovering what they really want, yet they shrink from doing anything about it. Plainly, people who develop their self-portraits ineptly or who fail to act on the judgments they obtain in autonomous reflection cannot be autonomous. Thus, diligence in the pursuit of autonomy does not guarantee a satisfactory result.

The only protection against disruptive factors like the ones I have just described is sensitivity to patterns of unfavorable self-referential responses and openness to the skeptical remarks of one's friends, on the one hand, coupled with a willingness to let one's imagination soar and to listen to others' inventive advice, on the other. Indeed, one's

responsiveness to problems and one's approach to solving them—
that is, whether one tries to ignore obstacles for as long as possible
and whether one tends to rely on prescribed solutions—are telling
signs of autonomy or its absence (Haworth 1986:23–24).

Moreover, it is important to recognize that self-correction is an
inextricable part of the process of autonomous living. No one is infallible, and no competency can guarantee success. Though a person
who has deliberated by deploying autonomy skills may subsequently
decide that he or she has taken an unsatisfactory course, this adjustment does not show that the earlier decision was not the best
exercise of autonomy competency that was possible at the time. Furthermore, whether or not it was, the dynamic interaction between
self-discovery, self-definition, and self-direction or, in other words,
the procedural conception of the authentic self entails that conduct
can only essay expression of the authentic self more or less approximately at any given time. For the authentic self is a moving target—
one that skitters away as soon as it is pinned down.

Still, autonomy competency, as I have explicated it, is compatible
with the utmost conventionality. (For detailed treatment of conventionality, see part 3, sec. 4.) Since this is so, it might be objected that
it is impossible to distinguish mimicry from autonomy on such an
account. As I have observed, people are normally in a position to
judge whether or not they have proficiency in the skills that make
up the competency of autonomy and whether or not they have used
these skills in arriving at their decisions. Since agents can recall their
own deliberation procedures to discover whether or not they have
used the skills of autonomy, and since anyone who has used the skills
of autonomy can examine his or her subsequent self-referential responses to ascertain whether or not these responses ratify the chosen
course of action, conventional people are not barred from assessing
the extent of their own autonomy or heteronomy. Some conventional
people may be liable to think that their social acceptability demonstrates their sober maturity and therefore their self-mastery; others
may be liable to think that their social acceptability demonstrates
their capitulation to social pressure and therefore their failure to assert control over their own lives. However, unconventional people
must make their self-assessments under obverse liabilities. No one is
ideally situated to judge the extent of his or her autonomy accurately,
but few are susceptible to impenetrable self-delusion.

Considering the matter now from the viewpoint of an independent observer, it is clear that a stranger cannot discern whether a thoroughly conventional individual is autonomous or not, upon first making such a person's acquaintance. However, when people know one another well, they are sometimes better situated to judge the extent of their associates' autonomy than these people are themselves. People who are driven by overwhelming passions but who have paused to deliberate before acting may be convinced that they have deployed their autonomy competency and are doing what they really want. (Daniel Dennett discusses some related cases of what he terms "local fatalism" [1984:104–105].) Yet, in the case of an obsessive conformist, an intimate may be able to see that this person's single-minded deliberations have overlooked concerns that are central to his or her life plans and that could have been accommodated by a mildly innovative but socially acceptable course of action. Also, since an observer has less reason to dismiss others' self-deprecatory responses as fleeting or trivial, such individuals may be quicker to recognize serious dissonance within others' selves. Thus, a friend might more readily identify ways in which ingrained social conformity frustrates another individual. On the positive side, it should be noted that intimates can sometimes reassure their conventional confidants of their autonomy. What the observer may be able to see that the agent cannot is that the latter's self-critical worries are manufactured and lack emotional resonance. Though opaque to strangers, autonomous conventionality may be evident to intimates.

To have autonomy competency, a person must use the repertory of autonomy skills enough to become and to remain proficient. This can be accomplished by charting a life plan and by making decisions for which the life plan does not provide with it in mind. In addition, autonomous people must be sensitive to intrapersonal tensions and dissatisfactions, and they must be willing to reassess their life plans in light of these disturbances. Moreover, they must recognize that life can go too smoothly, and they must be willing and able to overcome their reluctance to "mess with a good thing." Still, for the most part autonomy competency can remain in the background. Provided that people set their overall directions autonomously and are attentive to changes in and departures from their true selves, autonomy is more a matter of vigilance than a matter of plodding self-scrutiny and self-conscious choice.

\*    \*    \*

WITH THIS sketch of autonomy competency in hand, the nature of the authentic self can be clarified. I have claimed that people who are in control of their lives give expression to their authentic selves. But I have maintained that the authentic self should not be understood as a socialization-transcending core. Rather, it is the repertory of skills that make up autonomy competency along with the collocation of attributes that emerges as a person successfully exercises autonomy competency. To sharpen this conception, it is useful to compare it to the conceptions of the self that Michael Sandel has developed.

Part of Sandel's broad attack on Rawls' liberal conception of justice concerns Rawls' excessively sparse conception of the self. Sandel dubs the Rawlsian conception the *voluntarist self* (Sandel 1982:58). On this view, the self is a will. As such, it lacks ends until it chooses them, and it chooses them solely on the basis of its preferences (Sandel 1982:58, 159). Sandel calls his alternative conception the *cognitive self* (1982:58). In this view, the self is a faculty of critical reflection and a plethora of socially given ends. Whereas Rawls' view makes the problem of identity formation a problem about how to acquire some ends—a matter of decision-making—Sandel's view makes it a problem about how to distinguish oneself from one's environment— a matter of understanding (Sandel 1982:152). Moreover, Rawls' view establishes an unbridgeable gap between the self and its ends—each person *has* a conception of the good. Since the self does not embrace ends from within itself—ends that have accumulated in the course of experience—the Rawlsian self is "disembodied." In contrast, Sandel's view conflates the self with its ends—each person *is* a conception of the good. As a result of social experience, the self is full of ends—it is "radically situated"—and adopts ends which it already contains (Sandel 1982:21, 62).

Sandel has two major objections to the Rawlsian self. First, it has no constitutive ends, and therefore no blow to its adopted ends could impinge on its identity. Second, it is incapable of examining its preferences, and therefore its ends, critically. In short, Sandel accuses the Rawlsian self of shallowness. I shall not digress to ask whether the charges Sandel lodges against the voluntarist, disembodied self are warranted as criticisms of Rawls. Rather, I wish to ask whether either of the conceptions Sandel presents is adequate by itself.

Sandel analyzes the self along two dimensions: 1) its operational capability—will or critical reflection; and 2) its relation to social experience—disembodiment or radical situation. Moreover, he couples will with disembodiment and critical reflection with radical situation and treats these pairs as if they were the only possible combinations. But if the account of autonomy competency I have outlined is correct, these conceptions rest on a false dichotomy.

Sandel conceives of the two types of self in a puzzling, almost paradoxical, way. His construal of the voluntarist, disembodied self denies that any attributes are constitutive of the self. Accordingly, the self is fixed through insubstantial; yet personality, which is generated by the self's choices, is maximally malleable. Nevertheless, since Sandel denies that this self has any rational basis for embracing this or that end or, in other words, for changing its personality, the plasticity of personality is unavailing. By contrast, the cognitive, radically situated self has nothing but constitutive qualities. Since social experience implants ends in the self, the self is maximally open to the vicissitudes of circumstances and, conversely, minimally under the control of the individual. While its powers of critical reflection endow this self with a rational basis for change, change is limited to orchestrating preexisting elements. Thus, this self's cognitive powers seem unavailing, as well.

For Sandel, there is a trade-off. On the one hand, the self may have control but lack depth. As Edmund Wilson wrote of T. S. Eliot, "He gives you the creeps a little at first because he is such a completely artificial, or, rather, self-invented character." (Wilson's letter is quoted in "Eliot without Words," by John Updike in *The New Yorker*, March 25, 1985.) Or, on the other hand, the self may have depth but lack control. The narrator of Ralph Ellison's *Invisible Man* illustrates this state of affairs:

> I am an invisible man . . . I am invisible, understand, simply because people refuse to see me . . . I learned in time though that it is possible to carry on a fight against them [the people who refuse to see him] without their realizing it. For instance, I have been carrying on a fight with Monopolated Light & Power for some time now. I use their service and pay them nothing at all, and they don't know it. Oh, they suspect that power is being drained off, but they don't know where. All they know is that according to the master meter back there in their power station a hell of a lot of free current is disappearing into the jungle of Harlem . . . . I myself, after existing some twenty years, did not become alive until I discovered my invisibility . . . . All sickness is not unto death, neither is invisibility. (pp. 7–16)

Or, in more individualistic terms, consider Roger Shattuck's comment on Henri Rousseau, Erik Satie, Alfred Jarry, and Guillaume Apollinaire: "When our entire life stems from our deepest self, the resulting personality is usually so startling and abnormal as to appear a mask or a pose" (*The Banquet Years*, p. 40). Surely, these extremes are caricatures of human autonomy. It may be possible for a self to be disembodied and to pick its ends from an array of options it finds outside itself, and it may be possible for a self to be radically situated and to function as a conduit for overwhelming ends. But these conditions border on pathology, and, I shall argue, neither is intelligible as an account of autonomy.

Taking the voluntarist, disembodied self first, it seems that Sandel implicitly acknowledges the limits of self-creation. The voluntarist self chooses its ends on the basis of its contingent preferences. Many of these preferences are ones that the self has previously chosen. But, if a vicious regress of preference choosing is to be avoided, not all of the self's preferences can be chosen. Some preferences must be innate, or some preferences must have been incorporated into the self in the course of social experience. In either case, using Sandel's parlance, these nonvoluntary preferences would be constitutive. Now consider the cognitive, radically situated self. It embraces internal ends on the basis of critical reflection. But, if the criteria that critical reflection deploys are nothing more than prevailing social norms, critical reflection will be reduced to an arbitrary shuffling and reshuffling of equally constitutive ends. For the criteria available to critical reflection are no more integral than the array of ends it is charged with judging. Critical reflection needs an anchor—an individual standpoint marked by a set of endorsed preferences, traits, and so forth. Thus, voluntarism without some degree of situation and critical reflection without an independent base of choice are equally untenable.

But this line of argument seems to strand us. For autonomy to get going, it looks as if there must be such a thing as chosen, constitutive ends, but, in Sandel's view, this would be a contradiction in terms. By definition, chosen ends are external possessions, and constitutive ends are instilled by socialization. But I think this polarity is not borne out by experience.

There are two ways in which constitutive qualities can be chosen. Either a decision is made to accentuate an already established one, or a decision is made to replace an established one with one that the agent does not yet possess. Whichever kind of decision is taken, the mechanisms of self-definition are basically the same. To illustrate: having enrolled in nursing school with the aim of becoming a surgical nurse, Ellen realizes that she is more squeamish about gore than most of the other students. She has not chosen to become fainthearted in this way. Socialization into femininity with the premium this gender norm places on fragility and helplessness has imparted this quality to her, and so her squeamishness is constitutive in Sandel's sense of the term. Still, in order to achieve her career goal, Ellen might choose to overcome her squeamishness by witnessing additional operations. If her desensitization program is successful—that is, if she reaches a point where she could only fake being upset by the sight of an open wound—Ellen will have eradicated a constitutive quality, and she will have replaced one constitutive quality with a chosen, yet equally constitutive one.

Though people cannot choose directly to change their constitutive characteristics, they can choose to place themselves in situations and to act in ways designed to bring about such changes. No doubt, everyone has some qualities that would resist all attempts at deliberate change, and, no doubt, some of these intractable qualities stem from socially constructed categories, such as race and gender, or from immersion in special relationships, such as motherhood and daughterhood. While it would be a mistake to insist that people can control all of their qualities, it is clear that people can indirectly choose to transmute at least some of their constitutive qualities and that they can contrive to alter many others to some extent. (For related discussion of the possibilities and limits of self-definition, see Elster 1983:44–60.)

Here, Sandel might object that the trouble with this kind of choice as the basis for autonomy is that it is irremediably accidental. People have preferences which are given in experience, but they have no reasons which would give them a critical perspective on their inclinations. It is evident, however, that preferences and reasons mutually influence one another and that critical reflection and volition can be coordinated. In deciding to become a nurse, Ellen might have renounced a desire for the prestige of being a physician for a variety of reasons including such personal ones as disapproving being seduced by the lure of social stature and such social ones as wanting to get into a position to organize nurses to fight for comparable worth. Now, it is undeniable that the reasons Ellen accepts and brings to bear on her preferences are themselves influenced by prior social experience. But Sandel's view of critical reflection assumes that people's reasons are as much a product of their social environment as their desires are. Thus, he is in no position to claim that socially conferred reasons cannot be genuine reasons.

Still, it is also undeniable and much more important that, alone or in concert with others, people sometimes conceive novel reasons—the idea of comparable worth has not always been around—and they sometimes conceive innovative ways of putting novel or familiar reasons into practice—elective single-parenthood is a recent phenomenon. Though we often use language to mouth banalities or to repeat well-worn ideas, language competency enables us to utter new propositions. Similarly, exercising autonomy competency can reinforce established reasons and courses of conduct, but it can also propel people in new directions. Sandel overlooks this latter form of self-definition.

Although it is true that will without critical reflection divorces change from thought and reduces action to behavior, it is also true that critical reflection without will severs thought from change and shackles the agent. Sandel's voluntarist, disembodied self models the true self on the wardrobe of a person who lacks any interest in style or utility. If the wardrobe turned out to have any merits, they would be fortuitous, and the casual decision procedures used to acquire the clothing would have no intrinsic or instrumental value. Yet, the cognitive, radically situated self is modeled on a wardrobe of uniforms supplied by institutional edict and accompanied by a rudimentary sewing kit that equips individuals to embroider their names on their outfits. Neither conception does justice to people's capacity for self-definition. Furthermore, these conceptions are unattractive because they give us little reason to count securing personal autonomy as a priority.

In contrast, the account of the authentic self that emerges from my treatment of autonomy competency is a self that is shaped by social experience as well as by individual choice. (For a similarly balanced view of the relation between the self and society, see Grimshaw 1986:180–183.) Presupposing, as it does, self-discovery, self-definition, and self-direction, this conception does not ignore or deplore people's socialization, but neither does it abandon people to it. This balance can be maintained because autonomy competency takes advantage of the reciprocity that can hold between one's self-portrait and one's personal ideals and, more broadly, between one's desires and conduct and one's life plans.

The authentic self and the social world interact, but autonomy competency constitutes a resource that makes innovation possible and that puts personal harmony under the control of the individual. Not only are people empowered to transform themselves in ways that may break the chafing bonds of their social backgrounds, but also people sometimes conceive life plans that sharply diverge from available social norms. Further, these endeavors can bring people the satisfactions of integrated personalities—integrated personalities that they endorse, not ones that happenstance creates without their assent or dissent. (For detailed discussion of the integrated personality, see part 2, sec. 3.) The voluntarist, disembodied conception of the self is ill-equipped to account for personal harmony, while the cognitive, radically situated conception of the self is ill-equipped to account for individual control and innovation. The richer conception of the self implicit in my treatment of autonomy competency is necessary to account for these phenomena, and these possibilities help to explain why we value autonomy.

# SECTION 5

# Interests, Self-Interest, and Autonomy

FORMALLY, AUTONOMOUS people structure their life plans so as to secure personal integration (part 2, sec. 3), and, procedurally, autonomous people conduct their lives using a repertory of skills that enable them to engage in self-discovery, self-definition, and self-direction (part 2, sec. 4). It remains to be considered what kinds of things can be the proximate objects of autonomous choices and how these desiderata are related to the individual's authentic self.

Many authors have maintained that all people share certain fundamental interests (Rawls 1971:62; D. Richards 1971:37). Let us say, following Richards, that basic interests are generalized means to various self-regarding ends. Though lists of basic interests vary, survival and well-being constitute the controlling principles for generating all such lists. Among the serious candidates for inclusion as basic interests are health, strength, intelligence, companionability, power, wealth, friendship, opportunities, and reputation. Since these goods enhance everyone's ability to obtain other goods, each person benefits from having at least some of them. Thus, all authentic selves seem to have these interests in common, and these interests seem to delineate the minimal content of self-interest.

Still, authentic selves are far from uniform. Different people have stronger or weaker interests in one basic good or another, and these different emphases mirror the contents of their life plans. An entrepreneur's interest in wealth is apt to be considerably more pressing than a nun's. Autonomous people consult their selves, discover their abilities, inclinations, and values, and organize their desires into life plans. Nevertheless, it can be urged that basic interests impose constraints on the content of life plans. On this view, no admissible life plan can fail to make provision for a duly adjusted measure of each of these fundamental goods. It is clear that many people's life plans would be self-defeating were they to neglect basic interests, for the principle of responsibility to self generally requires that people secure these interests (part 2, sec. 6). Still, I doubt that securing these interests is a sine qua non of autonomy, and I shall urge that autonomous individuals are engaged in self-interested activity regardless of whether their life plans promote basic interests.

To distinguish between pursuing self-interest and pursuing one's own life plan, we must show that it is possible for a person to have normal desires to secure basic interests and yet to think it best and to be willing to sacrifice some or all of these standard interests for other values. Such a predicament is easy to understand if morality is imported into the situation. A scientist, Jake, who thinks he should forget about his failing health in order to complete research that will provide the key to a new weapon that will overpower his country's fascist enemy can advert to justice (the enemy is evil) and reciprocity (others are losing their lives to fight the war) to support his decision. But here the conflict is between self-interest and moral values, not between self-interest and personal values.

In this context, it is crucial to recall that the subject of this study is personal autonomy. Assuming that people are concomitantly attending to their moral responsibilities, I am asking how their self-regarding affairs can be autonomously ordered. While it is undeniable that in practice the moral and the personal realms interpenetrate, they are being artificially isolated from one another for present purposes. (For further discussion of the relation between morality and personal choice, see part 1.) Admittedly, it is not uncommon for autonomous people to face conflicts between their moral duties and their personal life plans. Since morality usually supercedes private preference, self-interest must usually be set aside for the sake of morality in these situations. Moral autonomy and self-interest do not invariably coincide; however, it seems to me that personal autonomy and self-interest do.

Imagine an epistemologist named Ann whose work fascinates her and a few colleagues but whose speculation has no likely use. Suppose that this epistemologist discovers that she has an incurable cancer for which two ameliorative treatments are available. One is radiation therapy, which will make Ann nauseous and exhausted for most of her remaining life; the other is hormone therapy, which is less effective than radiation therapy but has no bad side effects. Since Ann will never be able to work on her epistemological opus if she is feeling ill all the time, she must risk shortening her life or give up her work. What could be the rationale for taking this risk? It can't be the hope that history will record her as the greatest epistemologist ever, for this aim assimilates her sacrifice to self-interest as it is ordinarily understood. Rather, the rationale must be something like Ann's believing philosophical inquiry, however obscure and practically inconsequential, to be intrinsically valuable, or her believing potential-realizing, active living to be more intrinsically valuable than quiescent, but prolonged life. If Ann has all of the usual intense self-preservative impulses which are constitutive of her self-interest yet believes in certain principles or values which have come into conflict with her self-interest constituting concerns, it seems that self-interest can conflict with personal values.

Two questions arise in connection with conflicts between basic interests and personal values. First, can a person rationally opt to sacrifice basic interests for the sake of personal values? Second, if personal values can take precedence, does this entail that personal autonomy can commit people to acting against their own self-interest? I shall argue that it can only be rational for Ann to uphold her personal values in the face of extreme self-sacrifice if she has autonomously adopted these values. Moreover, if she does not autonomously change her mind when these values come into conflict with her survival, she can rationally adhere to them. However, if all of the preceding is true, Ann is not upholding personal values as opposed to self-interest. For in the process of discovering that it is rational for her to adhere to values that apparently conflict with self-interest, she has discovered that what she really cares about is the completion of her work. If this is what matters most to Ann, I shall urge, it is in her self-interest to refuse debilitating medical treatments in order to continue her writing. In other words, Ann has an idiosyncratic interest profile.

Suppose that Ann's parents were ambitious for her and systematically inculcated achievement-affirming values in her while working to eradicate competing desires. Suppose further that Ann's autonomy competency is poorly developed and that she has never subjected her devotion to epistemology to any sort of critical scrutiny. Can it be rational for her to arrange to maintain a demanding work schedule at the probable cost of an early death?

If Ann's nonautonomous desire to live a longer life is stronger than her nonautonomous desire to live a philosophical life, few would question her taking the relative strength of the former desire as a sufficient reason to slacken the pace of her research. Yet, a stronger nonautonomous desire to live a philosophical life does not seem to present a symmetrical case. The rationality of Ann's acting on a slightly stronger desire to proceed with her research is plainly suspect when this desire is not autonomous. Since securing basic interests affords extensive and varied prospects of satisfaction, it is reasonable to discount a marginally stronger, conflicting nonautonomous desire. Perhaps, if Ann's desire to press on with her work were tremendously stronger than her desire to survive, and if she were neither subject to present coercion nor suffering from impaired faculties, the immensely greater strength of the former desire might be thought sufficient to outweigh the interest in survival. Still, such overwhelming, yet nonautonomous disproportionality could well be interpreted as evidence of a twisted personality brought about by the rigors of a frightfully exiguous childhood. In the absence of autonomy competency, the swollen proportions of one aspect of Ann's personality bespeak compulsion, not independent choice.[1] If Ann acted on this desire simply because it was stronger and without probing it in the least, she would seem to be cheating herself, for there would be no reason to believe that contributing a footnote to epistemology was what she really wanted. Indeed, Ann's nonautonomous philosophizing at the expense of her life would be reminiscent of the pitiable achievements of children who have been hectored into ceaseless study and who have thereby been deprived of normal play and companionship.

The rationality of satisfying the desire to survive does not seem similarly compromised when it is the stronger nonautonomous desire because the dominance principle—choose the plan that secures as many of one's desired ends as any other plan and at least one more—certifies the rationality of basic interests (D. Richards 1971:51). Most of the time, securing basic interests is compatible with or positively contributes to any other aims a person might have—regular exercise takes time away from study, but physical vigor helps people to think more clearly. Moreover, nonautonomous conflicting aims cannot usually controvert basic interests, for people typically have many other desires and values that require securing basic interests. Thus, basic interests constitute a default conception of self-interest. In the absence of autonomous choices to the contrary, it can be presumed that a person's self-interest requires that his or her basic interests be protected.

Nevertheless, it is possible for autonomy to defeat basic interests. Since the dominance principle presupposes that aims coincide and selects the course of action that maximizes aim fulfillment, this principle supplies no guidance regarding incompatible aims of comparable standing. When securing basic interests conflicts with autonomously adopted values or desires, and when those values or desires are autonomously ranked above other values or desires, dominance cannot justify opting for basic interests. Thus, from the subjective point of view, it is doubtful that basic interests are as invariably forceful as some thinkers have suggested they are. Like any other aim, it seems that these interests must submit to appraisal under some circumstances.

Now, the project of autonomously assessing the force of basic interests might seem doomed from the start. The chorus of protest might include the following motifs:

1. Human nature dictates attachment to . . .
2. Nothing could be as important as . . .
3. No one could be fulfilled without . . .
4. Autonomy would be impossible without . . .
5. No one is capable of making rational choices between . . .

Since the default conception of self-interest incorporates basic interests, morality requires that one presume that other people have these interests when one is deciding how to treat them. Still, the above lines of argument are unconvincing if they are taken to preempt the choices of individuals with respect to their own life plans.

The facts of human psychology and conduct belie the first three contentions. Although most people are powerfully attached to the goods classified as basic interests, regard these goods as supremely important, and feel frustrated and possibly desperate when they lack these goods, other people do not. Surely, everyone has met content people who place a very high value on one desideratum—say, family life—and who sacrifice certain other basic interests—such as achievement or friendship—in order to better realize their primary value. If the first three lines of argument amount to anything more than bald assertions, they illicitly import the imperatives of other-regarding morality into the realm of personal choice.

The claim that autonomy would be impossible without certain goods must be taken more seriously.[2] It should be noted, however, that people can be autonomous though they lack some elements of the standard interest profile. No doubt, friendship and reputation commonly contribute to autonomy, but they are hardly necessary for autonomy in all circumstances. Nevertheless, it is true that life, some degree of safety, a measure of individual liberty, some opportunities, and some material resources are necessary for autonomy. Still, it does not follow that people cannot rationally decline these goods.

Sometimes, autonomy is going to be lost or, at least, sharply curtailed. The only questions are how fast it will be lost (or curtailed) and what the interim will be like. Ann's terminal disease is a case in point. Now, if the reason it is impossible to choose rationally to forego basic interests is that they are necessary to autonomy, such predicaments would seem to leave people at the mercy of circumstances. In the name of autonomy, they must passively endure the ravages of disease, famine, despotism, and the like. Though the role of certain goods in sustaining autonomy undoubtedly creates a presumption against renouncing them, this presumption loses its force when autonomy itself cannot be fully and indefinitely sustained.

When coupled with the claim that people are not capable of making rational choices between basic interests and other personal desires or values, however, the observation that a set of goods is necessary for autonomy may seem more compelling. In an in extremis situation—that is, a situation in which it seems highly plausible that someone could rationally sacrifice a good that is necessary for autonomy—it might seem advisable to cling to those goods that support autonomy for as long as possible. Under such circumstances, it is understandable that people would distrust the reliability of their own feelings and the soundness of their own arguments and would place great stock in a formulaic solution, especially if one has the imprimatur of social consensus. However, it is doubtful that everyone would find a longer period of severely restricted autonomy to be superior to a shorter period of less constrained autonomy, social consensus on the value of autonomy notwithstanding.

Social norms regarding basic interests can be understood as reflecting the aggregated decisions of individuals or as encoding a synergistic conclusion reached through ongoing discussion and review. Since the former view presumes that individuals can make rational choices with respect to basic interests, I shall not pursue it further. In contrast, if one supposes that wisdom can only be achieved and preserved through a process of cultural evolution, there is reason to be skeptical that the independent contrary choices of individuals are rational. Thus, it is necessary to ask whether autonomous people who find themselves at odds with social norms regarding basic interests should surmise that there is something wrong with them and therefore that they should conform to those norms despite their own inclinations and convictions or that the social norms are inapplicable to them and therefore that they should follow their own inclinations and convictions.

The latter position would be indefensible only if individual deliberation regarding basic interests were inherently more misleading than social decision-making regarding this matter. Of course, people who must confront choices about basic interests are often under considerable emotional or physical strain. Opting to be guided by social norms is often a concession to one's perception of one's own rational deficiency—one's lack of dispassion, one's utter confusion, and one's overweening anxiety. Nevertheless, people sometimes face these decisions with remarkable lucidity and calm. Should they accede to social norms regardless of how aggravating they find this compliance?

Surely, not. In the first place, it seems clear that social consensus will settle on norms suited to the majority of people, for theirs (or their representatives') will be the dominant voices in the cumulative, collective conversation. Since the voices of atypical individuals will, by and large, be drowned out, social norms will sometimes fail to address these individuals' needs. Likewise, for the most part, social norms are designed to handle common circumstances—circumstances that can be anticipated and disposed of in advance. Thus, there is little reason to suppose that social norms can always be applied satisfactorily in extraordinary situations. In addition, social decision-making is no more free of distorting influences than individual re-flection. Particularly pertinent here is the tendency of individuals who are participating in collective decision-making processes to self-censor dissent for the sake of maintaining agreement (Mansbridge 1980:259). Though it would be foolish to dismiss cultural lore about basic interests out-of-hand, it is doubtful that it befits all individuals and their circumstances equally well, and it does not necessarily have a stronger claim to rationality than an autonomous individual's con-clusions.[3] After all, people who have autonomy competency are sin-gularly well-equipped to address personal issues on an individual basis.

Returning to my epistemologist, Ann, if her desire to complete her work were autonomous, she could not simply assume that her desire to survive for a longer period of time should take precedence. The autonomy of her competing desire ensures that it cannot be dismissed as a compulsion and confers on it a status comparable to her basic interest in survival. Although satisfying her desire to prolong her life would afford her the possibility of satisfying more secondary de-sires—some of which may be autonomous—as well as the possibility of suffering more frustrations, to satisfy her desire to complete her work would be to satisfy the paramount desire of her authentic self. Thus, Ann cannot accept the equal or greater strength of her non-autonomous desire to survive as a sufficient reason to undergo ra-diation therapy at the expense of her work. Since Ann's basic interest is genuinely contested—that is, contested in virtue of the autonomy of her commitment to an opposing value—this conflict necessitates an autonomous inspection of the basic interest. When the opposing value or desire is nonautonomously held, it lacks the connection to the authentic self that would place it in serious competition with ba-sic interests. Accordingly, it is only when the opposing value or desire is autonomously held that basic interests cannot prevail nonauton-omously.

If Ann has autonomously adopted values that run counter to the basic interest in survival, it is rational for her to take steps to satisfy a stronger desire stemming from these values when it conflicts with basic interests provided that she does not at this point autonomously decide that prolonged life is more important to her. Here, the dis-tinction between self-interest and personal values collapses. In au-tonomously embracing and acting on these values, Ann has taken the counsel of her authentic self, and she is doing what she really wants.

If anything is in one's self-interest, it is surely in one's self-interest to do what one really wants to do. Thus, an autonomous epistemologist who decided to jeopardize her health in order to advance her scholarship would be pursuing her own self-interest. Though this individual's interest profile is atypical, it is not impossible. Autonomous reflection makes rational satisfaction of non-moral desires that are apparently in conflict with self-interest possible, but, in so doing, autonomous reflection transforms these apparently interest-defeating desires into elements of idiosyncratic interest profiles.

There is a further complication, however, that must be considered. Since a person's best justified value does not necessarily match the person's strongest desire, values and desires can conflict. Suppose Ann has come to the conclusion that she should continue working but she still most wants to undergo radiation therapy in the hope of extending her life. If Ann has reached this impasse without the benefit of autonomy competency, it seems clear that the default status of basic interests should take priority, as it does in the case of conflicting nonautonomous desires. However, if Ann's belief in the superior value of continuing her philosophical inquiry has been autonomously arrived at, and if the basic interest in survival has been autonomously scrutinized, her autonomy competency has presumably reached its limit.

Apparently, Ann accepts a value that cannot be reconciled with a desire that she also accepts. Certainly this individual does not have a fully integrated personality, and evidently her use of autonomy skills has failed to remedy this dissonance. Under the circumstances, there is no basis for saying that it would be more rational for her to follow the value rather than the desire or the desire rather than the value. Still, her predicament does not show that autonomy can collide with self-interest, for both her desire and her value have been ratified through autonomous reflection. Rather, it shows—and surely anyone who has had to make many hard choices will confirm—that an individual's self-interest may not be ascertainable in advance. Sometimes people are obliged to plump arbitrarily for one alternative or the other and then to wait and see how things turn out. Under such circumstances, people either grow into their decisions and come to regard their chosen course as a solid basis for going on, or they find the results disappointing and seek ways to make amends. (For further discussion of the way in which autonomy competency functions in medias res, see part 3, sec. 3.) In life and death situations like Ann's, of course, people do not enjoy the luxury of such experimentation. However, in more ordinary predicaments, vacillation is best resolved, if it can be resolved at all, by trial and error.

Now, it might be countered that, faced with her dilemma, Ann would be well-advised to look after her basic interest in prolonged life. Ann must choose between disruptive treatment and continuing her work, and, since she has not found sufficiently persuasive support for her values to carry along desire, it might be urged that the default conception of self-interest should override her personal values. If one is convinced that Ann's autonomy competency is poorly developed or that distress about her deteriorating health has prevented her from using her skills with her usual sensitivity and acumen, this recommendation is well taken. However, by itself, the recalcitrance of desire is not conclusive evidence of impared autonomy. If there is no basis for impugning Ann's autonomy apart from her inability to resolve a life and death dilemma over which no philosophical consensus has ever prevailed, one can hardly presume that her rational powers have slipped and should yield to brute desire. But, again, this is not a plausible case of autonomy vying with self-interest. Ann's values and desires are both autonomous, but they are equipoised. Hence, her self-interest is unknowable, if not indeterminate.

No competency can guarantee that its adepts will be able to handle successfully every problem they encounter within the competency's domain. Many competent English speakers marvel at Shakespeare's facility for capturing emotions that they find ineffable. In regard to autonomy competency, it is not at all surprising that an individual's authentic self might lack the resources to settle perennial and profound philosophical controversies. Nevertheless, this competency provides the only possible access to the interests of the authentic self. People who lack this competency can gauge their interests as occupants of assigned social roles, as typical human beings, or as instinctive creatures. In contrast, autonomous people can guage their individual interests, that is, their *self*-interest. Autonomy and self-interest are thus inseparable.

If autonomous choice is definitive of self-interest, it is necessary to consider whether any principle captures this link between self-interest and autonomy. In section 4 above, I noted several principles of rational choice—postponement, greater likelihood of success, strict dominance, and effective means—that contribute to autonomous decision-making. At this point, I shall focus on the dominance principle.

This principle requires that one choose that plan from a selection of two or more plans which secures all of the desired aims that the other plans secure and at least one more. We have seen that dominance is implicated in the defense of a set of basic interests which constitute the default conception of self-interest. I shall now argue, first, that, in order to be definitive of self-interest, autonomous choice must comport with the dominance principle, and, second, that this relation between autonomous choice and self-interest does not entail that autonomous choice must comport with Rawls' stronger principle of self-realization, the Aristotelian principle.

Autonomous people cannot opt to satisfy fewer of their autonomous desires than possible. To do so would be arbitrarily to frustrate one's authentic self and thus to live out of harmony with one's authentic self. Accordingly, autonomy requires compliance with the dominance principle, and, inasmuch as satisfying one's autonomous desires guarantees that one is acting in one's self-interest, violating the dominance principle is contrary to self-interest. However, this is not to say that autonomous, self-interested people must satisfy as many of their desires as possible, for autonomous people may experience desires that they autonomously prefer not to satisfy and that it would be contrary to their self-interest to satisfy. Moreover, since potentialities do not necessarily constitute autonomous desires, autonomous, self-interested people may have potentialities that they do not activate. Though self-interest obviously requires that the dominance principle be applied to nonautonomous desires that do not compete with autonomous ones and that secure basic interests, the scope of the dominance principle is, first and foremost, autonomous desires.

People who persistently experience desires that they have autonomously decided against satisfying do not have perfectly integrated personalities. As a result, they need to exercise more conscious control over their actions in order to maintain their autonomy than people who have rid themselves of their unwanted desires need to exercise. Nevertheless, people with nonautonomous desires can be autonomous through alert perseverance. Sam, an autonomously cured alcoholic (a rarity, I admit), may occasionally want a drink, but he might muster sufficient resolve not to indulge this desire and thus stop himself from going on a binge. Though autonomy would be easier for Sam if he could extinguish this desire, and though Sam does not instantiate the ideal of the spontaneous autonomous personality, he is in control of his life, and there is no convincing reason to deny that he is autonomous. Moreover, Sam's exercising this control is plainly in his self-interest. Thus, Sam can only maintain his autonomy and promote his self-interest by excluding his nonautonomous taste for liquor from the ambit of the dominance principle.

Other cases leave the proper purview of the dominance principle open to doubt. Consider a banker, Kay, who cherishes an image of herself as a poet but who, unlike another banker, T. S. Eliot, never so much as attempts a quatrain. Let us grant that Kay wants to be a poet but that she also has reasons not to try to become one. Perhaps, Kay does not want her exquisite vision of the poetic life to be tarnished by the humdrum labors of actual composition, or she may enjoy tantalizing herself with the prospect of becoming a poet because resisting this desire reinforces her sense of self-mastery and her commitment to high finance. We may think this constellation of desires perverse, but it seems possible that it is autonomous. Yet, it appears to violate the dominance principle, and it is open to doubt whether satisfying these desires can count as securing Kay's self-interest.

It is a mistake, however, to accept Kay as a counter-example to the claim that autonomous people must comply with the dominance principle where their autonomous desires are at stake or as a counter-example to the claim that such compliance constitutes self-interested conduct. This romantically inclined banker does not really want to be a poet. Both her persistent refraining from writing and her contrary desires call the autonomy of her desire to be a poet into question. What Kay really wants is to want to be a poet, and her wanting to be a poet satisfies this second-order desire.[4] (For a related discussion, see Frankfurt 1971:9.) Thus, Kay's autonomously unsatisfied desire to be a poet does not constitute an abrogation of the dominance principle. On the contrary, her satisfying her autonomous second-order desire confirms that the dominance principle applies only to autonomous desires and to nonautonomous desires that do not interfere with autonomous ones.

Still, it is necessary to take account of the curious status of Kay's first-order desire to be a poet. Ordinarily, autonomy is transitive. When a person autonomously wants to do a certain act and does it, the autonomy of the wanting renders the doing autonomous, too. But, in Kay's case, if the autonomy of her second-order desire transfers to her sequential first-order desire inasmuch as the latter is the fulfillment of the former, it seems that her refraining from writing poetry will violate the dominance principle. Unless she takes up this additional vocation, she will be frustrating an autonomous desire and thus will be living at variance with her true self. However, if the autonomy of Kay's second-order desire is not transmitted to the first-order desire that satisfies it, or if the autonomy of the first-order desire is not transmitted to the action that satisfies it, an explanation of this blockage is needed.

These difficulties are created by Kay's conflicting desires. Kay, it must be remembered, autonomously wants to want to be a poet, but simultaneously she autonomously wants not to become a poet. Thus, we seem to have three autonomous desires—the desire to want to be a poet, the desire to be a poet, and the desire not to be a poet. The second two desires cannot both be satisfied.

In this connection, it is important to recognize that the transitivity of autonomy can fail in various ways. Someone could form a desire and conceive a plan to fulfill that desire, taking into account all relevant and ascertainable feelings, desires, beliefs, and values along with all relevant and ascertainable information about the world; yet, upon carrying out this plan, some unforseeable event might intervene in such a way as to bring about major consequences that one deeply deplores. Although it would not be appropriate to disavow one's original desire because of these consequences—they were no part of one's desire—it would be appropriate to disavow one's action—in the event, it proved to violate one's sense of one's self. Alternatively, the same pattern can be confined to an agent's psyche. Someone could form a desire and conceive a plan to fulfill that desire, taking into account all relevant and ascertainable feelings, desires, beliefs, and values along with all relevant and ascertainable information about the world; yet, upon carrying out this plan, unforseeable psychological results might occur—for example, desires or feelings might be engendered—that one abhors. Again, the desire remains autonomous—it was not a desire to bring about these results—but this autonomy does not transfer to the act that satisfies it—the action in its totality conflicts with one's true self. Since desiring such-and-such does not entail desiring all of the possible consequences of satisfying this desire, the autonomy of a desire can remain intact though the autonomy of the action that satisfies the desire may be partially or completely nullified.

A more extreme form of the divide between desire and action that can also block the transitivity of autonomy can be seen when someone has unfulfillable desires. People can have autonomous desires that they know circumstances will prevent them from satisfying. In 1935, an American, college-educated woman with exceptional mathematical aptitude could have had an autonomous desire to become an electrical engineer—she could have really wanted to pursue this career—while fully realizing that no school of engineering would admit her. Her desire would have been autonomous, and, in a spirit of defiance of this unjust discrimination and of faithfulness to her true self, she might have deliberately chosen to keep this desire alive, despite the bitterness it caused. There would be no question of its autonomy being transmitted to her becoming an electrical engineer, for no such course of conduct was feasible. At best, her autonomous desire could find circuitous expression, possibly in political activities or in her child-rearing practices. Plainly, the actions taken to vindicate such socially inadmissible, yet autonomous desires are less autonomous than the actions that would directly satisfy the desires would be.

A related possibility is that of an autonomous desire that can be partially satisfied. A woman from the same era whose aspirations to become a physician were squelched by discrimination might have settled for second-best and become a nurse instead. People can have authentic selves that cannot be completely expressed in a given social environment but that can find a closely related mode of expression. Plainly, autonomous people cannot always adjust themselves to fit into circumstances, and their compromises with circumstances may yield less than fully autonomous action. Since the autonomy of a desire does not entail the availability to the individual of a course of action satisfying the desire, autonomy is not transitive under all circumstances.

Although autonomous desire is ordinarily correlated with autonomous action that satisfies the desire, the autonomy of a desire is sometimes pried apart from the autonomy of the action satisfying the desire. Thus, there is no reason to insist that the autonomy of Kay's wanting to be a poet, never mind the autonomy of her writing poetry, must follow from the autonomy of her wanting to want to be a poet. Other factors can intervene between desire and action. In Kay's case, that factor is her countervailing, yet autonomous desire not to become a poet. Although it is unusual for the transitivity of autonomy to be blocked through such exquisite self-manipulation as Kay displays, it is common enough for the transitivity of autonomy to be blocked. Here, again, the individual in question lacks a fully integrated personality, and, as a result, this person's autonomy requires greater self-consciousness and willfulness than would that of someone who does not experience antagonistic desires. However, the precariousness of Kay's self-control does not entail that she is not at all autonomous. Provided that Kay is able to entertain both the desire to be a poet and the desire not to be a poet but only to satisfy the one that she autonomously prefers to satisfy, she is autonomous and does not abrogate the dominance principle.

Still, since Kay's pair of incompatible desires ensures that she will always be to some degree frustrated, it seems to follow that she is not behaving self-interestedly. Though she satisfies only her autonomous desires, and though she satisfies all of her autonomous desires, in so doing she creates a desire that is perpetually excluded from satisfaction. This configuration hardly seems consonant with self-interest. But notice that, if Kay's desire to want to be a poet and her desire not to be a poet are autonomous, she has reasons for cultivating each of them. Perhaps, in order to avoid complacency, she persists in testing her commitment to banking by sustaining her desire to become a poet. Whatever her reasons, they explain why Kay's combination of desires is in her self-interest, as she conceives it. Unlike most ambivalent people, Kay is not a victim of indecision. She has values that can best be realized by taxing her equilibrium, and there is no reason to think that her values are incompatible with self-interest. Again, adherence to the dominance principle would not assure self-interested conduct unless the scope of the dominance principle were restricted to autonomous desires and nonautonomous desires that are innocuous to autonomy.

Still, Kay's case might be elaborated to highlight another difficulty for the dominance principle. Suppose that this banker has an undeveloped potential to become a poet. Her desire to be a poet is not pure whimsy: she has a gift for verse which she has never developed. In view of this additional background information, one might say that this talent is part of Kay's authentic self and therefore constitutes an autonomous desire that must be satisfied if autonomy is to coincide with self-interest. Indeed, even if she did not experience any desire to be a poet, it might be said that this potential constituted an autonomous latent desire. In either case, dominance would require that this potential be actualized if possible.

Rawls' Aristotelian principle states that people "enjoy the exercise of their realized capacities (their innate or trained abilities), and this enjoyment increases the more the capacity is realized, or the greater its complexity" (Rawls 1971:426). As Rawls understands it, this principle entails that it is rational for people to realize as much of their potential as they can before they reach a point where the frustration of further learning and practice offsets the joy of performance (1971:428). This extension of the dominance principle implies that people who are content to leave some of their realizable potential undeveloped are less true to themselves than achievement-oriented people are and that they undermine their self-interest in ways that achievement-oriented people do not. It is therefore necessary to ask whether an individual's potentialities form autonomous latent desires that should come under the dominance principle in autonomous deliberation.

I believe that the preponderance of reasons argues against granting potentialities this status. When issues of this kind arise, there is a temptation to think of potentialities as discrete mental entities, like little pellets that, when dropped into water, fizz and dye the water some attractive hue. This picture of potentialities lends itself to their assimilation to desires. For it suggests that, like many desires, potentialities are themselves determinate as well as determinate in their realization and also that, like many desires, failure to act on them impoverishes the individual's life. But, on reflection, it becomes apparent that human potentialities are nothing like this.

An individual's genetic makeup endows him or her with a distinctive but inchoate combination of potentialities—manual dexterity, verbal aptitude, reasoning ability, and so forth. But the application of these elemental potentialities to particular activities depends on the culture into which people are born, as well as on their personal inclinations. (For a similar view of human potential, see Scheffler 1985:10–16, 46–67.) Verbal aptitude might be funneled into fundraising or journalism. But there is no such thing as a fund-raising potentiality or a journalism potentiality. Thus, there is no such thing as a suppressed talent for fund-raising or for journalism. Still, a person could fail to fully realize his or her verbal aptitude. People who are endowed with diverse potentialities often fail to take full advantage of all of them. Does this entail that selective potentiality realization is a betrayal of the true self and an abrogation of self-interest?

Most people's innate potentiality would support their taking up countless types of activity. Nevertheless, people cannot profitably attempt to do everything they are capable of doing. All that autonomous people can be expected to do is to harness their background potential to a project (or, more likely, a set of projects) that they deem worthwhile. For to hold that anyone who does not pursue every activity he or she is in principle capable of taking up is thereby betraying his or her authentic self is to render autonomy unattainable to mortal beings.

Nevertheless, there seem to be people whose chief goal is stress reduction and who hew to a policy of avoiding potential-developing activities in preference for time-wasting activities in order to minimize tension. Could an autonomous and self-interested person adopt this sort of life plan? Plainly, it is unlikely that any autonomous person would choose this course. Possession of autonomy skills tends to expand people's horizons. Since people who have autonomy competency can picture themselves engaged in various projects and playing various roles, and since they can figure out how their options mesh with their authentic selves and how to apply their distinctive resources to attain their goals, they can allow themselves to range freely over possibilities without dreading failure and disappointment. (For an account of autonomy competency, see part 2, sec. 4.) Thus, autonomous wastrals are improbable, for autonomous individuals do not suffer from the insecurities and deficiencies that commonly lead to severe self-limitation.

Still, it seems possible that people could autonomously decide to neglect their potential in favor of more hedonistic pursuits, and it is arguable that this drives a wedge between autonomy and self-interest. Yet, with respect to choices about leisure time, it seems clear that neither autonomy nor self-interest requires compliance with the Aristotelian principle. Suppose that Sandra is exceptionally good at playing the cello but that she loves disco dancing and lets her musical talent languish. Sandra does not find playing the cello frsutrating or otherwise unpleasant, and she does not justify her preference for disco dancing by saying that she wants to meet new people or that she needs the exercise. She just finds disco dancing more fun. Surely, she could autonomously choose to devote her leisure time to this activity. There is no reason to assume that the true self is serious through and through. Moreover, her self-interest does not dictate that she join an amateur trio instead of stepping out at fashionable clubs, nor, for that matter, does her self-interest dictate that she allot some time to practicing the cello. Part of what we mean when we talk about leisure time is that there is nothing wrong with using it simply to amuse oneself or to loaf. If the realm of leisure does not exclude the application of autonomy skills, and if sheer relaxation can be in people's self-interest, it follows that, from the standpoint of autonomy as well as from that of self-interest, the Aristotelian principle is suspended where leisure time is at issue.

What about the rest of life? Do autonomy and self-interest require compliance with the Aristotelian principle in one's vocational decisions? Again, it seems doubtful that they do. Not only does it seem possible for autonomous and self-interested people to opt to minimize the demands their vocations impose in order to pursue engrossing avocations, but also it seems possible for them to opt to minimize striving in all areas of life. An authentic self with strong aversions to exertion and to overmastering challenges seems entirely possible. Provided that these aversions do not obstruct expression of a person's other autonomously held beliefs, values, feelings, desires, and so forth, an autonomous person could give them full rein. Though I suspect that most people who choose life plans along these lines lack autonomy skills or suffer from deep-seated anxiety about their abilities, I can see no necessary connection between full possession of autonomy competency and maximization of potential-realization. Moreover, to warn such people that they are sacrificing their self-interest is to indulge in misplaced and paternalistic moralism. The Protestant Ethic— itself a possible object of autonomous choice—cannot serve as the arbiter of autonomy or of self-interest.

For any aspect of a person's potential to count as a latent desire which should not be frustrated, it must be distinguished from the innumerable other aspects of the individual's potential which inevitable temporal and material constraints will not permit him or her to realize or which countervailing attributes bar him or her from realizing. Only if someone feels unfulfilled and can trace this frustration to a previously unnoticed desire can it be meaningfully said that this person has a latent desire which calls for satisfaction. Thus, Johan, an eighteenth-century peasant with a flair for melody, could have an incipient desire to compose sonatas that his social class would prevent him from satisfying. Nevertheless, if Johan is capable of composing music yet never experiences the slightest urge to do so or dejection at not having done so, he can ignore this potentiality without compromising his autonomy and, with it, his self-interest. Autonomous people must be prepared to recognize latent desires and must apply the dominance principle to such desires as they appear; however, they are not obliged to concern themselves with every aspect of their potentiality that they could bring to fruition.

Still, it is undeniable and troubling that many people who apparently elect uncomplicated lives and who do not avail themselves of much of their potential are not autonomous. I shall address their plight from the vantages of social psychology and justice in parts 3 and 4. At this point, it is important to appreciate that their lack of autonomy and their failure to promote their self-interest is not due to their failure to comply with the Aristotelian principle. It is due to their lack of autonomy competency, if not to their society's repressive policies.

Violating the Aristotelian principle is compatible with autonomy. Unless qualified to say that only unrealized potentialities that somehow disturb people count as the authentic self's desires, the Aristotelian principle is too strong. But, qualified in this way, the Aristotelian principle does not exact more than the dominance principle. However, people who fail to realize much of their potential face a problem anterior to applying the dominance principle, for autonomously applying the dominance principle presupposes a knowledge of one's autonomous desires. This is precisely what escapes many people who squander their potential. They do not know how to figure out what they really want. They do not know how to recognize a potentiality crying out for fulfillment. Not knowing their real desires, they cannot use the dominance principle to determine what course to take. Thus, autonomy eludes them, and their pursuit of self-interest is confined to securing minimal satisfaction while avoiding as much frustration as possible.

A mediocre life can be autonomous if the individual realizes that he or she does not really want to take on challenges and endure the stress that accompanies them. In applying the dominance principle to their occurrent desires and ignoring their unactualized inchoate potential, these people autonomously pursue their own self-interest. No one else is in a position to pronounce their lives out of step with their authentic selves. Conversely, people who lack autonomy competency, regardless of whether they stick in the mud or get up and go, are in no position to determine where their self-interest lies.

# Responsibility for Self

THINKERS WHO sharply contest one another's views in other respects generally agree about one principle underlying autonomy. Rawls dubs this principle the principle of responsibility to self and states it as follows: "the claims of the self at differing times are to be so adjusted that the self at each time can affirm the plan that has been and is being followed." (1971:423; also see Fried 1970:158–161, 170–176). The idea is that people are enduring entities capable of pressing new claims as time passes and that people should provide for their futures. They should not so squander their resources—in this context, resources include such goods as talent and vitality along with financial wherewithal—in the present that they are left destitute at a later time.

Most people would concur that prudence does require providence of this sort. Indeed, it initially seems obvious that living for the moment without a care for the future is almost certain to diminish a person's control over his or her life in the long run. However, Derek Parfit has recently mounted a concerted attack on this bit of conventional wisdom. Parfit's approach is to question the rationality of temporal neutrality—that is, a posture of caring as much about the past and the future as one cares about the present in deliberations regarding personal matters. Though Parfit does not maintain that he has demonstrated the irrationality of the principle of responsibility to self, his arguments sharply undercut complacent acceptance of this point of view and warrant a reply. Though I shall take up Parfit's major arguments in turn, I shall not address an important dimension of Parfit's argument, namely, his contention that defending temporal neutrality presupposes certain assumptions that an amoralist cannot accept. Since my investigation is operating within the confines of morality, that is, I am assuming that personal autonomy concerns the realm of morally indifferent choice (part 1, sec. 1), this aspect of his argument is not germane to the topic at hand.

Parfit begins by suggesting that there are few situations in which anyone would think it rational to try to satisfy past desires (1984:152–53). If temporal neutrality with respect to the past is silly, Parfit implies, temporal neutrality with respect to the future is suspect. Why should people expend any of their resources trying to satisfy future desires as the principle of responsibility to self requires? Why not concentrate exclusively on satisfying present desires?

Parfit urges that, when a person's desires concern values that can be justified, as opposed to mere preferences, the principle of responsibility to self is incoherent (1984:154–156). For, in this case, this principle requires people to give the same weight to what they now believe to be justified and to what they now believe to be unjustified but in the future may come to believe justified (Parfit 1984:155). If justification has any force at all, it rules out this form of crazed even-handedness. Parfit then entertains the counter-argument that people might rationally decide to take possible future beliefs into account on the grounds that they are becoming wiser as they are growing older. But he dismisses this argument by asserting that people who now believe that a future belief of theirs will be justified in fact have this belief now (1984:155).

Although it is true that under some circumstances to acknowledge the justifiability of a future belief is to accept it now, there are circumstances in which this inference cannot be made. Suppose that

Jane now knows that in ten years she will regard Roman Catholic dogma as fully justified and can now articulate the justification she will then accept. Assuming that the justification is impersonal—that is, it makes no essential reference to the special needs or proclivities of the individual—Jane's refusal to espouse Catholicism now would be incomprehensible. In regard to someone like Jane, Parfit is right. However, this hypothetical is predicated on two very unrealistic assumptions. First, people rarely, if ever, are able to predict precisely what their future beliefs will be, and, second, they rarely, if ever, are able to supply the justification for future beliefs before they come to hold them.

More realistically, suppose that Frank has spurned Orthodox Judaism and become an atheist. Having changed his mind about the existence of a divine being once, Frank knows that he might change his mind again, and he believes that time brings greater wisdom. Frank does not know what his religious convictions will be and certainly does not know what reasoning he will use to support those convictions, whatever they turn out to be. Not knowing what his belief will be, Frank cannot now hold this belief. But Frank can reasonably think it advisable not to foreclose the possibility of future worship by, say, working to ban religious observance. People can anticipate the possibility of marked changes in justified beliefs which they cannot specify in any detail. Though they cannot now believe these later beliefs, their belief in their growing insight justifies them in making provision for these beliefs by avoiding unnecessary over-commitment to present beliefs.

Still, many people have a pretty good idea of the shape their justified beliefs are likely to assume at a later time. Yet, they hold different beliefs now, and they do not necessarily believe that they are getting wiser as they get older. For example, some young people realize that, although they now think a life of risk and excitement is best, they will probably come to believe in the supervenient importance of security. (This is Thomas Nagel's example, which Parfit cites [Parfit 1984:154].) Does this predictable change of heart entail that these people now rank security highest or that they would rank security highest if they were honest with themselves? Does it entail that they should now adopt a security-oriented style of behavior?

Surely not. What is appropriate for and justified at one age may not be the same as what is appropriate for and justified at another age. For example, the elderly face a greater likelihood of illness and disability, and this may properly influence their deliberations. When the justification for a belief is personal, that is, it makes essential reference to the needs or desires of an individual, age can make a rational difference. Here, again, a person can rationally make provision for justified change without embracing future beliefs and, in this instance, without striking a Pollyannaish pose towards the wisdom of old age.

Now, it might be observed that people cannot always reconcile their justified present beliefs with their possible justified future beliefs. Acting on their present beliefs may preclude being able to act on some possible future beliefs, either because the present activity will change the world in ways that will bar conduct expressing the possible future belief or because the present activity will alter their health, mental capacities, or other resources in ways that will constrain their ability to act on possible future beliefs. Consider Martha, who does not merely become an atheist but also becomes convinced that religion is "the opiate of the people." If Martha joins like-minded comrades in spearheading a communist revolution that gains power and outlaws religion, Martha's faithfulness to her current belief severely limits her ability to honor a possible later religious conversion. Similarly, Scott might become persuaded that his religious disillusionment is a fall from grace and that no greater tragedy could befall him. If Scott decides to rekindle his spirituality by frequently taking huge doses of hallucinogenic drugs, he may jeopardize his sanity and thus his ability to abide by possible future beliefs. In both cases, temporal neutrality seems to be incoherent, not because it entails that Martha's and Scott's present beliefs must now be nullified by those they will think justified in the future, but rather because there is no way that they can do justice to their present beliefs as well as to their possible future beliefs.

It is a truism that every path taken represents indefinitely many paths forgone. Bridge burning sometimes takes on an aura of high drama, but more often it takes the form of unnoticed, slowly accumulating limitations. People cannot do everything, and they cannot even keep open the option of doing everything. It is obvious, then, that the principle of responsibility to self cannot require people to maintain a constant, if not an ever-expanding, supply of possible activities. In this respect, there is nothing extraordinary about the scenarios featuring Martha and Scott. Like everyone else, they are making choices in the present that restrict what they will be able to do in the future. What distinguishes them in most people's minds, I suppose, is that their choices seem fanatical or extreme and rule out courses of action that are widely considered reasonable. However, it seems dubious that this could be Martha's or Scott's view of the matter. Surely, in contrast to the scenario in which Frank loses his faith yet reckons another religious reversal possible, the second two scenarios make sense only if the protagonists reject the possibility of a reversal. If they do not reject this possibility, they would not be justified in holding the beliefs they do, nor would they be justified in acting as they do.

Now, it might be countered that Martha's political beliefs and Scott's theological beliefs are irrational and cannot be justified; hence, their refusal to admit that they might change their minds is irrational and self-destructive. But I fail to see what distinguishes Martha and Scott from the great ballet dancer, Peter Martins, who gave up dancing at the height of his career to devote all of his time to choreography and to the directorship of the New York City Ballet after George Balanchine's death. Martins can no more return to performing than Martha can take up religion or Scott can stop his drug-induced mystical visions. Though balletomanes lamented Martins' irrevocable decision and some, no doubt, thought it irrational, Martins presumably weighed his responsibilities and desires and decided to sacrifice those that were least important in his estimation. In the end, one cannot second-guess him. Similarly, I would urge, no one is in a position to denounce the imprudence of Martha's and Scott's decisions unless they lacked or failed to use the skills of autonomy competency.[1] (For further discussion of conflicts between personal values and basic interests, see part 2, sec. 5.) Only then would there be a presumption that their beliefs were unjustified; only then would paternalistic intervention be justified. After all, their convictions may well remain firm.

Alterable, but justified beliefs are compatible with the principle of responsibility to self. Such beliefs commonly warrant circumspection in the present with an eye to the future. However, such beliefs may require commitments in the present that permanently modify a person's constellation of future options. When this is so, the principle of responsibility to self does not require that people disavow their beliefs, but rather that they ask themselves how likely it is that they will change their minds later in life and how miserable they would be if they did change their minds after acting on their present beliefs.

This very inquiry may lead them to conclude that their present beliefs are excessively risky, or it may confirm them in their convictions. Whatever the outcome, they have given the future its due without betraying the present.

Still, Parfit maintains that other features of rational deliberation undermine this comprehensive approach to life. Parfit claims that much practical reasoning exhibits two biases. The bias toward the near leads people to prefer a smaller pain in the near future even if it means undergoing a greater pain in the distant future, and the bias toward the future leads them to prefer a greater pain that is over with and consigned to the past to a lesser one that lies ahead in the future (Parfit 1984:159, 160). According to Parfit, the advocate of the principle of responsibility to self must show that the bias toward the near is irrational though the bias toward the future is not. Most people think it rational to be more concerned about the future than about the past and thus think it rational to be relieved when terrible suffering is past, however horrific it was. Why, Parfit demands, is it irrational to be more concerned about nearer experiences than about farther ones? (1984:167) The principle of responsibility to self requires that we regard this bias toward the near as irrational. But, says Parfit, people do in fact favor the present over the future, and there is no reason to think them irrational.

A crucial feature of Parfit's argument is that the bias toward the near is a bias that causes people to discount events in the distant future simply because they are remote and not because they are (or are thought to be) less certain (Parfit 1984:162). The principle of responsibility to self does not require people to concern themselves equally with all parts of their lives, but rather it requires them not to arbitrarily ignore some parts of their lives. Whereas choosing to suffer more pain if only it will be postponed would violate the principle of responsibility to self, taking a chance on a more distant and less probable, though greater, pain would not necessarily violate this principle. One problem in Parfit's argument, I shall suggest, is that people do not have a bias toward the near of the sort Parfit requires, that is, a bias in favor of the present simply because it is at hand and a bias against the future simply because it is distant. And if people neither live by this bias nor think it rational to do so, there is nothing for the upholder of the principle of responsibility to self to explain away.

It is doubtful that the phenomenon of preferring greater suffering to be inflicted in the distant future in order to reduce suffering in the near future would survive if people did not think that, given more time, they could avert the worse pain. Behavior that appears to comport with the bias toward the near often results from realistic probability calculations or from systematic miscalculations. In either case, the bias toward the near does not explain the conduct.

In many situations, people correctly think that additional time improves their chances of preventing impending suffering. Barring other obstacles to a favorable tenure decision, a person whose publication record is less than splendid but who has nearly completed a book would be wise to request a delay in the tenure review, even though a negative tenure decision later might well cause this individual to suffer more. Not all postponements of possible suffering are irrational. Delay sometimes gives people the time they need to bring their efforts to fruition or to devise an original way to elude the expected misfortune. When this is so, delay does not reflect a bias toward the near and does not violate the principle of responsibility to self.

Still, it is undeniable that people's probability assessments are vulnerable to error. Tversky and Kahneman have argued persuasively that people typically rely on heuristic devices that lead them astray when they are asked to judge probabilities. For example, people tend to suppose that possibilities that they can readily recall or imagine are more likely to occur (Kahneman, Slovic, and Tversky 1982:11–13). Thus, people who have trouble picturing themselves in terrible pain will be disposed to discount the risk of ending up in agony. Parfit, it should be noted, rejects this explanation of the bias toward the near. Although he grants that limited imagination may sometimes account for people's preoccupation with the present, he insists that a bias toward the near survives vivid imagination of the distant future (1984:161).

A second source of error where suffering is concerned is inveterate optimism. Hope often distorts probability calculations—people tend to overrate their own ability or the ability of other people to influence favorably the course of events (Abramson and Alloy 1981:439). Still, these apparently irrational exaggerations may function beneficially. As Jonathan Adler points out, embarking upon marriage fully cognizant of the gloomy divorce statistics and duly cynical about one's own chances for success will undermine the emotional commitment and sense of responsibility necessary to maintain the relationship (1984:176). Similarly, by temporizing despite an objectively pessimistic prognosis, people may effectively use the time gained. If they can subdue their anxiety, for example, they may eventually be able to withstand distant greater pain better than they could withstand immediate though smaller pain. Again, such strategies are consonant with the principle of responsibility to self, for they do not subvert the needs of one's future self.

Estimating probabilities and hoping for the best, people seem to be biased toward the near. However, if people could be convinced that the threatened long-run calamities were inevitable and that nothing could be gained through delay, their apparent bias toward the near would vanish. In sum, people do not have a bias toward the near that can be explained simply by the remoteness of later events; their procrastination depends on their belief in the relative uncertainty of these later events. To the extent that the belief in this uncertainty is warranted or is necessary to gain a secondary but substantial good, it is rational to put off suffering, that is, to appear to be biased toward the near, but to observe the principle of responsibility to self in fact.

Parfit might reply by saying that, when great pain is certain and a person chooses to get it over with, this individual is only displaying another bias—the bias toward the future, which mandates a preference for putting bad things in the past (1984:160). Though it seems true that people often want to get pain over with as soon as possible—"Do the root canal now, Doc; I can't take a week thinking about it"—it is not clear that this desire manifests, properly speaking, a bias toward the future. Paradigmatically, one exhibits a bias toward the future when one prefers a greater pain that is in the past to a lesser pain that is in the future. But, when one opts to suffer a pain as quickly as possible, the pain one is taking on is still in the future; one is sacrificing one's immediate future for the benefit of one's extended future.[2] Still, Parfit's explanation captures a strong tendency in human psychology, and it cannot be dismissed. Nevertheless, it is plainly not the whole story, for it does not explain why the bias toward the future prevails in one kind of situation and the bias toward the near prevails in another kind of situation.

What makes the difference, I think, is the perceived likelihood and manageability of the pain. The greater its perceived certainty and manageability, the more likely people are to concede defeat and opt to undergo whatever is in store for them sooner. In Parfit's phraseology, the bias toward the future takes precedence over the bias toward the near. However, the greater its perceived uncertainty or un-manageability, the more likely people are to hope for the best and to gamble on trying to prevent the pain. As Parfit would say, the bias toward the near takes precedence over the bias towards the future. Since it is sometimes rational to give in and sometimes rational to fight back, there is no reason to believe that hastening to endure pain results from the operation of an irrational bias or that it is always irrational to postpone pain. Insofar as there is an irrational bias toward the near, it is a product of excessive optimism or miscalculation, not a product of concern with immediate experience as such.

Only if the bias toward the near is treated as a full-fledged prejudice does it conflict with the principle of responsibility to self. Indeed, the principle of responsibility to self could prescribe a strategy of postponement designed to manage, if not to avert, fearsome pain. It only forbids self-destructive procrastination. Thus, this principle is vindicated against the charge that it endorses arbitrary temporal distinctions. It allows that relative indifference to past events is rational (I am leaving aside Parfit's fascinating, but extremely counter-intuitive challenge to the bias toward the future [1984:174−177]) and condones only rational forward-looking attitudes. Moreover, it affirms those "biases" with respect to time that people would actually defend.

As I mentioned at the outset, Parfit does not claim to defeat the principle of responsibility to self, decisively. In fact, he provides an intriguing argument in support of this principle. As Parfit notes, "All these later times *will,* at some time, be a *now* for you" (1984:188; for a complementary argument, see Fried 1970:171−173). To ignore this fact about the passage of time is to reject impartiality—is arbitrarily to prefer one now to another now—and to reject impartiality is to be irrational. I doubt, however, that an appeal to impartiality can ground this line of argument. Though interpersonal impartiality often needs no defense, intrapersonal impartiality is precisely what is at issue.

A better way to develop this argument, I think, would be to draw out the implications of an assymmetry between past desires and future desires. The bias toward the future—that is, concerning oneself with future desires and ignoring past desires—seems rational because it is impossible to satisfy past desires. If one has ceased to have a desire, one can behave in a way that would have satisfied that desire when one had it, but, since one no longer has this desire, behaving this way cannot satisfy it now. The logic of desires entails that temporal neutrality with respect to the past is irrational.

Against this view, Parfit maintains that the satisfaction of some desires is not conditional on the persistence of the desire (1984:151). Only when the fulfillment or nonfulfillment of a desire would bring the person who has the desire satisfaction or frustration is the satisfaction of the desire conditional on its persistence (Parfit 1984:151). If Rita wants lobster for dinner tonight but none is available, it will not help matters to give her a lobster for breakfast tomorrow morning, unless she still feels like eating lobster. Moreover, if Rita wants and succeeds in getting lobster for dinner two weeks later, she is not simultaneously satisfying her earlier unsatisfied desire. This type of case is familiar. But Parfit claims that many past desires can be satisfied.

He gives a series of examples of unconditional desires. The first involves a chance encounter with a stranger who shares her ambitions, hopes, and fears with you during a train journey (1984:151). When the two of you part, you very much want her to succeed despite the fact that you will never meet again. Your desire does not last, yet, Parfit maintains, your desire would be satisfied if she succeeds. Here Parfit conflates a wish with a desire. It would be understandable if you left the train wishing the amiable stranger well and hoping that she succeed. However, unless you planned to take steps to further her aims or hoped to find a way to further these aims, it would be odd to say that you wanted her to succeed.[3] As we know from fairy tales, wishes can come true whether one wants them to or not.

Parfit then turns to the desires of people who die before their desires are satisfied. A dying man might want his daughter to continue making donations to Dance Theater of Harlem, a company he had supported throughout his lifetime, but he might never ask for or receive any assurance from her that she will do so. Suppose that after her father's death the daughter spontaneously decides to duplicate his philanthropic practice. Parfit contends that, although the father's desire no longer exists, she is satisfying his past desire. The question of our relations to the dead is a complicated one that I cannot adequately explore here. Nevertheless, it seems to me that there are a number of reasons to doubt Parfit's conclusion. Although Parfit assumes that death is extinction and therefore that the father's desire does not persist, it seems likely that, to the extent that we are inclined to agree that the daughter's activities satisfy his desire, our inclination may reflect a deeply entrenched cultural belief in the immortality of the soul. Although one may not believe that doctrine, it has been pervasive for many centuries, and it would not be surprising if it had ramifications in our intuitions about our treatment of the dead. Also, this example is hard to separate from promises made to dying persons. It is too easy to slip into thinking that there must be an unspoken pact between the father and the daughter and that she is abiding by that understanding. Of course, a promise can be fulfilled although the promisee does not want it to be fulfilled.

Finally, Parfit offers the case of an individual who has spent fifty years working to save Venice (1984:152). During this time, this individual's two strongest desires are that Venice be saved and that he be among its saviors. Moreover, he wants Venice to be saved and to be among its saviors even if he ceases to have these desires. After fifty years of dedication to this cause, he ceases to have these desires. Parfit maintains that, despite his change of heart, his former desires constitute a reason to continue giving to the Venice Preservation Fund, for doing so helps to satisfy two of his former desires. Here, Parfit seems to be overlooking the reasons that support the individual's desires. It seems doubtful that this person could intelligibly want Venice to be saved and to be among its saviors regardless of whether he continued to have these desires unless he thought that the desirability of these states of affairs was independent of anybody's (or at least his) wanting them to be the case. If it is rational for him to contribute to the Venice Preservation Fund although he has lost interest in this cause, it is not because he will thereby satisfy his past desires. Rather, it is because powerful reasons to save Venice still obtain.

Satisfying desires appears to be conditional on their persistence. Desires can be continuing, but they are not timeless. No past desires can be satisfied, for none has persisted.

From one point of view, future desires present a parallel case—trying to satisfy them in advance of their inception is as irrational as trying to satisfy past desires. Since one does not now have one's future desires, no action that one now takes can satisfy any of those desires. Suppose that Christa will want to make love to Vincent two weeks from now but that she does not now want to do so. Suppose also that Vincent is prescient. Vincent cannot satisfy Christa's future desire by forcing her to have sex with him today. If anything, this rape would lead Christa not to form her predicted future desire and instead to form a desire never to encounter Vincent again. Still, people sometimes act contrary to their plans but later affirm what they have done. Have they satisfied their future desires? Everyday locutions suggest that they do not. Such people do not think to themselves, "What luck! I've already satisfied a desire I didn't have until now." Rather, they think, "So that's what I really wanted all along. I just didn't realize it until now." If no one has a desire, the desire cannot be satisfied. To try to satisfy such a desire is not merely irrational in the sense of being undesirable; it is irrational in the sense of Alice-in-Wonderland nonsensicality.

Yet, future desires differ from past desires inasmuch as one will eventually have one's future desires, whereas one's past desires are gone forever. Of course, one can come to want the same sort of thing that one once wanted, but one cannot have the desire that one once had. In contrast, at some point one will actually have one's future desires. Consequently, there is a sense in which it is not irrational to take into account the eventual satisfaction of these desires. Since it is generally desirable that one be able to satisfy one's desires, it is rational in the sense of desirable that one not preclude their satisfaction. Parfit is right: "All these later times *will*, at some time, be a *now* for you." But no past time will ever again be a now for you.

Parfit's argument against the principle of responsibility to self plays on an ambiguity in the term "irrational." When Parfit allows that everyone considers the bias toward the future rational, we readily agree, for the alternative orientation—temporal neutrality with respect to the past—would be nonsensical. When he goes on to suggest that the bias toward the near must also be rational, he implies that the alternative orientation—temporal neutrality with respect to the future—is likewise nonsensical. If the principle of responsibility to self were understood to require attempting to satisfy future desires now, this conclusion would be correct. But no one understands the principle this way. On the contrary, we understand the principle of responsibility to self to require making provision for the satisfaction of future desires when they occur. At worst, this principle is irrational in the sense of undesirable; it is surely not irrational in the sense of nonsensical. Similarly, we regard the bias toward the near as irrational, not because it is nonsensical, but because it is undesirable.

Richard Wollheim puts this point in the language of subjectivity, as opposed to Parfit's language of social relations. Wollheim maintains that each person stands in a relation of "self-concern" to himself or herself (1984:236). Self-concern is neither egoism nor selfishness (Wollheim 1984:242−244). Rather, self-concern is what makes the difference between my learning (and believing) that some calamity is about to befall me and my learning that the same calamity is about to befall anyone else (Wollheim 1984:237−241). According to Wollheim, empathy with others cannot bring about the same sense of stricken dread that self-concern can. Whereas each person's responses to others depend on who the victim is and how one feels about this individual—is it someone close to me? is it someone I like or someone I dislike? is it someone who likes me or someone who dislikes me? and so on—one's responses to one's own situation do not depend on one's attitudes toward oneself—barring pathology, I shall be upset to learn that I am about to suffer whether or not I am currently pleased with myself (Wollheim 1984:240−241). Since self-concern is an attitude toward one's existence as an ongoing being, and since it seems to be a primitive ingredient of human psychology, to reject the principle of responsibility to self is to controvert the basic structure of consciousness.

If these arguments are correct, the principle of responsibility to self emerges from Parfit's attack more plausible than ever. It is irrational not to take an interest in the desires of one's future self, for, as I have argued, there is nothing inherently irrational about this concern and, as the present arguments show, rationality requires due regard for one's continuing well-being.

Now, it might be objected that the principle of responsibility to self is exceedingly conservative. At one point, Rawls remarks that people should avoid "substantial swings up and down" (1971:421). But, if this advice were taken seriously, people might become so risk averse that they would hardly accomplish anything and they would find their lives boring. Does the principle of responsibility to self enjoin people to approach life with extreme trepidation?

In this context, it is important to keep in mind that the principle of responsibility to self recommends an approach to living. As Charles Fried puts it, "we are considering as rational persons only those whose life plans involve some use of their lives" (1970:167). Neither the compulsively suicidal person nor the person who prefers maximum safety over every possible pursuit is interested in living. Not only do these orientations exclude such major values as love and learning, but also they rule out the trivial pleasures and concerns that are constitutive of distinctive human personalities (Fried 1970:179−180). Living necessarily imposes risks. Accordingly, the question raised by the principle of responsibility to self is not whether to assume any risks, but rather which risks any given person finds worthwhile to assume.

Courting disaster is ill-advised for everyone, but this restriction leaves a great deal of latitude in which people can freely conceive their life plans. What must not be overlooked is that different individuals are more or less insouciant. In other words, they are more or less prone to suffer in the present over possible setbacks in the future. Worrywarts may be justified in spending extra time on train travel if flying makes them nervous, whereas less anxious people may be better off enduring a brief bout with fear rather than a long and tedious train ride. Furthermore, different individuals have different values and goals, and they place more or less importance on them. Consequently, what counts as disaster varies from person to person. Minor career setbacks will not faze people who are content with their present jobs or who have other sources of fulfillment, but similar setbacks may greatly disturb people who are trying to get ahead or who totally identify with their work. In view of this diversity and in view of the fact that the principle of responsibility to self must be applied in the context set by the individual self, there is no reason to suppose that adherence to this principle will crimp people's aspirations.

One must not forget after all that taking great risks can prove worthwhile. Consider Siegfried Sassoon's reflections on his heroic exploits in World War I:

> My real reason for seeking trouble like this was my need to escape from the worry and responsibility of being a Company Commander, plus annoyance with the idea of being blown to bits while sitting there watching Velmore inditing a nicely-worded situation report. I was tired and overstrained, and my old foolhardiness was taking control of me.
>
> To be outside the trench with the possibility of bumping into an enemy patrol was at any rate an antidote to my suppressed weariness of the entire bloody business. I wanted to do something definite, and perhaps get free of the whole thing. It was the old story; I could only keep going by doing something spectacular.
>
> So there was more bravado than bravery about it, and I should admire that vanished self of mine more if he had avoided taking needless risks. I blame him for doing his utmost to prevent my being here to write about him. But on the other hand I am grateful

to him for giving me something to write about. (*Sherston's Progress*, 645)

Plainly, Sassoon is not holding his youthful self up as a model of autonomy. He realizes that he was being driven by forces over which he had little control, and he accuses himself of abrogating the principle of responsibility to self. Still, he also concedes that time vindicated the risks he impetuously took as a soldier. Though Sassoon did not assume these risks autonomously, it is important to acknowledge that someone could have assumed them autonomously.

The principle of responsibility to self requires people to be frank with themselves about their emotional capacities, their talents, and their values when formulating their aims and deciding how to pursue them. In providing an occasion to speculate about one's future self, this exercise also provides an occasion to conceive and evaluate present desires about that future self. As a result, conscious compliance with this precept is conducive to the emergence of forward-looking desires—these may prove to be cautious or daring in tenor—that must themselves figure in a person's deliberations and may balance a conservative, excessively tentative drift.

To have control over their lives, it is evident that individuals must honestly scrutinize their own traits, abilities, and values and must choose activities and projects that they are capable of fulfilling and that they deem worthwhile. As I have urged, personal autonomy requires adherence to a life plan congruent with one's self-portrait (part 2, sec. 4). Since people are dynamic, it follows that no satisfactory life plan can be static. Nevertheless, it would be unreasonable to suppose that the natural tendency of people's lives is toward ever-narrowing interests requiring fewer and fewer resources. Though people cannot reliably predict exactly what resources they will need later in life, they can avoid depleting many of the resources available to them, and they can acquire resources that are apt to prove useful. While these precautions should not consume people's lives in the present, failure to take them can prevent people from doing what they really want in the future. Thus, people can deprive themselves of personal autonomy by defying the principle of responsibility to self.

I have argued that the principle of responsibility to self does not entangle people in self-contradictory belief systems, does not commit people to arbitrary temporal distinctions, and does not impose undue conservativism on their choices. Therefore, contrary to Parfit, I conclude that this principle is neither destructive nor perverse. But, more importantly, I would urge that compliance with the principle of responsibility to self is necessary for ongoing autonomy. As such, this principle should be seen as enhancing individuals' ability to fulfill themselves and thus as enriching their lives.

# PART III

# Obstacles to
# Personal Autonomy

Women have served all these centuries as looking glasses possessing the magic and delicious power of reflecting the figure of man at twice its natural size.

Anything can happen when womanhood has ceased to be a protected occupation, I thought, opening the door.

*A Room of One's Own* by Virginia Woolf

# Theories of Socialization

I HAVE argued that our understanding of personal autonomy is not advanced by positing an innate or self-generated inner self which autonomous action must express. Not only is socialization inescapable; it is also beneficial. Thus, inquiry into the nature of autonomy is seriously impeded when the true self is taken to be an asocial core. A better approach is to understand autonomy as the successful exercise of a competency—a repertory of coordinated skills which enables people to control their own lives.

To understand autonomy as the exercise of a competency is to acknowledge that autonomy is impossible without socialization. People are born with the potential to become competent in various ways, but it is only through education that these potentialities are realized. Nearly all human infants are capable of learning a language. But they cannot become competent speakers unless they are exposed to a language, and writing skills do not develop without systematic instruction. Similarly, one would expect autonomy competency to languish if it were not cultivated.

Interestingly enough, while philosophers have been questing after the holy grail of free will, social psychologists have been studying sundry phenomena bearing on autonomy. Though they have not always conceived of autonomy as a competency, students of human development have examined assorted self-regulatory behaviors along with the social and psychological contexts in which they occur. Their cumulative research reports supply a picture of those social practices which tend to enhance and those which tend to defeat autonomy.

Strongly suggested by this literature is one striking conclusion: socialization does not foster the same capacity for autonomy in men and women alike, at least not in the dominant cultures of Western industrialized nations. Indeed, it is almost a platitude of the socialization literature that men are encouraged to act more autonomously than women. Men are taught to be more independent and to exert greater control over situations. Of course, it is important to recognize that independence and control over situations do not necessarily entail that people are doing what they really want. Interpersonal domination or emotional and economic self-sufficiency can easily be mistaken for autonomy. Nevertheless, keeping this caveat in mind, we can learn a great deal from socialization theory.

Psychologists have proposed a number of theories to account for the genesis of autonomous conduct. These theories fall into three main types: psychoanalytic accounts, behavioristic social learning accounts, and cognitive development accounts. Before considering how socialization can promote or suppress autonomy, it is useful to review the main features of these three models.

Psychoanalytic theory, which Freud originated but which generations of analysts have developed in various ways, stresses the interaction between biological conditions and unconscious mental processes in personality formation. Although Freud maintained a fatalistic view of the significance of biology in human development, other psychoanalysts have treated the significance attaching to biology as a social construction. Nevertheless, in all variants of psychoanalysis, human biology establishes a sequential schedule through which individual development proceeds and which poses a series of problems for the developing individual.

On the one hand, the oral, anal, phallic, and genital stages represent the infant's suckling followed by the child's toilet training and discovery of sexual differences culminating with the youth's sexual stirrings. But, on the other hand, these stages represent periods of prominence for three erogenous zones. As children develop, their psychic energy—in psychoanalytic parlance, their libido—is transferred from one location to the next, and these shifts are accompanied by struggles with anxiety and frustration. At the unconscious level, this drama is played out through an array of mechanisms including condensation—collapsing several ideas into one; displacement—separating the emotion connected with an idea from the content of the idea or focusing the emotion connected with an idea on one part of the idea; identification—modeling oneself on qualities attributed to someone else; externalization—assuming that one's relations to others take a form that in fact holds between one part of oneself and another part of oneself; and reaction formation—e.g., converting a response into its opposite or denying that something is important. By these and other similar means, children unconsciously defend themselves against threats to their psychic stability. In the process, their personalities take shape.

What is distinctive about psychoanalytic theory is its emphasis on unconscious processes—its emphasis on a concealed, yet determinative psychic realm. As the basis for their claims about the structure and contents of this realm, psychoanalysts rely primarily on information provided in the course of clinical interviews. Thus, critics of psychoanalysis have often objected to the construction of a theory purporting to account for all human psychology on the basis of discoveries about disturbed individuals. Moreover, because of the improvisational conversational methods of psychoanalytic therapists, the evidence for this theory is limited to anecdotal materials extracted from sessions with patients together with these patients' testimonials to the efficacy of the "talking cure." Since this evidence is unsystematic and open to divergent interpretations, the psychoanalytic theory of development has been accused of failing to allow for rigorous empirical testing.

A second approach to the problem of socialization has its roots in behaviorism. Though some variants of social learning theory do not presuppose acceptance of the philosophical position that the mind is reducible to outward behavior, social learning theory sees reinforcement as the prime force in the socialization process. According to behavioristic social learning theory, children observe and store up various patterns of behavior, and they imitate many of the behavior modes they observe. Societies capitalize on these inclinations by rewarding acceptable conduct and by punishing unacceptable conduct. Moreover, through canalization—a process in which people persist in those behaviors which are familiar because they like what is familiar—certain behaviors become self-reinforcing.

Whereas psychoanalysis regards the web of emotional bonds between parents and their children—especially, children's identification with their same-sex parent—as the indispensable extra-psychic impetus to development, behavioristic social learning theory sees these emotional relations as one more form of positive or negative reinforcement. The withholding of parental love, according to the latter theory, is no different in kind from the withholding of lollipops. Another departure of social learning theory is its conception of mental life as an unmediated exchange beween individuals and their environment. This conception contributes further to social learning theory's exiguous treatment of mental processes—experience is reduced to satisfaction and deprivation while motivation is reduced to the pursuit of satisfaction and the avoidance of deprivation. Throughout the life cycle, then, people respond to cues issued by their parents, their peers, and the media, and they try to model themselves on social expectations.

According to cognitive development theory, children take a much more active part in personality formation than they do according to behavioristic social learning theory. On the former view, children are motivated by a desire for competence and high status. In order to obtain these goods, they must figure out how to fit into their social environment. Yet, their interaction with their social world is limited by the stage of cognitive maturity they have reached. Thus, socialization is an interaction between a society and a child's developing cognitive apparatus.

Throughout the graduated process cognitive development theory envisages, children receive input from their cultural milieu and assimilate it to the extent that they can with the concepts they have at their disposal. Based on their understanding of what is appropriate for them, they imitate what they take to be suitable conduct. When they are successful, society reinforces their conduct with approval. But they eventually confront anomalous experience which the schema they have acquired cannot handle, and this discovery leads them to generate more sophisticated conceptions of their social roles and to model themselves accordingly. As before, society rewards approved adjustments.

Unlike social learning theory, cognitive development theory does not reduce people to receptacles for social influences. On this view, social rewards do not create children's curiosity and mimicry. Rather, these are natural dispositions which equip children to take advantage of the information society furnishes. Moreover, children actively collaborate with society's wishes for them because they want to succeed. Consequently, they revise their views and adjust their behavior as their capabilities mature and as they encounter increasingly subtle and complex situations. The socialized individual, then, is not wholly a socially manufactured product. Society provides direction, but children interpret and assimilate it.

One difficulty with socialization theory that should be evident from this brief overview is that the field is divided among hostile camps. Each model posits different mechanisms of socialization and directs investigators to different phenomena. Thus, each theory gives pride of place to a different aspect of human development.

Yet, to the lay reader, none of the theories can easily be dismissed. A possible explanation of the intuitive plausibility of all of these theories is that each of them, taken alone, is unacceptably unidimensional. Psychoanalysis probes the intra-psychic evolution of personality but neglects the broad social setting in which this process takes place.[1] Social learning theory depicts the impact of social stimuli but dispenses with the child's motivation. Cognitive development theory exhibits children's active curiosity about their place in society but leaves out individual temperament. Still, it seems obvious that youthful eagerness to grow and learn, social reinforcements of crude as well as subtle design, and a richly meaning-laden inner life are all part of the process of human development. Thus, it seems reasonable to suppose that each of these theories is telling part of the story.

In the context of the present inquiry, a further reason to take an eclectic view of human development concerns the salience of differential masculine and feminine developmental tracks with respect to the issue of personal autonomy. Each type of theory has weaknesses, as well as the strengths I have mentioned, with respect to its ability to account for the dichotomy between masculinity and femininity. In view of its emphasis on girls' and boys' identification with their mothers and fathers respectively, psychoanalysis predicts that children will grow up to resemble their same-sex parent. But this prediction is not borne out except insofar as children generally fit into sex roles (Frieze 1978:103). Behavioristic social learning theory maintains that gender identity is only as compelling as the strength and the persistence of the reinforcements that secure it. However, on this view, it is hard to understand the deep commitment to motherhood that women commonly feel and the singular adaptation of typical feminine personalities to the relational tasks of parenting (Chodorow 1978:33). For cognitive development theory, a major difficulty is that children prefer gender-appropriate toys at the age of two although they do not yet grasp the concept of gender constancy—that is, they do not realize that they will always be male or female, even if they know what sex they are (Hyde 1985:68). If cognitive development theory is correct in maintaining that children imitate gender-appropriate conduct because they know what sex they are and want to fit into that role, their preference for gender-appropriate toys at this age is inexplicably precocious.

This sampling of criticisms that have been raised against the three major models of development should make it clear that none can claim to have produced an altogether convincing explanation of gender-typing. But, as I stated earlier, this phenomenon is central to my inquiry, for men are thought to be more autonomous than women. In order to understand how child-rearing practices can contribute to or detract from personal autonomy, then, it is necessary to understand the differences between the ways in which boys and girls are typically brought up. In view of the limitations and the insights of each theory of development, I shall sketch an account of these processes using an eclectic approach.

# Feminine and Masculine Socialization

THE PROBLEM of feminine and masculine development presents two subsidiary problems. First, how are girls and boys socialized? Second, what are adult women and men like? We need to know both how children are treated and what kind of adults are produced.

Both of these issues have sparked heated controversy. Although everyone is intimately acquainted with feminine or masculine socialization, people's conceptions of these processes and their outcomes are commonly skewed by stereotypical prejudices about women and men. Thus, many studies have produced data that have proved impossible to replicate. Moreover, earlier researchers invariably detected sizeable differences in feminine and masculine development, but more recent reviews of these studies have questioned the dimensions of the demonstrable differences. A further complication arises because social-psychologists are presently investigating feminine and masculine development during a period of marked social change. Thus, discrepant data may be attributable to shifts in child-rearing practices and popular gender ideals rather than to faulty research design or misguided interpretation. In sum, the perennial difficulties of social psychological research—e.g., relying on subjects' recollections, generalizing from laboratory settings and experimental tasks to everyday life, characterizing average individuals while losing sight of diversity, and inferring causal connections between childhood experience and adult personality structure—are exacerbated in studies of feminine and masculine socialization.

I mention these difficulties here because it is important to appreciate the gap between "common knowledge" and social scientific documentation in the area under study. The claim that women are less autonomous than men is a bit of common knowledge backed by a body of fragmentary, though suggestive, social psychological evidence. Nevertheless, if the claim that women are not autonomous is taken in an unqualified and extreme form, the extant research does not support it. The outlets for women's autonomy and the degree of autonomy women display vary in comparisons among socioeconomic, ethnic, and racial populations, as well as in comparisons within these populations (Gerson 1985:11–22; Hyde 1985:138–141; Weitzman 1984:177–183, 215–218). Moreover, there is reason to believe that the forms in which women's autonomy have been manifest have not always been recognized as such (see part 3, sec. 3). Still, the widespread belief in the inferiority of women's autonomy is not without foundation, and I shall examine the evidence for this view in the rest of this section.

Before considering the socialization practices that compromise women's autonomy, it is necessary to consider wherein this lack of autonomy consists. In her classic study of women's subordination, *The Second Sex,* Simone de Beauvoir diagnoses two prime characterological obstacles to women's autonomy: narcissism and altruism. Though de Beauvoir stresses that these qualities are consequences of remediable social arrangements, she stridently condemns them (de Beauvoir 1953:xxvi, 249). Women are "mutilated," she repeatedly asserts (de Beauvoir 1953:274, 295, 306, 451, 642). Thus, they cannot exercise control over their own lives.

According to de Beauvoir, women are raised to be excessively self-conscious and excessively dependent on others' approbation. This narcissism prevents women from single-mindedly pursuing their aims, for they always have one eye on the reception their activities are getting. The result of this distraction is that women are unable to fulfill their potential (de Beauvoir 1953:660–661). A second impediment to autonomy is altruism. Women are raised to over-identify with others' interests and to neglect their own. As a result, women suppress their own values and needs in deference to others' and forego the possibility of forthrightly expressing themselves (de Beauvoir 1953:484– 489, 496, 550). In combination with discrimination against women in education and employment and the institution of marriage, these implanted characteristics bar women's autonomy.

In the treatment of feminine socialization that follows, I shall grant de Beauvoir's diagnosis of the sources of women's heteronomy. Also, though I shall trim it and supplement it in light of current research, I shall follow the main outlines of de Beauvoir's seminal narrative account of feminine socialization. Despite the fact that in the 1940s when *The Second Sex* was being written the social-psychological literature on gender development was very primitive, de Beauvoir anticipated many of the conclusions later studies substantiated. Also, her treatment is illuminating because it synthesizes disparate child-rearing practices and the developmental strands that correspond to them into a single conception of the evolving gendered personality.

De Beauvoir sees the divide between the feminine and the masculine mentality occurring at about the age of three. Before that point, she maintains, girls and boys behave and are cared for roughly the same way (1953:250–251). However, accurately dating the onset of gender socialization and gender consciousness has spurred controversy. Girls and boys are color-coded pink and blue respectively from the moment of birth. Furthermore, there is some evidence that parents handle male babies more than female babies and that, in experimental situations in which adults are asked to play with a baby that has been identified (sometimes misleadingly) as a boy or a girl, they are inclined to give toy trains or footballs to babies they believe to be boys and dolls to babies they believe to be girls. Yet, students of early socialization dispute the extent of gender socialization in infancy. Some doubt that, over all, parents respond to infants in strongly sex-stereotyped ways, while others have challenged this conclusion on the grounds that the differential treatment accorded babies may be too subtle for crude social-scientific techniques to pick up (Hyde 1985:156–157; Weitzman 1984:160–163). Nevertheless, there is a consensus that differential socialization gradually becomes more overt and more intense as the child grows older (Wietzman 1984:163).

The crucial initiation period, according to de Beauvoir, begins as children become capable of greater independence or, in psychoanalytic terms, as they reach the phallic stage—around the age of three. At this point, boys are subjected to what de Beauvoir aptly calls a "second weaning." Of course, all breast-fed babies suffer the trauma of separation from the woman who is nursing them. But a further withdrawal of intimacy is imposed on boys a couple of years later. Whereas little girls are still allowed to cling to their mothers and are still petted and protected, little boys are encouraged to play by themselves and are denied the tender caresses they had been accustomed to receiving (de Beauvoir 1953:252). Girls continue to garner attention for their cute turns of gaiety and pouting, but boys discover that they can only please their parents by giving up these stratagems. Otherwise, they will be chided as sissies.

We have already seen that adults are disposed to interact with children on the basis of sex-stereotypes. Although it is unclear what, if any, impact this disposition has on babies, one study suggests that differential treatment may have had a discernible effect as early as the age of thirteen months. By that time, boys start spending less time in close proximity to their mothers, but girls continue to talk with and gaze at their mothers (Hunter College 1983:145). These observations lend support to de Beauvoir's contention that boys become more independent earlier than girls, but they also indicate that boys' independence emerges well before de Beauvoir timed it. Nevertheless, it is debatable why this difference appears. Contemporary researchers may be studying essentially the same phenomenon that de Beauvoir detected in boys' behavior when they look at activity levels. There is some evidence that boys are more active than girls (Hyde 1985:149), and greater activity would help to explain boys' more extensive forays. However, their greater activity is probably stimulated, at least in part, by social forces, though the nature of these forces remains obscure.

That boys at all ages are more aggressive than girls is frightfully well established (Hyde 1985:143; Weitzman 1984:175). Here too, we may have experimental confirmation for de Beauvoir's contention that little boys are pressed into independence. One student of male aggression maintains that the difference between female and male aggression is most marked among preschool-age children (Hyde 1985:144).

Yet, it appears that aggressive behaviors are often inadvertently sustained as boys mature. According to one theory, if sanctions meant to deter aggression are administered by a figure with whom the child does not identify, they tend to instigate further aggressive behavior. Boys receive more punishments for verbal and physical attacks than girls. But since these punishments are mainly inflicted by women (mothers and elementary school teachers) while boys identify with men (primarily their fathers), these attempts to restrain boys actually promote aggression (Hyde 1985:144–146). Thus, a prime component of the masculine stereotype may be unintentionally reinforced. Since aggression is a form of self-assertion—albeit a degenerate one—early socialization plainly does not detract from boys' bumptious spirit.

A final line of inquiry that supports de Beauvoir's view concerns social attitudes toward gender-stereotype violations. Though recent investigations of adult toleration for men who do not display traditionally masculine characteristics yield mixed results—some suggest increasing openmindedness; others suggest strong disapproval—studies of children's attitudes reveal a rather fierce loyalty to the stereotypes (Hyde 1985:109–110). Thus, there may be considerable diversity in parental attitudes towards their children's conformity or lack of conformity to gender standards. Still, children themselves partially negate this latitude. Especially where boys are concerned, they enforce strict adherence to these stereotypes (Hyde 1985:110). Since the period de Beauvoir is describing is one in which children have begun to play with one another, there is good reason to believe that boys will be penalized by their peers, if not by their parents, for "sissyish" behavior.

Let us grant, then, that, although de Beauvoir may have been mistaken about the timing of this event, she is correct in claiming that young boys undergo a "second weaning"—that they are severed from the security and warmth their mothers have hitherto provided. To compensate boys for this harsh loss of maternal warmth and affection, de Beauvoir contends, their fathers welcome them into the masculine realm.

There they are assured that they belong to a superior world of manly tasks and manly prerogatives and that their penises gain them entrance to this priviledged world (de Beauvoir 1953:253). From then on, boys learns to take pride in their genitals and to associate their anatomy with their masculinity. Thus, the phallus becomes the symbol of their status as males, and little boys come to identify with their penises. Meanwhile, little girls have been given dolls—inert toys that are anatomically separate from them and that they are supposed to take care of (de Beauvoir 1953:260). Whereas the boy projects himself into a vital part of himself, the girl projects herself into a passive object of solicitous attentions. Thus, the boy's infantile narcissism is purged—he ceases to view himself as an object destined to be inspected and approved or disapproved—but the girl's is reinforced—she becomes incapable of viewing herself as a subject of experience and an author of action (de Beauvoir 1953:261). Not incidentally, the girl also learns that her station in life is that of the domestic caretaker who is responsible for maintaining the family's emotional bonds and for keeping the household running smoothly (de Beauvoir 1953:264).

Studies of paternal behavior support the broad outlines of de Beauvoir's account. After the first birthday, fathers begin to pay more attention to their sons, thus leaving their daughters largely in their mother's hands (Hyde 1985:122). Moreover, fathers and mothers treat their children differently. Whereas mothers engage in caretaking, fathers play with their children, frequently in exciting ways (Hyde 1985:122). The upshot is that boys have access to more vigorous, stimulating activities than girls have. Accordingly, boys have good reason to identify with the masculine world—it is more fun.

Whatever inclination boys may have to identify with the masculine role is likely to be compounded by paternal sanctions. Fathers evidence greater concern with gender stereotypes than mothers. They have more stereotypical conceptions of how their children should behave, and they impose these conceptions on their children consistently (Weitzman 1984:164). Moreover, they use different enforcement methods to deal with their daughters and their sons. They tend to reward their daughters for feminine behavior, but they are apt to punish their sons for behavior inappropriate to their sex (Weitzman 1984:164). In view of the theory cited above that children are more compliant when punishments are administered by people with whom they identify, there is reason to believe that this mode of paternal insistence that boys be masculine is very effective. How responsive girls are to their fathers' approbation is an open question.

One thing is clear, however. Preschool-age girls and boys alike express strong preferences for gender-appropriate toys. While girls elect stringing beads or playing house, boys opt to play with guns or trucks or to build structures (Hyde 1985:158). Furthermore, these preferences are strongly ingrained, especially in boys. When nursery school teachers urge boys to switch to feminine activities, they refuse to go along (Hyde 1985:116). Seconded by their school mates, children are disinclined to cross gender lines.

But as they grow up, de Beauvoir points out, girls make a dreadful and humiliating discovery. All children initially seek to retain their ties with their mothers and to identify with their mothers because they seem to be the most powerful figures around—this is why the "second weaning" is so distressing for little boys. But lucky girls get their wish—they are not pryed away from their mothers. A grave disappointment awaits them, however. Both girls and boys soon realize that men are actually in command, and the girls realize that they have marched into a cul-de-sac and cannot turn back (de Beauvoir 1953:267). The books they read along with the regimentation of their activities endlessly reiterate the lesson that the feminine role is a sharply circumscribed one of passivity, objectification, and routine chores (de Beauvoir 1953:266–269).

Although both girls and boys distinguish feminine and masculine toys and prefer gender-appropriate toys by the age of three, there is evidence that boys become firmly attached to the masculine ideal while girls become ambivalent about femininity. At the onset of the period de Beauvoir has singled out—age three—both girls and boys want to be like their mothers (Weitzman 1984:168). But by the age of five, boys have transferred their aspirations to the masculine role. Studies show this reorientation to be almost universal and unwavering (Weitzman 1984:168). Girls, needless to say, are not called upon to switch their gender identification. But, despite the relative directness of girls' developmental course, their gender identities are less firmly established at this stage. A significant proportion of girls express a desire to be boys, and the girls who prefer the feminine role evidence a weaker preference for this role than that of boys for the masculine role (Weitzman 1984:168). Thus, de Beauvoir's affirmation of girls' disillusionment is borne out by empirical research.

Nevertheless, women rarely defect from the feminine role, and social expectations, as conveyed by various media, help to account for this allegiance. A survey of award-winning children's books reveals portrayals of passive, doll-like girls and active, adventuresome boys coupled with portrayals of women as "housebound servants" and men as workers of all kinds (Weitzman 1984:165). Evidently, children's literature has failed to keep pace with the recent influx of women, including mothers of young children, into the workforce. Television redoubles the starkly differentiated gender images found in books. When children's television programs show any females at all, they are apt to be depicted as deferential while men are depicted as aggressive and constructive (Weitzman 1984:166). This same pattern is repeated in elementary school textbooks (Weitzman 1984:184).

Throughout their childhood, girls and boys are exposed to a barrage of unrealistically polarized images of women and men. Since children are modeling themselves on these extreme portrayals (in conjunction, of course, with the examples set by adults whom they know), they can deviate quite a lot from the stereotypes they are given and yet remain well within conventional expectations regarding feminine and masculine personality and conduct. Nevertheless, by providing such an extreme model of femininity, the media may curb the effects of girls' attraction to the masculine role.

An interesting sidelight in regard to children's media concerns their presentation of reactions to female characters. Whereas male characters are commonly shown being rewarded for their activities, female characters are simply ignored (Weitzman 1984:165–166). Female characters only elicit significant responses when they violate gender stereotypes and are punished for their transgressions (Weitzman 1984:166). When books and television shows are not threatening girls with ostracism for gender-crossing behavior, they are communicating the message that girls should stay in the background and acquiesce in anonymity. It is hardly surprising, then, that girls become reluctant to assert themselves.

De Beauvoir allows that girls' rankling at their confinement and their resulting ambivalence about femininity sometimes find a temporary outlet. They may rebel by idolizing independent women—actresses or favorite teachers—or by becoming tomboys (de Beauvoir 1953:275). Indeed, a survey conducted in 1977 reports 63 percent of the sample of junior high school age girls describing themselves as tomboys and 51 percent of the sample of adult women remembering having been tomboys (Hyde 1985:159). But, in de Beauvoir's view, socialization has already done its work.

Girls have acquired a personality structure that suits them to assume the duties of housewife and mother and that impedes their doing anything else. Specifically, de Beauvoir notes three ways in which feminine socialization has debilitated women:

1. women have been made incapable of living free of convention
2. they have been made incapable of dedicating their lives to a constructive social purpose

3. they have been made incapable of supporting themselves economically (1953:334, 441, 560, 654–655)

In view of the lack of employment opportunities for women and the social and economic advantages of marriage, few girls will fail to conform to the feminine role (de Beauvoir 1953:405). Thus, while boys are beginning to prepare themselves for careers, girls spend their adolescence waiting—waiting to be chosen by a marriageable man in order to take up responsibilities which require no further intellectual or personal maturation (de Beauvoir 1953:307).

A number of recent studies specify in more detail the nature of girls' preparation for subordination. For example, it has been found that girls who are attuned to social approval are likely to be popular with their peers, but boys who are other-directed in this way are likely to be unpopular (Hunter College 1983:153). Whereas boys benefit from independence, girls pay a price for going their own way. Thus, girls' self-interest strongly commends compliance with feminine norms of passivity and conventionality.

Still, other mechanisms are plainly at work. Studies of students' expectations regarding their performance have examined populations ranging from nursery school through college, and they reveal that males tend to overestimate the merits of their performance while females tend to underestimate the merits of theirs (Hyde 1985:147–148). Though the difference between these levels of self-confidence is reduced when females are asked to estimate their success on traditionally feminine tasks or when no competition is taking place, it is clear that women are at a disadvantage in a wide variety of situations.

Further corroboration for girls' low self-confidence is provided by research on a syndrome called "learned helplessness." When children believe (rightly or wrongly) that their poor performance is a result of fixed, uncontrollable factors—e.g., lack of ability as opposed to lack of effort—they stop trying because they infer that additional effort will prove futile (Weitzman 1984:186). The classroom is the prime environment in which learned helplessness develops, and, in this context, the problem is most pronounced in girls (Weitzman 1984:186). Moreover, past accomplishment does not shield girls from learned helplessness. Unlike boys, girls who are proficient at a given task are prone to attribute unsatisfactory work to their lack of ability (Weitzman 1984:186). Since low expectations and learned helplessness can reciprocally reinforce one another, this combination is particularly damaging to self-confidence. Statistics show that women are more likely than men to be afflicted by this double liability.

A further hindrance to women's activities is fear of success. Discovered by Matina Horner in 1969 and studied extensively since then, fear of success is found in talented women whose career prospects are excellent. These women fear success because they regard achievement as masculine and therefore associate success with loss of femininity (Hyde 1985:204–205; Weitzman 1984:202–203). Not surprisingly, the problem is aggravated when women are performing gender-inappropriate tasks or when women are competing with men.

Though many people find fear of success an intuitively appealing explanation of women's failure to gain demanding and prestigious political and economic positions, controversy over this phenomenon has mounted. The design of Horner's experiments has been criticized for conflating people's responses to others with their feelings about themselves—women may be distressed by other women's success but not by their own—and also for conflating a realistic assessment of societal attitudes toward gender with individually internalized norms—women may recognize that successful women are likely to be penalized socially without believing that they should capitulate to these forces (Hyde 1985:206; Weitzman 1984:203–204). Thus, it is not clear that fear of success significantly limits women's potential for advancement.

In addition, many men test positively for fear of success; however, the reasons for their aversion seem to be different. While men air worries about whether hard work is rewarded and about stress-related health problems, women worry about projecting a masculine image that will undermine their social lives (Weitzman 1984:203). If this is so, women's fear of success evidence their captivity in gender stereotypes, but men's fear of success evidences their sensible reservations about the value of success as it is conventionally defined.

Self-esteem is closely related to achievement, and it has been found that femininity is detrimental to self-esteem. Both women and men who have androgynous personalities—personalities that combine desirable traits from the feminine stereotype with desirable traits from the masculine stereotype and eliminate the undesirable traits associated with these two stereotypes, as measured by the Bem Sex Role Inventory—exhibit the highest levels of self-esteem (Puglisi and Jackson 1980–1981:136). They are followed by masculine, feminine, and undifferentiated individuals, in that order (Puglisi and Jackson 1980–

1981:136). Thus, these investigators conclude that masculinity is a far better predictor of self-esteem than femininity. Their view is borne out by another study that found that "appropriate" sex role identification is not necessarily correlated with high self-esteem. Rather, the women and men with highest self-esteem scored high on both achievement motivation and masculinity (Steriker and Johnson 1977:25). To the extent that traditional feminine socialization succeeds in instilling a stereotypically feminine personality, it diminishes women's self-esteem. Low self-esteem is positively correlated with depression, and depression poses a serious obstacle to carrying out one's plans (Rosenberg 1979:55).

Consonant with the conclusions regarding fear of success and self-esteem are the results obtained in studies of identity formation in high school and college women. A number of these inquiries suggest that young women hold personal identity formation in abeyance in anticipation of their eventual marriages. In order not to rule out a desirable match, young women often postpone career commitments and decisions about broad life plans until they know whom they will marry and what preferences and expectations their husbands will have (Hyde 1985:164; Weitzman 1984:200–201).

This flexibility makes women well-adapted to patriarchal marital relations, but it renders them maladapted in the event that they fail to marry or lose their husbands. Furthermore, as mores in regard to married women working outside the home move toward approval, women who fail to establish their career directions early are becoming vulnerable to social disapproval for their inability to get a good job (Hyde 1985:165). Although there is anecdotal evidence that these conditions are leading some women to reverse their priorities, no broad-based trend has been documented (Weitzman 1984:201).

If social pressure on women to achieve in the work world becomes pervasive enough and if most men come to expect this sort of achievement of their wives, another aspect of women's personality structure would militate in favor of such a trend. Women are more easily influenced than men; that is, women are less willing to resist challenges to their opinions (Hyde 1985:146–147, 149). Though the gender difference in regard to influenceability is not as pronounced as the difference in regard to aggression, it nevertheless makes women more susceptible to the vagaries of social fashion as well as to the demands of individuals.

Recent research supports de Beauvoir's theses that, compared to men, women are insecure about their own abilities and worth and that they are less well prepared to function outside the home. Women are more sensitive to others' opinions of them; they are less self-confident and more easily influenced than men; they have less self-esteem than men; their fear of success may help to confine them to traditional feminine occupations; their identities and life plans are dependent on their husbands. However, our account of how these outcomes come about is incomplete. As yet, we lack systematic longitudinal studies analyzing the processes that conspire to consolidate feminine personalities and to induct girls into the feminine role.

Despite the overwhelmingly gloomy prognosis for women's autonomy implicit in de Beauvoir's social psychological biography, it is worth noting that there is a ray of hope in her account. De Beauvoir claims that women have a richer inner life precisely because feminine socialization creates conflicts for girls. Except for the "second weaning," masculine socialization conforms to boys' natural bent, and men fit comfortably into the masculine role (de Beauvoir 1953:643). In contrast, girls have the same impulses as boys, but theirs are suppressed: girls yearn for freedom but are constrained; they seek prestige and power but find themselves doomed to subordination; they desire accomplishment but are coopted by a volatile mix of self-absorption and devotion to others. Thus, women are never at ease with the destiny society assigns them, but the confines of the feminine role are such that their dissatisfaction with it can only be expressed in indirect, often harmful ways (de Beauvoir 1953:494).

Still, this predicament has at least one compensation. The tension-fraught, frustration-ridden psychological brew instilled by feminine socialization sparks girls' curiosity about themselves and draws them into introspection (de Beauvoir 1953:337). Thus, compared with men, women are more aware of their feelings, more sensitive to nuances of psychological meaning, and more skilled in understanding other people, as well as themselves (de Beauvoir 1953:589). Although it is obvious that the cultivation of these capabilities adapts women to function as society's emotional shepherds, it is important to notice that these capabilities enable women to gain greater insight into themselves. Since self-knowledge is indispensable to autonomy (part 1 and part 2, sec. 4), de Beauvoir's account of feminine socialization—her disgust with femininity notwithstanding—gives women an advantage with respect to one of the critical ingredients of autonomy.

Women's receptivity to others' needs and desires has been widely remarked. Both Carol Gilligan's research on moral development and Nancy Chodorow's research on personality development conclude that women are more other-directed than men. Despite doubts in some quarters about the superiority of women's empathic powers (Hyde 1985:151), the theories advanced by Gilligan and Chodorow help to explain women's adaptation to the traditional feminine role and highlight women's focus on the psyche.

Gilligan maintains that moral development can proceed either according to the logic of the Justice Tradition—a system of universalizable, equal rights which abstract reason recognizes and deploys—or according to the logic of the Care Perspective—taking responsibility for preventing harm, ministering to needs, and maintaining interpersonal connections (1982:173–174). Although virtually all people can understand and use both of these approaches to morality, men typically resort first to the ethic of justice, whereas about one third of all women rely primarily on the ethic of care (Gilligan 1987:25). Gilligan's research does not bear out the claim that all women take their moral cues from their immersion in interpersonal relations, but, in keeping with de Beauvoir's view, it does reveal that virtually all of the exponents of this orientation are women.

Gilligan cites Chodorow's psychoanalytic treatment of feminine development to account for this difference in feminine and masculine moral perspectives (1982:7–8). According to Chodorow, the configuration of girls' and boys' relations to their parents is the decisive factor in the creation of gender difference. Chodorow starts from the psychoanalytic premise that all infants form a primary attachment to their main caretaker. Initially, they do not realize that their caretakers are independent individuals; thus, a gradual process of separation from one's original caretaker is central to ego development (Chodorow 1978:61, 69). How this process takes place is critical to the formation of gender identity.

On Chodorow's view, the most salient feature of the emotional environment in which the self evolves is female responsibility for child-rearing. In sum, because all children begin life by forming an exclusive attachment to a woman, but because girls and boys are supposed to become feminine or masculine heterosexuals, girls and boys must follow different developmental routes.

Specifically, boys must altogether renounce their identification with their mothers if they are to achieve masculinity. For the sake of their gender identity, boys' ties to their mothers must be broken and re-

placed with ties to their fathers (Chodorow 1978:165). Yet, boys retain their original sexual orientation. Although they must concede
defeat in their oedipal rivalry with their father for their mother's love,
boys are nonetheless expected to continue to desire females. In the
psychoanalytic idiom, the crucial, yet most elusive, and therefore most
anxiety-inducing oedipal goal for the boy is the formation of a masculine personality.

The situation of girls is the mirror opposite of that of boys. Girls'
feminine identity allows them to maintain their identification with
their mothers. Thus, girls experience the emergence of their gendered
selves in the context of an ongoing, intense emotional bond; however, boys can only achieve suitably gendered selves by breaking away
from this relationship (Chodorow 1978:166). Although girls are obliged
to shift their sexual orientations to male objects, Chodorow maintains that girls expand their emotional lives to include an attachment
to their fathers without denying their attachment to their mothers
(1978:167). Thus, girls are spared the experience of shattering deep
emotional ties and enduring emotional isolation.

According to Chodorow, this difference in girls' and boys' oedipal
resolutions accounts for the differences in their relational capacities.
In commonsense terms, boys' break with their mothers is emotionally
crippling, and they never get over it (Chodorow 1978:181–183). But
girls get through this period with the support of an intact attachment
to their mothers and without repression of their new attachment to
their fathers (Chodorow 1978:168–169). What may be problematic
for girls at this stage is an overweaning, relentless maternal affection—their mothers' refusal to accept their need for independence
(Chodorow 1978:100). But barring pathological distortions of the
mother-daughter relation, Chodorow concludes that women develop
a rich inner life and do not feel threatened by intimacy (Chodorow
1978:168–169). Thus, as de Beauvoir stressed, feminine personalities
facilitate close interaction with other people.

Ironically, de Beauvoir discerns the germ of female autonomy in
women's attentiveness to their inner lives coupled with women's exclusion from public life. Because women are not obliged to secure a
niche in any public institution, they can afford to adopt a critical
perspective on these institutions that would be too costly an indul-
gence for most men (de Beauvoir 1953:590). Still, de Beauvoir despairs
over women's prospects for autonomy given the persistence of feminine socialization, and many of her conjectures about the organi-

zation and effects of this process are supported by current research. Made dependent on others' approval and expected to be dedicated to others' interests, women are caught in a self-perpetuating, yet demeaning, social role. In short, declares de Beauvoir, "As long as she [woman] still has to struggle to become a human being, she cannot become a creator" (1953:672).

# Autonomy and Feminine Socialization

WE HAVE seen that Simone de Beauvoir detects a distinctive potential for autonomy in women—a potential implanted by the lifelong process of feminine socialization coupled with the subordinate socioeconomic status of women. Nevertheless, she considers this potential to be entirely unrealized (see part 3, sec. 2). To fully understand why de Beauvoir reaches this dire conclusion, we must go beyond her social psychological account of feminine and masculine development and consider her conception of autonomy. Moreover, to see that de Beauvoir's complete denial of women's autonomy is unwarranted but that most women's autonomy is more limited and precarious than most men's, it is necessary to explore a partial form that autonomy can take and to examine the impact of feminine and masculine socialization on autonomy competency.

According to de Beauvoir's diagnosis, women are not autonomous because they are overly conformist (1953:330, 336, 660–661, 667), strongly identified with others' interests yet either unconcerned with social issues or wrongheadedly active in politics (424–425, 449, 484, 558–560, 563), and economically parasitic (xx–xxi, 430, 448). The feminine role stipulates that women must be devoted to their husbands and children. This devotion has a psychological dimension as well as an institutional one, and these two aspects of women's situation are reciprocally reinforcing. Psychologically, women are socialized to be altruistic; they are taught to care more about their family's welfare than they care about their own. Institutionally, marriage traditionally assigns the wife the domestic tasks of child-rearing and housework and reserves gainful employment outside the home and political participation for the husband. The marital role provides an outlet for women's altruism, and women's altruism leads them to embrace the marital role gladly. Indeed, women's altruism joins forces with their conformist desire for others' approval to disqualify them from any other vocation.

In de Beauvoir's view, women are incapable of transcendence, for they are trapped in immanence (1953:422, 591). Their psychological makeup suits them for a social role that epitomizes "maintenance" as opposed to creativity (de Beauvoir 1953:430). Women, according to de Beauvoir, perform jobs that are essentially repetitive and unproductive. The children must be admonished for the same shortcomings time and time again; tidied rooms are in disarray all too quickly; the freshly washed laundry gets dirty in no time. Homemaking is a cyclical routine. The work never varies, and, as the plaint goes, it is never done. Moreover, the objective is not to create something new. Rather, it is to maintain the status quo. Even in regard to child-rearing, de Beauvoir insists that women function merely as adjuncts to the natural process of maturation. They are necessary facilitators, to be sure, but they are not creators. Women live to serve others; and feminine work strangles women's spirit (de Beauvoir 1953:431). Thus, they are unfree in a diabolically constricting way. A woman exists solely as an Other for someone else; she never exists as a Subject for herself (de Beauvoir 1953:xvi). This is the state of immanence, which de Beauvoir dubs antithetical to autonomy.

As de Beauvoir construes autonomy, an autonomous person disregards convention when necessary (1953:xxviii, 667, 671), is economically self-sufficient (448, 455), and is dedicated to constructive social purposes (404, 638, 640). She does not offer many models of autonomy. But her image of an autonomous person seems to be either the iconoclastic, leftist worker who is socially aware and active in his union or the politically committed artist or intellectual (de Beauvoir 1953:588, 667–669).

There can be no doubt that women rarely satisfy de Beauvoir's conditions for autonomy, but these requirements are beholden to a masculine bias that renders them much too stringent. Although it is evident that autonomous people must be capable of flouting convention when their own convictions, emotional bonds, or interests call for it, autonomy requires neither economic independence nor social responsibility. Admittedly, economic self-sufficiency is usually desirable from the standpoint of autonomy, for this kind of independence can make one feel entitled to act on one's own preferences, and it can make it easier to refuse to comply with others' demands. Nevertheless, some benefactors intrude so little in their dependents' lives that these individuals are in no way constrained and can attain autonomy as easily as anyone else. (For additional discussion of economic autonomy, see part 1.) Were it not for the assumption that men's lives supply the model for autonomy, de Beauvoir, who herself occasionally accepted Jean-Paul Sartre's financial support in order to free herself to write, could hardly have overlooked the fact that economic dependence need not be oppressive. As for de Beauvoir's stipulation that autonomous people must further the public weal, it is evident that this position merely glorifies the heroism of the leftist political activist, for there is no reason to believe that human selves are so uniform that none could be fulfilled in family life or in other private vocations. Nor is it credible that autonomous participation in the public sphere must assume a politically progressive tenor. Again, de Beauvoir overstates her position. Undeniably, confinement to domestic chores has undercut the autonomy of many women, and an option to enter public enterprises supports autonomy. Nevertheless, whether people are autonomous depends on whether their lives match their authentic selves, and there is no reason to suppose that one form of life befits all selves.

Still, women typically labor under a double psychic dependency. As de Beauvoir contends and recent studies confirm, not only are girls taught to put others' interests ahead of their own, but also they are taught to judge themselves by others' approbation. In sum, girls are brought up to be so preoccupied with the impression they are making on others that women are incapable of devoting themselves single-mindedly to socially approved projects, never mind defying convention to pursue their own ideals. (For detailed treatment of feminine socialization, see part 3, sec. 2.) Also, de Beauvoir accurately depicts various ways in which the privatized regimen of largely menial services that make up the feminine role crushes women's creative initiative. Though it is undeniable that autonomy does not preclude devotion to other people, it is clear that heteronomous altruism pervades distinctively feminine life plans. For successful feminine socialization ensures the externality of the conduct imperatives that guide a woman's everyday life along with the standards that shape her self-concept. A woman who critically appraises and freely subscribes to traditional feminine obligations is not a traditional woman, for she lacks this role's characteristic heteronomy (Sher 1983:48). Although de Beauvoir's conception of autonomy far overreaches these social psychological insights, it is important to appreciate that her treatment of feminine socialization highlights genuine obstacles to autonomy.

But none of this should be taken to imply that de Beauvoir imagines most men to be free spirits. She is well aware that many men conform to societal expectations and work at tedious jobs (de Beauvoir 1953:588). How, then, can she celebrate male autonomy?

Whereas many authors identify personal autonomy exclusively with occurrent self-realization, de Beauvoir discerns two forms that autonomy can take. A person may be choosing and acting autonomously, or a person may have a developed capacity for autonomy which he or she is not presently exercising. Conversely, a person may be born with a potential for autonomy which forever remains latent. Women, de Beauvoir contends, are in the latter position. Their socialization blocks the development of their potential into an exerciseable capacity. By contrast, male socialization awakens this potential and grooms boys' capacity for personal autonomy. Though few men's lives are consistently directed by autonomous reflection— most men are mere drones in the work world, and they acquiesce in customary marital arrangements as automatically as women—this capacity is a resource men have at their disposal, one they are sometimes moved to utilize. Over and above the conspicuous masculine bias in her conception of personal autonomy, then, de Beauvoir's conviction that women have only a latent potential for autonomy but that men have a developed, abeit sometimes disused, capacity compounds her underestimation of women's autonomy.

To link autonomy to transcendence, as de Beauvoir does, is to deny the possibility of an autonomous pedestrian life. Furthermore, to link autonomy to a unitary capacity for transcendence is to deny the possibilities of intermittent or tentative autonomy. For de Beauvoir, a person is either capable of scorning convention and seizing an opportunity to transcend the clutch of circumstances, or not. That different people could be capable of resisting different social pressures and therefore of mastering different social entanglements is not a possibility she systematically explores.

If, instead, personal autonomy is construed as the exercise of a competency, it is evident that the assorted skills that constitute the competency can be honed more or less finely, that these skills can be coordinated more or less smoothly, and that they may be exercised more or less frequently and with more or less success. Though proficiency in this area requires both aptitude and practice, the skills this competency comprises are common enough. (For detailed explication of autonomy competency, see part 2, secs. 3–6.) Furthermore, since virtually all social roles afford some degree of latitude with respect to the manner in which they are carried out, few people can rely entirely on socially given formulas to fulfill their responsibilities. Accordingly, one would expect most people to lead at least partially autonomous lives.

This conclusion gains support from a thesis Marilyn Friedman has advanced. Friedman observes, "autonomy is always realized in the context of some substantive choice or other and, so, requires the skill for that substantive choice as well as the skill for making it autonomously" (Friedman, unpublished paper; Lawrence Haworth advocates a similar position, 1986:22). Though basically correct, this characterization is potentially misleading in two respects. Some substantive choices do not presuppose skills apart from autonomy competency, though many do. Also, some choices are so constrained by the enterprise of which they are a part that considerations of autonomy do not apply.

Compare the decision not to have (or to have) children with the decision to feed a child this meal or that and with the decision whether to cook the bacon before eating it. The first of these decisions concerns general life plans. While a decision about becoming a parent cannot be made autonomously without some familiarity with the burdens as well as the joys of childcare, the requisite knowledge is rudimentary and hardly presupposes an independent competency. Since general life plan formulation rarely involves a second competency, a person's proficiency with respect to autonomy competency and the opportunities available to that individual are the sole determinants of global programmatic autonomy. In contrast, specific life plan elaboration and carrying out particular plans frequently call upon independent competencies. Whether the second decision—what meal to serve a child—concerns a single menu or a general dietary policy, supplying healthy and enjoyable food for a child presupposes independent competencies. One must be knowledgable about nutrition and complementary flavors as well as proficient in cooking techniques. But in addition, making autonomous choices about feeding a child presupposes judgments about the merits of vegetarianism, the time consumed by home cooking, the pleasures of fresh foods, and so forth—that is, reflection on one's own needs, values, goals, and the like. Thus, this kind of autonomy involves the coordination of autonomy competency with several independent competencies, and people who lack those latter competencies will not be able to achieve autonomy in this area. However, the third decision does not call upon autonomy skills at all; an independent competency forecloses autonomous reflection. In view of the dangers of trichinosis, it would be stupid not to cook the bacon, regardless of whether one has a penchant for raw meat. Some choices afford little or no scope for self-expression.

That autonomy competency must sometimes collaborate with other competencies to secure autonomous conduct suggests that some degree of autonomy can be achieved without global programmatic autonomy—that is, without control over the basic direction of one's life—and that global programmatic autonomy can fail to ensure the autonomy of particular acts. (For discussion of how the autonomy of life plans is transmitted to actions taken to carry them out, see part 2, secs. 2–4.) To see this, it is important to distinguish doing *that which* one really wants from acting *as* one really wants. To be doing that which one really wants is to be engaged in a type of activity or a project which one considers to be consonant with one's authentic self. To be acting as one really wants is to be conducting oneself in a manner that expresses one's authentic self. Doing that which one really wants does not entail acting as one really wants, nor does acting as one really wants entail doing that which one really wants. Amy has autonomously become a movie director, but she may find that she lacks the technical know-how to capture some of her most important ideas on film. As a film director, Amy is doing that which she really wants without succeeding in shooting particular scenes as she really wants. Contrariwise, unable to obtain an abortion, Edith had a baby against her will, yet she may succeed in projecting her true self in the manner in which she raises the child. As a parent, Edith is acting as she really wants despite the fact that she is not doing that which she really wants.

Deficiency with respect to independent competencies can sabotage episodic autonomy, and proficiency with respect to independent competencies can be an enabling factor in the episodic exercise of autonomy competency. A possible interpretation of the studies of fear of success cited in the previous section would be that independent competencies are instrumental in salvaging a measure of autonomy for women. When women are asked to perform traditionally feminine tasks, they do not exhibit the same reluctance about achieving excellence that they exhibit when assigned traditionally masculine tasks. Although these data are undoubtedly explained in part by the absence of tension between the assigned tasks and the subjects' self-concept, they may also reflect women's greater confidence in regard to tasks in which they are well-versed. However, the autonomy enhancing effects of independent competencies are not only to be found in women. A similar phenomenon can be seen in the world of the arts. Robert Lowell was clinically insane much of his life, and his everyday affairs were hardly under his control. Nevertheless, his extraordinary literary talents enabled him to write poetry which many critics admire and which satisfied him as the embodiment of his ideas. Lowell was autonomous in his art, though not in his mundane concerns.

Through the confluence of elemental autonomy skills and a well-developed independent competency, behavior may evidence a considerable degree of autonomy even though the person's conduct is not usually autonomous and even though the overall plan that subsumes the behavior is not autonomous. There can be pockets of autonomy—particular actions—and threads of autonomy—policies addressing specific problems—in a person's life. The possibility of such pockets and threads raises the question of whether these outcroppings of autonomy can be conjoined so as to mitigate the need for global programmatic autonomy in a person's life.

Since carrying out an autonomous programmatic decision consists of doing all of the actions needed to fulfill the plan, it could be urged that autonomously doing each of the actions must add up to autonomously fulfilling the plan. Just as programmatic autonomy transfers to the actions subsidiary to the plan, serial episodic autonomy should transfer to the life plan implicit in the particular actions.[1] Though not altogether without merit, this conception of the relation between episodic and programmatic autonomy is seriously flawed.

Understanding the difficulties of this route to autonomy turns in part on the distinction between nonautonomous and autonomy-defeating life plans. A nonautonomous life plan is a life plan that one pursues without assessing whether or not it matches one's authentic self, most likely a conventionally expected and automatically accepted life direction. When people adhere to nonautonomous life plans, they experience no psychological discord centering on the activities the plan dictates. In contrast, an autonomy-defeating life plan is a life plan that one undertakes knowing that it partially or completely conflicts with one's authentic self, usually a project that one has been sucked into against one's will. When people are engaged in actions subsidiary to an autonomy-defeating life plan, they experience friction between their true selves and their behavior. The amount of friction varies with the severity of the conflict; however, the plan would not be autonomy-defeating if there were no opposition.

Now, someone might observe that, if a person autonomously persists in acting in a manner that implies an autonomy-defeating life plan, the friction may eventually stop. People adapt. This cessation of symptoms of intrapersonal dissonance, it might be contended, should be interpreted as an outward sign that the person's true self has been transformed. Through episodic autonomy, what had been an autonomy-defeating life plan has become an autonomous life plan.

If not incoherent, this is an extremely counter-intuitive line of argument. The only way in which a person could perform particular actions known to coincide with his or her true self which also follow from a life plan known to conflict with this person's true self would be if the particular action stems from one attribute (or set of attributes) that does belong to the person's true self but contributes to a life plan that presupposes an additional attribute (or set of attributes) that is excluded from his or her true self. Consider Bill, a political consultant who, despite his right-wing leanings, sells his services to liberal candidates. In fulfilling his contractual obligations, he gives expression to his enthusiasm for politics and to his ingenuity at manipulating electorates—both authentic traits; but simultaneously and unavoidably he promotes a political platform he deplores—an inauthentic overarching plan. As a result of his work on behalf of liberal politicians, Bill's conservative principles are slowly eroded, and Bill is eventually converted to liberalism.

Arguably, the consulting activities that precipitated Bill's conversion were never episodically autonomous. Since his work conflicted with his autonomously held principles, the advice he furnished and the tactics he implemented gave expression to selected components of his authentic self while suppressing others. It is doubtful, then, that there can be autonomous episodic conduct that serves an autonomy-defeating life plan.

If it turned out that such autonomous episodic conduct were possible, however, it would seem as reasonable to say that acting in this way would destroy the agent's authentic self as to say that such conduct would generate his or her authentic self. Of course, if Bill were ambivalent about his conservative political affiliation, and if his work afforded opportunities for debating current issues and for probing his principles, and if Bill were sufficiently stalwart not to be seduced by the excitement of political campaigns and the glamor of his growing political power in liberal circles, his consulting activities might be seen as autonomously testing and ultimately supplanting his original convictions. (For related discussion of the possibility of retrospective autonomy, see part 2, sec. 2). However, in the absence of ambivalence about one's life plans, or in the presence of irresistable inducements to betray one's life plans, episodic autonomy has no priority over programmatic autonomy.

Still, since a nonautonomous life plan has an indeterminate relation to the individual's authentic self, it might be thought that the accumulation of autonomous particular actions could render the nonautonomous life plan implicit in them autonomous. It is conceivable, though quite dubious, that people following nonautonomous life plans would regularly exercise autonomy competency in making particular decisions. Would this episodic autonomy allay the heteronomy of their life plans?

On my view of autonomy, the answer must be no, for autonomy is a function of exercising autonomy competency and by hypothesis this competency is never deployed to assess these people's overall life plans. The problem here is that people are supposed to move from situation to situation consulting their authentic selves, yet they are never supposed to examine the big picture in light of their authentic selves. But obviously, people can be satisfied with their conduct considered in this fragmentary way and nevertheless reject it decisively once they have an overview of it. Within the constraints of circumstances, Victoria, who has nonautonomously become a television news reporter, may be projecting her own values, traits, and so on. Nevertheless, if Victoria ever stepped back and asked whether she really wanted to be a news broadcaster, she might discover that she wanted to be a carpenter instead. Episodic autonomy, then, is no guarantee of programmatic autonomy; doing particular actions as one really wants does not translate into doing that which one really wants. Until a person's life plans have been subjected to autonomous scrutiny, they cannot be presumed to be autonomous.

Beyond the philosophical considerations I have been sketching, there are psychological reasons to doubt that a life plan implicit in a series of separately autonomous actions is autonomous. For two main reasons, people are less defended against admitting to themselves that their particular actions fail to coincide with their true selves than they are against admitting to themselves that their overall life plans fail to coincide with their true selves. First, since most people have fairly conventional life plans, their commitment to these plans is reinforced by social acceptance. (For further discussion of the attraction of conventionality, see part 3, sec. 4.) This social approbation forms a barrier to their acknowledging that their plans do not mesh with their selves. But, since a good deal of individual variation in the way these plans are executed is socially tolerated, people can monitor their day-to-day performance with a view to autonomy without risking social ostracism. Second, overhauling one's life plans commonly involves material insecurity, if not sacrifice, and such radical change may rupture friendships and family relations, as well. In contrast, fine tuning one's quotidian behavior can be accomplished without disrupting one's financial and emotional equilibrium. It is not surprising, then, that many people are not disposed to allow autonomous reflection to penetrate to their basic life plans. If their life plans do not match their true selves, they have ample reason not to want to know it. Accordingly, episodic autonomy without a background of programmatic autonomy does not warrant the inference that people's life plans are in harmony with their true selves.

It is reasonable to suppose that most people—women as well as men—sometimes do what they really want, believe in, care about, and the like, but that they sometimes pliantly follow societal norms regardless of whether the prevailing norms are consonant with their selves. A measure of proficiency in the self-reading and self-projecting skills that make up autonomy competency is commonplace, and most people have some independent competency (or competencies) which in conjunction with their autonomy skills foster episodic autonomy, though not the more comprehensive forms of programmatic autonomy. The difference between men and women with respect to personal autonomy, then, is best understood as a difference of degree coupled with a difference with respect to the orbits in which autonomy skills are activated, rather than as a difference between having and lacking a competency (Meyers 1987a:624–626).

De Beauvoir is right to distinguish the latent potential for autonomy from a developed capacity for autonomous choice and to recognize that a person can have such a capacity without always exercising it successfully. But she is mistaken in analyzing this capacity as one that, once developed, can be used equally well in all situations. Autonomy competency comprises a number of skills (part 2, sec. 4). Each of these skills may be more or less developed in different people, and the diverse skills may be more or less smoothly coordinated. Furthermore, since independent competencies are necessary for people to make many decisions autonomously, and since no one can master every competency that he or she might ever need, a developed capacity for autonomous choice can only be deployed selectively.

Though it is important to appreciate that de Beauvoir's epithets condemning women's autonomy overstate the case, it is also undeniable that there is abundant evidence to support the claim that differential socialization and segregated social status curtail personal autonomy in women to a greater extent than they do in men. Whatever the liabilities of masculine socialization, men are not taught to be as thoroughly other-regarding as women. Though independence of mind may not be encouraged in all boys as much as it should be, neither independence of mind nor self-assertion in action is incompatible with ideals of masculinity, and in some contexts both are fostered in boys. (For a helpful treatment of class differences in regard to these qualities, see Chodorow 1978:186–187.) Furthermore, since boys are traditionally reared to take up various roles in the public sphere and a dominant role in the private sphere while girls are traditionally reared to assume one narrow, privatized, subordinate role, men's programmatic choices have been less constrained, and men have had more opportunities to piggyback autonomy skills with their independent competencies to produce episodic autonomy. Women may be more sensitive to their inner lives, but their vulnerability to others' influence and their concern with others' opinions of them prevent them from consistently acting on what they know about themselves when their self-portraits do not comfortably fit with social expectations. Though exceptional patterns of socialization—e.g., fathers who make their affection contingent upon their daughters' level of achievement—and inconsistencies in feminine socialization—girls are encouraged to be self-effacing, yet they are rewarded for good grades in school—may relieve women's conformist tendencies, few women have defied entrenched norms despite the substantial disadvantages these norms impose on women (Weitzman 1984:218–221).

Still, it might be urged that childhood socialization has little predictive power. Rather, the shape of a person's life is determined by the pattern of opportunities and constraints that the individual confronts as an adult. Taking issue with the emphasis many feminist social scientists have placed on child-rearing practices, Kathleen Gerson maintains that women's choices regarding reproduction and gainful employment are not positively correlated with their upbringings and their childhood self-images, but are positively correlated with their adult circumstances. Thus, women who had always expected to become housewives but whose marriages ended in divorce and who stumbled upon opportunities for advancement at work became intensely committed to their careers (Gerson 1985:89–91). Similarly, women whose girlhood plans had focused on careers often switched directions when they found themselves stuck in dead-end jobs and when they established happy marriages with men who could afford to support them and who wanted them to stay at home (Gerson 1985:92–115). Gerson contends that these reversals show that the impact of early socialization is much more muted than many have assumed.

To properly interpret Gerson's results, it is necessary to note, first, that she studied a small group of women from a transitional generation. Her sample consisted of San Francisco area women whose ages ranged from twenty-seven to thirty-seven (average thirty-one) in 1978 and 1979 when she conducted her interviews (Gerson 1985:41). These women were young enough to have been influenced by the women's movement starting in the late 1960s, but they were old enough for many of them to have received traditional feminine upbringings. Plainly, the women in Gerson's study had been exposed to powerful opposing forces. Since socialization continues throughout life, neither the recent valorization of self-realization doctrines nor the recent ferment in relations between men and women can be dismissed as factors in their choices. Thus, these subjects' experiences in their teens and young womanhood may have eclipsed their earlier socialization to a large extent.

Second, Gerson examined the broad outlines of women's lives—the choices between careerism and domesticity and between childlessness and motherhood. Since she has little to say about the details of the ways in which individuals live, her study highlights those aspects of people's lives that are most explicable in terms of salient social and economic circumstances. Obviously, whether a person works for pay or not will probably depend on need and opportunity. This has always been true of men and women alike. In the past, the difference has been, on the one hand, that no woman was thought to need to work as long as a man was providing for her and, on the other hand, that many men have had attractive opportunities and therefore have opted to work, even when they have not been prodded by need. Of course, crippling socialization can prevent a desperately needy individual from functioning in any job. However, apart from such extreme cases, the influence of past socialization is more likely to appear in the particular choices made—e.g., the sort of job the individual seeks—and in the individual's experience of working—e.g., the individual's feelings of pride, embarrassment, or disappointment when she tells friends that she is working. Gerson's assessment of the minor influence of early socialization in the lives of the women she studied may well be correct, as far as it goes. But Gerson's work leaves a great deal to be investigated.

Most importantly, autonomy was not the focus of Gerson's project. What she studied were choices in favor of traditional versus nontraditional life plans. Both types of life plan can be embarked upon autonomously or nonautonomously, and Gerson simply does not address the dimension of autonomy. Consider the following exchange:

Q: What happened to your plans to become a policewoman?
A: I got married and my husband said no. . . .
Q: Were your plans for becoming a policewoman serious at that time?
A: They were at the point where I realized I had to make a choice, and they became less. I didn't particularly *like* it, but I didn't have much choice. (Gerson 1985:97).

Undeniably, almost no one would opt for divorce in a situation like this if work were unavailable. But assuming that this informant's plan to become a police officer was realistic, why did her husband's withholding permission to proceed with this plan settle the matter for her? Gerson never asks what the difference is between this informant, who declares that she had no choice, and someone who would say that she finally realized that she loved her husband too much to leave him or someone who would leave her husband at this point.

Still, Gerson's records of her interviews provide many tantalizing hints of differential autonomy among the women she interviewed. Compare, for example, the following pair of remarks from different informants:

> "Sometimes I feel like I was gypped, even though I wasn't gypped. It was my own choice, but I feel, why did I choose this? What made me choose to not have children when I really in my heart want to have children?"

> "But it's something eventually you weigh out and see that that was really the best decision, that I was really responsible in my decision, that I chose not to have children because I couldn't be the kind of mother I wanted to be, and that was good." (Gerson 1985:144, 156)

Without more extensive quotation from the interviews, it is impossible to draw definitive conclusions about the autonomy of either woman. Nevertheless, what we may have here is testimony to the intractable confusion and frustration attendant upon unconventional heteronomous choice and to the gradual clarification and gratification attendant upon unconventional autonomous choice—a difference that cuts through the similarities between these two individuals' marital and financial situations, that is, through the structure of their opportunities and constraints.

Childhood socialization, particularly in the present atmosphere of changing gender mores and expanding career opportunities, does not predetermine anyone's life direction. But that concession does not entail that this early experience is altogether negligible. Not only does socialization establish dispositions that facilitate or hinder certain enterprises, thus making some more eligible and more manageable than others; but also it nurtures or suppresses autonomy competency. Accordingly, early socialization influences both the options that are pursued and the way in which they are pursued. Since attitudes towards gender have not been so revolutionized as to eradicate feminine and masculine socialization, it would be premature to discount the effects of this formative experience.

Brute power and dominance behavior are easy to confuse with autonomy, and men often exhibit the former without consulting their authentic selves. Moreover, it is tempting to take conventionality for heteronomy and thus to be blinded to the forms that women's autonomy has often assumed. Although it would be wrong to suppose that most men are completely autonomous or that most women are not autonomous at all, masculine socialization is more conducive to autonomy than feminine socialization. The impact of differential socialization is best summed up in terms of a spectrum of autonomous lives.

I shall say that someone is *minimally autonomous* when this person possesses at least some disposition to consult his or her self and at least some ability to act on his or her own beliefs, desires, and so forth, but when this person lacks some of the other skills from the repertory of autonomy skills, when the autonomy skills the person possesses are poorly developed and poorly coordinated, and when the person possesses few independent competencies that could promote the exercise of available autonomy skills. I shall say that someone is *fully autonomous* when this person possesses a complete repertory of well developed and well coordinated autonomy skills coupled with many and varied independent competencies.[2] *Medially autonomous* people range along a spectrum between these two poles.[3]

These definitions may not be amenable to operationalization. Thus, it may not be possible to draw sharp lines between minimal and medial autonomy and between medial and full autonomy, and it may not be possible to calculate precisely an individual's level of achievement. However, these definitions do specify the factors relevant to autonomy with sufficient clarity to allow approximate evaluations of people's autonomy. Social psychological studies suggest that, whereas women are most likely to rank in the area of medial autonomy closest to minimal autonomy and are more likely than men to be minimally autonomous, men are most likely to rank well within the bounds of medial autonomy and are more likely than women to be fully autonomous. (For detailed exposition of the developmental constraints on women's autonomy and the enhancement of men's autonomy, see part 3, sec. 2.)

This discrepancy between men's and women's autonomy raises three questions. First, is autonomy a realistic goal for all people? Second, how might personal autonomy be equalized between men and women? Third, does justice require that efforts be made to eliminate gender differences in autonomy? The first two questions will be addressed in the remainder of this part. The last of them is the subject of part 4.

# Full Autonomy—An Attainable Ideal

I HAVE considered a number of ways in which feminine socialization undermines autonomy and leaves many women minimally autonomous. Though I have urged that masculine socialization is more conducive to autonomy, I have stressed that masculine socialization typically produces only a medially autonomous individual. It does not aspire to bring about, let alone ensure, full autonomy. Now, it is undeniable that full autonomy is an unrealistic goal to set for all people. Autonomy competency involves skills for which different people have more or less innate aptitude. Regardless of what socialization process they undergo, people will never be equally insightful, inventive, and strong. Moreover, some people's personalities make them more vulnerable than others to such departures from rationality as wishful thinking, compulsiveness, and the like. Cultural patterns of gender socialization present a major obstacle to autonomy, but reforming these practices would not guarantee full autonomy for everyone.

Still, it might seem that masculine socialization should do better; that is, it should produce more people who are fully autonomous than it does. In section 5, I shall argue that masculine socialization is by no means the ideal form of socialization for autonomy. But, before proceeding to that discussion, I should like to consider an obstacle to autonomy that burdens men and women alike—conventionality, that is, thinking and doing what is usual in one's social milieu. Apart from individuals' specific weaknesses with respect to the various skills that make up autonomy competency, assorted modes of irrationality conspire to enforce conventionality and to pervert, if not suppress, the exercise of autonomy skills. In what follows, I shall consider how different forms of irrationality are implicated in conventionality, whether these forms of irrationality are amenable to correction, and how full autonomy should be conceived in light of these psychological factors.

Psychologists have inventoried a distressingly large number of failings which appear to be endemic to human thought. Some of these might be characterized as departures from lucidity—people do not have access to pertinent information, or they distort accessible information. Others are departures from cogency—people use faulty reasoning methods to reach their conclusions. The list of these defects is too long to be fully presented here; however, I shall sample several which are particularly helpful in understanding conventionality. By sketching a scenario in which some commonplace psychological mechanisms converge on conventionality, I shall exhibit some of the ways in which human psychology resists autonomy both in particular perceptions and choices and in the construction of overarching life plans.

The "availability heuristic" shapes people's judgments about the frequency of a class or the probability of an event by leading them to suppose that instances which are easier to recall or imagine are more likely to be the case (Tversky and Kahneman 1982:11–12). But, of course, availability need not reflect relative frequency; instead, it may reflect familiarity or vividness. Applying this prevalent heuristic to the enterprise of self-discovery, it is evident that those of one's attributes and actions that are socially accepted are apt to stand out, for social approval simultaneously confers familiarity and desirability. Well acquainted with their socially approved characteristics, then, people looking for explanations of their own conduct and relying on the availability heuristic will advert to these characteristics. As a result, they will develop conventional self-concepts. In other words, they will see themselves as society thinks they should be.

But it might be thought that, since such conventional self-concepts are merely hypotheses which are open to testing in the light of subsequent experience, they do not make people any more conventional than they actually are. However, this view of the matter underrates the extent to which prior theoretical commitments control people's assimilation of subsequent evidence. Both data collection and attributions of causality are biased by expectations set up by previously established beliefs (Nisbett and Ross 1980:29, 41). Specifically in the area of self-knowledge, Hazel Markus has shown that, when people have schematized their self-concepts along a particular dimension (in her studies, the dimension of independence-dependence), they can readily recall behavioral evidence in support of their self-concepts, and they resist the implications of countervailing evidence (1977:71, 74). Accordingly, it would be a mistake to dismiss conventional self-concepts as innocuous hypotheses. Once accepted, they are hard to dislodge.

Still, psychologists disagree about the foundations of self-concepts. Markus maintains that people's self-concepts are generalizations based on observation of their past behavior (1977:64). In her view, I take it, if people have conventional self-concepts, it is because socialization has imparted to them standardized desires which have issued in socially approved behavior. If Markus is correct, conventional self-concepts are realistic summations of people's experience of their own conduct. However, Timothy Wilson's studies demonstrate that people's self-concepts are often contaminated by culturally learned elements that do not capture their experience and yet that have effects that are by no means negligible.[1]

Wilson maintains that the human mind is furnished with a dual self-monitoring system. On the one hand, there is direct introspection of one's attitudes and feelings (Wilson 1985:101). On the other hand, there is a system of theories—composed in part of personal insights and in part of cultural lore—that enables people to draw inferences about their psychological states when they do not have direct access to these states (Wilson 1985:102–104). Wilson's investigations show that self-reports relying on inferential explanations rarely coincide

with unregulated behavior (1985:108). Those aspects of people's behavior that are not under conscious control belie the theory-based
explanations they supply for their conduct. Thus, Wilson concludes
that people's motivational systems are commonly out of sync with
their self-concepts (1985:111; for a related treatment of fantasy, acting out, and rationalization, see Wollheim 1984:155–158). Their self-
concepts are incomplete, if not just plain wrong.

Returning to the effects of theory formation on people's lives, we
have seen that people gain self-knowledge by applying a theory to
their behavior when they cannot tap their feelings, attitudes, and desires directly. But obtaining an inferential explanation of their conduct is not the end of the story. Once people have articulated such
an explanation, they not only confidently predict future behavior
consonant with the theory, but also they often adjust their consciously controlled behavior to fit the account they have endorsed
(Markus 1977:72; Wilson 1985:109). Though Wilson has found that
a residue of unregulated behavior often conflicts with conventional
self-concepts, people are unaware of such tensions. To the extent that
people subscribe to explanations that embody conventional norms,
they are not merely telling themselves that they are like other people;
they are making themselves as much like other people as
they can.

But now it might be objected that there must be limits to people's
plasticity. However much one may yearn to conform, one may be
different, and one's differences are bound to surface sometime. Though
this claim is not without merit, studies of self-deception advise against
too much optimism regarding people's ability to correct their misconceptions about themselves.

Jill Millham and Richard Kellogg have found that people who have
a strong need for social approval are able to maintain unrealistically
positive self-concepts through defensive denial of negative feedback
(1980:455). Moreover, Daniel Gilbert and Joel Cooper have developed evidence of the tactics people deploy to elicit feedback from
others that is congruent with their self-concepts. To protect their self-
concepts, people will contrive to receive ambiguous evaluations of
their performances, and they will avoid comparisons with those individuals whose superior performance would be most damaging to
their self-concepts (Gilbert and Cooper 1985:86–88, 90). It is common
for people to manipulate themselves along with their associates in
order to preserve questionable, if not fragile, self-portraits. Thus, there

is little reason to assume that distinctive individual attributes will overwhelm conventionality. Once in force, conventionality is highly tenacious.

The cognitive mechanisms I have considered influence all kinds of inquiry, but their effects are magnified in reflexive inquiry. In this domain, intense ego-involvement combines with a presumption that introspection is reliable—expressed in the adage that individuals are the best judges of their own needs—to compound what are already serious deficiencies. In sum, the most casual acquaintance with the catalogue of human foibles which I have invoked would easily persuade one that any occurrence of full autonomy would be utterly amazing. Yet, the preceding account of how psychological mechanisms and socialization collaborate to ease people into conventionality opens the possibility that people can think and do what is usual for different reasons. Therefore, it is important to distinguish several species of conventionality and to consider whether any of them affords autonomy competency an opportunity to put self-knowledge on a lucid and cogent footing.

Conventionality founded on a lack of sophistication and imagination is conventionality by default. Paradigmatically, this form of conventionality is nothing more than the by-product of subjecting an individual with unexceptional potential to powerful, narrowly focused socialization in an environment offering limited opportunities. The predictable result is unreflective acceptance of prevailing beliefs and practices. Unable to plumb their selves and accustomed to understanding society in fixed schemas, such people can see no alternative to what is expected of them, and they remain dependent on society for direction. While no one picks up every cue emanating from his or her self, and while everyone filters experience to some extent through inculcated schemas, the more conventional people are by default, the less need they have for such distorting mechanisms as self-deception and the availability heuristic. Such people come closest to fitting Markus' model of the conventional self-concept based on cogent generalizations from past experience. However, Wilson's data about the frequency of behavioral leakage of unorthodox feelings, attitudes, and desires suggest that everyone has psychological reserves that elude such pedestrian self-concepts.

A second type of conventionality is founded on the value individuals place on others' good opinion and the value they place on fitting into their social context. Since no one wants to be despised or lonely, everyone presumably shares these values somewhat. What distinguishes other-directed conventionality is that these people elevate this pair of values to the paramount position in their hierarchy of concerns and pursue them to the detriment of their integrity. Instead of forecasting how other people will react to their conduct as part of the process of figuring out what they really believe and want, they concentrate on predicting others' preferences in order to comply with them. When this process takes place unconsciously, or when the individual's desire to do as others wish is sincere, other-directed conventionality is innocent. But when these calculations are undertaken for ulterior motives, or when the individual knows that he or she does not really want to satisfy others' desires, other-directed conventionality is hypocritical. In either case, the information encoded in culturally transmitted cognitive schemas is indispensable to this enterprise; these schemas function as tacit rules of thumb that guide the individual's interpretations and decisions into socially approved channels. Moreover, it is evident that the agent's overweening desire to obtain others' esteem and to be accepted would render these schemas all but immune to refutation.

Paradoxically, it might be thought that this form of conventionality could constitute a programmatically autonomous life. Provided that people had adopted and glorified these values—i.e., being liked and being included—using the skills of autonomy competency, their conventional lives would revolve around their own convictions. However, such lives must be viewed as abdications of autonomy on two grounds. First, since there is no reason to assume that what others believe and want coincides with what one really believes and wants, there is no reason to assume that a life lived entirely in deference to others will embody one's true self. Indeed, a self stripped of every attribute except the desire to be liked and included would be too amorphous to count as a self. This is not to say that people cannot autonomously identify with other individuals and autonomously pursue these individuals' interests as their own, but it is to say that blanket self-subordination to social convention nullifies autonomy. Second, such deliberate pandering to other people rules out being attuned to oneself for signs of discord and dissatisfaction, and it rules out being willing to correct one's life plans in response to such signals. In reducing self-definition and self-direction to compliance with societal demands, such servile conventionality, however principled it may be, blocks self-discovery and makes a mockery of self-definition and self-direction. Without reasonably accurate self-portraits, people cannot be self-governing.

Self-deceived conventionality represents a third form of conventionality. Here, one professes that one's real desires and convictions match the beliefs and practices of one's milieu while unconsciously knowing it is not so, or one maintains that one's attributes measure up to social norms while unconsciously knowing it is not so. People may repress their own desires and convictions or unconsciously alter their self-portraits for a variety of reasons. Prominent among them are anxiety about their shortcomings and fear of the consequences of acting on their abiding convictions and inclinations. Instead of confronting their selves, self-deceived people substitute a commitment to conventionality that can marshall heuristics like the availability heuristic to further block access to the true self.

The assortment of cognitive failings I sketched earlier predisposes people to nonautonomous conventionality. Moreover, a variety of motivations often reinforce such conventionality. To be conventional in this way, one's orientation must be overwhelmingly social. One thinks and does what is usual given one's social milieu, and one proceeds in this way because one is so dominated by social forces that one loses sight of one's self and cannot envisage oneself thinking and acting in any other way. Asked for their views about some issue or about the best course of action, nonautonomous conventional people often begin their replies with the self-effacing phrase, "They say . . ." Such individuals appeal to an unspecified, unquestioned social authority to back up their beliefs and to justify their actions. Being wrong is being mistaken about what "they" think is appropriate. Unlike autonomous people who often see possibilities where others see only constraints, thoroughgoingly conventional people are so locked into inculcated patterns of thought and action that they cannot fathom alternative interpretations or recognize opportunities for self-expression.

I have argued that various commonplace psychological mechanisms conspire with traditional socialization practices to promote conventionality. Yet, I have maintained elsewhere that people can be conventional and autonomous (part 2, sec. 4). Autonomously conventional people think and do what is usual in their social milieux, but they embrace these typical attitudes, values, goals, and so forth, autonomously. For this to be possible, their autonomy competency must be well-developed, and they must have used it to embrace what coincidentally are popularly accepted life plans. Thus, autonomous conventionality might be characterized as crypto-autonomy or as pseudo-conventionality, for the individual's adherence to socially approved beliefs and practices hides his or her underlying freedom from social domination, and this person's self-governance belies his or her apparent conformism. By trying to understand how autonomous conventionality might occur, we can begin to grasp how the psychological forces militating towards nonautonomous conventionality might be overcome.

In this connection, it is important to recognize the limits of introspection and memory. People can sometimes directly discern how they are feeling or what they are desiring. However, introspection often yields inconclusive or ambiguous information about people's inner lives. Moreover, people often delay inquiring into what brought them to perform actions until after the constellation of motivating factors has disappeared. Thus, self-knowledge should not be identified exclusively with introspective revelations. Of necessity, people sometimes resort to their self-concepts to understand their conduct and experience. Memory, too, is at least partially opaque. People cannot store all of the information—whether about themselves or about the world—to which they are exposed, and they cannot recall all of the information relevant to each problem they face. Selection mechanisms are at work in regard to acquisition, retention, and retrieval. Thus, it would be pointless to identify self-knowledge with a synoptic grasp of all autobiographical facts.

The problem, then, is not to figure out how people can become fully knowledgable about themselves and their environment. This is impossible. Rather, the problem is to clarify the difference between introspection and self-conception that are so misleading that they compromise autonomy, and introspection and self-conception that are sufficiently revealing to support autonomy. Also, it is necessary to clarify the difference between a memory so empty or so skewed that it compromises autonomy, and one that is sufficiently comprehensive and responsive to support autonomy.

Richard Nisbett and Lee Ross specify a number of circumstances that are conducive to accurate self-knowledge, and they suggest a number of remedies for the psychological mechanisms that often lead self-discovery astray. As a broad caveat, they emphasize that cognitive strategies like the availability heuristic can be helpful and, in addition, that the operations of various cognitive strategies may cancel one another out (Nisbett and Ross 1980:259, 263–264, 267). For example, insofar as people's true selves actually coincide with social expectations, the availability heuristic streamlines the process of self-discovery and generates an accurate self-portrait. Still, happenstance cannot be relied on to counteract the ill effects of such shortcuts. Moreover, lucky guesses about oneself hardly constitute autonomous self-knowledge. Thus, it is necessary to ascertain what enables people to understand themselves correctly while retaining an acceptable degree of control over the process of self-discovery.

Nisbett and Ross note that, when people are asked to explain why they did something that they have been trained to do, their self-reports are reliable (1980:212). However, this may seem cold comfort to anyone seeking a route to autonomy. The reason people can account for such behavior so well is that, having been socialized to follow a certain procedure when making a determinate type of decision, they can refer to this procedure as a theory which explains their conduct. Since this model of self-knowledge concerns relatively mechanical decisions—ones that can be made using a decision-procedure that can be taught—it seems confined to those attributes that people share with others and that lack emotional complexity.

In considering human conduct, however, it is easy to mistake similar form for identical content and, consequently, to exaggerate the pervasiveness of social conformity. To a great extent, people express themselves through culturally transmitted behaviors. Of course, people can deploy these behavior modules to meet others' expectations, and they can enact them as orthodox routines. But they also can deploy them in response to their expressive needs, and they can vary them to suit their personalities. Still, they remain grounded in shared theories.[2] While it is important to keep in mind Wilson's discovery that people's reliance on cultural rules can obstruct their access to those parts of their emotional life that are not congruent with these rules, shared theories must be adaptable to the purpose of explaining people's distinctive relationships and attributes. Otherwise, self-knowledge would be impossible.

Think of Stephen Dedalus being bullied by Wells:

—Tell us, Dedalus, do you kiss your mother before you go to bed?
Stephen answered:
—I do . . .
—O, I say, here's a fellow says he kisses his mother every night before he goes to bed . . .
—I do not . . .

He still tried to think what was the right answer. Was it right to kiss his mother or wrong to kiss his mother? What did that mean, to kiss? You put your face up like that to say goodnight and then his mother put her face down. That was to kiss. His mother put her lips on his cheek; her lips were soft and they wetted his cheek; and they made a tiny little noise: kiss. Why did people do that with their two faces? (James Joyce, *A Portrait of the Artist as a Young Man,* 14–15)

Stunned by Wells' incredulous and combative questioning and torn between masculine sangfroid and filial tenderness, Stephen is reduced to dissecting physical behavior, which baffles him precisely because he cannot apprehend the emotional dimension of kissing. The "emotion rule of kissing," as the psychologist would have it, and its application to Stephen's feelings for his mother elude him. He is at a loss to account for himself, for no one can do without the behavioral theories that cultures supply. The difference between autonomous self-knowledge and conventional self-stereotyping, then, cannot be that the former is independent of cultural practices.

At this juncture, it is important to stress that, by itself, the fact that socialization was instrumental in the genesis of someone's practices does not demonstrate that the person is not autonomous in that respect (part 2, secs. 1, 2, and 4). Thus, the fact that kissing is a conventional expression of affection does not impugn the geniuneness of Stephen's love for his mother. Moreover, there is no reason to believe that only nonautonomous conventional people can understand themselves through theories derived from learned procedures. What seems crucial to this approach to self-knowledge is that people explicitly learn how to undertake the conduct to be explained and that the link between the procedure and their feelings, attitudes, and desires not be broken.

Unconscious assimilation of cultural practices exacerbates people's difficulty in deciphering their real motives. When cultural practices insinuate themselves into people's lives unawares, people then tend to conflate shared understandings with inviolable imperatives (Wilson 1985:103). In regard to gender, for example, people have typically evolved conventional images of themselves, and they have come to associate the conventional with the natural.[3] Once such a wedge of mandatoriness has been driven between people's real attributes and their conduct, layers of rationalization begin to encrust people's self-concepts, and their self-concepts become immune to change. Rationalization of this kind can take a number of forms, but all of them involve subscribing to reasons for accepting a self-concept that do not originate in the authentic self. Such reasons are inimical to flexibility because they make contrary dispositions, feelings, and the like seem bad—not merely different or surprising, but bad. Rather than confront these "bad" parts of themselves, people cling to inaccurate self-portraits; behavioral forms take on a life of their own; and participation in shared practices becomes nonautonomous conventionality.

After they have undergone straightforward training, Nisbett and Ross contend, people's self-reports are accurate. The experience of being explicitly taught cultural practices enables people to articulate what they have learned, and they are less prone to split off their inner lives from their outward behavior. Yet, since autonomous people sometimes modify cultural practices in accordance with their peculiar needs, and since they call upon these practices on this occasion or that in accordance with their peculiar needs, self-knowledge must go beyond the theories of cultural practices.

Nisbett and Ross list a number of ways in which individuals can supplement these general theories with personal information. Sometimes, they note, people know facts about their personal lives—such as their past behavior, their values, their aversions, and the meanings they attach to events—and they have organized this information into plausible causal theories (Nisbett and Ross 1980:223–225). These are the idiosyncratic elemer : that Wilson says complement the cultural elements in the verbal explanatory system (1985:103). Unfortunately, Wilson's studies to date do not distinguish between explanations that rely on conventional wisdom and ones that rely on idiosyncratic conceptions. It is important to learn whether people who work out their own self-portraits are usually better able to infer their own attitudes and desires than people who adopt conventional self-portraits. Since people who devise distinctive self-portraits are as vulnerable to problems of lucidity and cogency as people who adopt conventional self-portraits, the greater adeptness of the former is by no means a foregone conclusion. Furthermore, it is important to ascertain what strategies people use to generate accurate self-portraits.

In this connection, two of Nisbett and Ross' recommendations for reducing error in judgment are apposite. They maintain that, when people deliberate in groups, there is a better chance that someone in the group will notice cognitive abuses and convince their fellows that their reasoning has gone awry (Nisbett and Ross 1980:266–267). Applied to the enterprise of self-discovery, this insight argues for a less privatized, more conversational approach. Instead of pretending that self-knowledge depends exclusively on one's privileged access to a strictly private realm of mental states, people need to solicit and attend to others' impressions and suggestions. Still, in view of people's ability to elicit the feedback they prefer and in view of people's inclination to maintain social harmony by expressing concurrence with their associates, an interactive approach to self-discovery will not improve self-knowledge unless safeguards against these tendencies are incorporated into the conversational process. For example, Irving Janis maintains that designating a devil's advocate authorizes someone to raise objections and propose alternatives that would otherwise be suppressed on the grounds that they were socially untoward (1983:267–268). It is easy to imagine how well-meaning friends could informally adopt such a corrective practice.

But people may yet contrive to elicit responses from others that confirm their own self-concepts, and their self-concepts function as filters that shunt aside disconfirming evidence. In view of this, Nisbett and Ross are frankly pessimistic about the prospects for self-knowledge (1980:288). However, they do defend education as a palliative, if not a total, solution to the problem. Since mistakes in reasoning contribute to people's misconceptions about themselves, schools should incorporate statistics and probability theory into their curricula, and students should be instructed about how common informal reasoning practices can lead to serious error (Nisbett and Ross 1980:296). Though knowledge of formally correct reasoning and of human propensities to subvert it cannot altogether prevent error, it does provide people with some tools they need to monitor their own reflection.

Now, it might seem that the evidence I have rehearsed for the fallibility of self-discovery procedures commends relativizing full autonomy to the capacities of individuals. That is, fully autonomous people are not those who succeed on an objective scale applicable to everyone; rather, they are people who have developed their potential as much as they can and who have exercised their capacities as well as they can. Christopher Cherniak's defense of a conception of minimal rationality—rationality constrained by individual capabilities— lends support to this relativization of full autonomy to the individual.

Against the view that human rationality must be seen in ideal terms,

Cherniak persuasively maintains that a conception of minimal rationality makes sense of the way we attribute beliefs to people. Cherniak details minimal requirements for deductive ability and for the ability to eliminate inconsistencies. For example, his "minimal inference condition" requires that people make some, but not necessarily all, of the sound inferences from their belief sets which would tend to satisfy their desires (1981:167). But, in this view, the question immediately arises as to how many of these inferences suffice to constitute minimal rationality. Cherniak acknowledges that it must be established that the individual has some logical ability, but, apart from that, Cherniak insists that qualifying as minimally rational depends on the "cognitive psychology of the particular subject"—for example, this individual's deductive proficiency and memory structure (1981:168, 177). Thus, a person with great deductive acumen will be required to make more sound and appropriate inferences in order to be counted minimally rational than a person with moderate deductive capabilities will be required to make.

While this result may not undermine Cherniak's epistemological project, it cannot plausibly be transferred to a theory of autonomy. Suppose that Justin has excellent deductive ability and memory retrieval and that Rebecca has mediocre deductive ability and memory retrieval. Furthermore, both have identical beliefs and desires in a given situation and make the same inferences about how they might satisfy their desires. It would seem that our assessment of their autonomy would depend on whether there are any additional feasible inferences that would contribute to their satisfaction, as opposed to the extent to which each has utilized his or her capacity.

If there are no such inferences, that is, if both of them have deliberated as much as is worthwhile, then they are both maximally autonomous with regard to this episode. However, if there are more feasible inferences which, had they made them, would have increased their satisfaction, then it seems that neither is fully autonomous. Even if these inferences exceed Rebecca's deductive powers, she cannot be considered fully autonomous since she can only discover how to give partial expression to her true self. In other words, she cannot satisfy the dominance principle as well as Justin can. (For further discussion of the relation between autonomy and the dominance principle, see part 2, sec. 5.) Also, it would be odd to declare Justin less autonomous than Rebecca on the grounds that he could have made the additional inferences but did not do so while she made all of the inferences she could have made, since both have satisfied the desires of their true selves to the same degree. Finally, if we alter the assumptions of this case and assume that Justin has made the additional inferences and thus increased his satisfaction, surely we would want to claim that Justin is more autonomous than Rebecca, for he has fulfilled more of the desires of his true self than she has.

To be autonomous at all, people must succeed in living in harmony with their authentic selves to some extent. Although the authentic self is an evolving collocation of desires, values, emotional attachments, goals, traits, and the like, it nevertheless provides a touchstone against which exercise of autonomy competency can be gauged. Consequently, the autonomy of any given choice cannot depend merely on whether a person's autonomy skills have been exhausted in the process of deliberation, for previous exercise of autonomy competency might have ratified components of the self which poorly developed autonomy skills then prevent the individual from taking into account. An additional reason for considering people who do not fully avail themselves of their autonomy competency less autonomous than people with equally developed competencies who do stems from the relation between autonomy competency and the authentic self. Since autonomy competency is part of the authentic self, not to live up to one's potential in this respect is to ignore part of one's authentic self—in other words, to violate the dominance principle (part 2, secs. 4 and 5). Moreover, since the authentic self is disclosed through the exercise of autonomy competency, less than maximal use of one's powers yields less than maximal self-knowledge and therefore a decline in autonomy. (However, for an account of why maximal exercise of autonomy skills does not entail constant, self-conscious self-monitoring, see part 2, sec. 4). Still, none of this entails that people who have exceptional, but under-utilized autonomy skills automatically fall below or fall to the level of people who have mediocre, but fully utilized skills. The formers' casual use of their well developed skills may give them more control over their lives than diligent exercise of comparatively weak skills can give the latter.

Full autonomy is not relative to individual powers, but neither is it an absolute standard disregarding all human frailty. Full autonomy is relative to two factors. People can be fully autonomous if their lack of control over their own lives is a result of inevitable human limitations or if their lack of control contributes to a psychic economy that is programmatically autonomous. The questions of which psychological constraints are universal human limitations and how these limitations can serve the purposes of self-governance are largely empirical ones which have yet to receive conclusive answers. However, some conjectures are supported by persuasive evidence, while others are supported by the logic of mental concepts. I shall review only a few of the relevant parameters.

First, people can assume control over the selection devices that structure memory only to a limited degree. Undeniably, people can become aware that retrieval mechanisms are distorting their understanding of the situations they face, and they can try to curb the gross biases these mechanisms produce by deliberately entertaining alternative interpretive schemata. Nevertheless, the press of time often obliges people to rely on whatever information they happen to recall, and, while the utmost leisure does allow people to compile a larger stock of information, it cannot afford them direct consciousness of the operations of memory. Thus, full control over this pivotal faculty necessarily eludes people, and their intractable memory patterns must be regarded as brute facts definitive of their individuality.

Second, the psychology of intellectual and emotional shortcuts is an expanding field, and evidence that people cannot be altogether weaned from these shortcuts is rapidly accumulating. For example, Tversky and Kahneman report that, although researchers who regularly work with statistics do not make the elementary errors that many of the rest of us make, they are nonetheless prone to use misleading heuristics when asked to form intuitive judgments about somewhat complex problems (1982:18). Though these devices sometimes produce efficiencies, they often lead to excessive conservativism or excessive optimism. Yet, people sometimes need to be unduly fretful in order to protect themselves from serious hazards, and people sometimes need to believe that they will achieve a great deal in order to achieve anything at all (Elster 1983:158). Although these heuristics can undermine autonomy, they can also create a background of caution or confidence that enhances self-governance.

Furthermore, when people do not measure up to cultural or personal standards, they avail themselves of sundry defense mechanisms and cognitive schema to sustain their self-esteem. Obviously, these mechanisms must be calibrated to prevent people from so inflating their self-concepts that they undertake projects sure to bring failure and disenchantment with themselves. However, as Gilbert and Cooper have observed, under some circumstances people predictably move to conceal from themselves information damaging to their self-esteem (1985:91; also see Coopersmith 1981:37, 247). Thus, self-deception can supplement honest self-assessment to maintain the individual's sense of personal worth and competency.[4] Although people who are almost never candid with themselves about their attributes can have little control over their lives, it is hard to believe that anyone lives entirely free of self-deception. Inasmuch as a firm sense of personal identity depends in part on a person's belief that he or she can fulfill a chosen set of aims and can live up to a preferred ideal, properly modulated self-deception can reinforce personal identity.

Likewise, self-concepts order people's lives. Functioning as self-perpetuating cognitive filters, they lead people to disregard anomalous behavior and to fasten exaggerated importance on confirming behavior. Thus, it may seem that people are either fixated on a self-portrait that is not entirely warranted by the evidence, or else, for want of a self-portrait, they are uncertain and confused about themselves. Both states of affairs are uncongenial to autonomy.

To be without a self-portrait is, indeed, to lack autonomy. Though self-portraits are worked out retrospectively as well as prospectively (part 2, sec. 2), people cannot ask themselves what they really believe and want without developing some conception of who they are and what matters to them. Moreover, without such a conception, people would have no stable criteria to guide their programmatic decisions. Self-concepts thus play a central role in the formation of integrated personalities and long-term life plans. In addition, the unconscious operations of self-concepts facilitate spontaneous autonomy since they obviate people's need to consult their self-concepts each time they take action (part 2, sec. 2). Thus, the problem self-concepts pose for autonomy is not how they can be jettisoned, but rather what enables people to regard them as sufficiently provisional to be able to monitor and adjust them as needed.

Broadly speaking, what I have been urging is that full autonomy is compatible with the influence of unconscious forces. Some of these forces, for instance, people's cognitive styles, are best understood as constitutive of the uniqueness of persons—they underpin the distinctive ways in which each individual thinks and acts. Others, for instance, people's defense mechanisms, are best understood as shielding the integrity of persons—they allow people to sustain ongoing identities despite the vicissitudes of experience. That these types of forces should govern people's lives and that, for all their moment, these forces should remain occluded from consciousness are elemental facts about the human condition. People are not as malleable as they sometimes wish they were, and part of the reason they resist change is that they are not and cannot be made transparent to themselves. Since the springs of our individuality can only be partially exposed to conscious scrutiny, the self cannot be brought completely under control.

Plainly, however, unconscious forces can be antipathetic to autonomy. Some sabotage the use of autonomy skills to formulate life plans—the unresolved oedipal complex that leaves the individual timid and dependent. Others splinter the personality—the obsession that drives the individual to perform a secret ritual that frustrates consciously adopted plans. Still, the relation between unconscious forces and autonomy must not be oversimplified. When unconscious forces overwhelm the individual, they enforce heteronomy. But since unconscious forces can play various constructive roles, they can contribute to an autonomous life.

Full autonomy does not presuppose total self-control, for that is impossible. Yet, social-psychological knowledge has not advanced far enough to certify clear boundaries between individual limitations and universal human constraints on self-regulation. Only social experimentation and empirical inquiry can reveal which obstacles to autonomy are inherent in the human condition and which are caused by childhood socialization. One point is indisputable, however, and that is that current educational practices and social and economic arrangements are not designed to enhance autonomy. To ascertain the limits of autonomy, it will be necessary to stop gearing socialization to role preparation, and it will be necessary to dismantle those social and economic institutions that depend on docile acquiescence in preordained roles. Rather, socialization practices aimed at awakening and cultivating autonomy competency must be coupled with a social and economic climate that supports the exercise of this competency. Though it may turn out that a substantial measure of alienation and mystification are part of the human condition, in the absence of decisive arguments against the viability of autonomy, it seems advisable to seek better socialization methods (part 3, sec. 5) and to try out social and economic reforms (part 4).

# Autonomy-Enhancing Socialization

ANYONE CAN fall prey to self-deception and other departures from rationality, and conventionality exerts a certain pull on most people. However, to see through such autonomy-defeating mechanisms and in general to live in harmony with one's authentic self, a person needs the self-reading skills of autonomy competency (part 2, sec. 4). Since differential socialization cultivates boys' autonomy competency more than it does girls', it is natural to seek a remedy for this inequality in the socialization process. In this regard, three main proposals can be found in the literature. Simone de Beauvoir suggests socializing girls the same way boys are socialized. Nancy Chodorow recommends co-parenting—mothers and fathers sharing equally in child-care responsibilities. Janet Radcliffe Richards advocates pluralism in socialization—exposing all children to the widest possible variety of ideas and lifestyles. All of these proposals must be taken seriously; implementation of each would help to alleviate the disparity between women's and men's autonomy. However, since none of them is designed to address the specific problem of cultivating autonomy competency, each requires modification and supplementation.

Since masculine socialization develops autonomy competency more fully than feminine socialization, de Beauvoir concludes that girls must be brought up with the "same demands and rewards, the same severity and the same freedom, as her brothers, taking part in the same studies, the same games, promised the same future, surrounded with women and men who [seem] her undoubted equals . . . " (1953: 683). Still, de Beauvoir recognizes that overhauling socialization practices is not enough. Institutional changes, such as child-care facilities, equal opportunity in education and employment, and giving married women control over their property, are also necessary. Moreover, she appreciates the difficulties posed by gradual change—aggressive, ambitious women will be considered freaks until most girls receive masculine upbringings (1953:683). Yet, universal masculine socialization coupled with social and economic reform holds out the only hope of freeing women from immanence.

An insuperable problem with de Beauvoir's program is that it is impossible for girls and boys both to receive masculine socialization since this includes raising them to believe that they belong to the superior sex (part 3, sec. 2). In the same communities and often in the same families, girls and boys would soon discover that they were both being encouraged to believe that they have superior genitalia and belong to a privileged sex-defined class. Obviously, the members of at least one of these groups would eventually conclude that they had been misled and relinquish this belief. At most, both sexes could be raised to believe that there is nothing wrong with belonging to either sex.

Unfortunately, in de Beauvoir's account of the development of autonomy, this egalitarianism would be a poor substitute for instilling a belief in one's social and biological superiority. The purpose of inculcating this peculiarly masculine hauteur is to reassure little boys about their own worth and importance, and the reason this reassurance is needed is that these children have been discouraged from clinging to their mothers and pushed into independent play (part 3, sec. 2). To prevent them from feeling unwanted and inadequate, they are initiated into the masculine world and encouraged to take pride in their sex. As a result of this "second weaning," little boys not only learn to occupy themselves on their own, but also they gain sufficient self-confidence to go ahead and carry out their own projects.

Plainly, if it is necessary to soften the blow of apparent parental rejection by convincing children that they belong to the superior sex, it will not be possible to bring autonomy to girls without sacrificing the autonomy of boys. Taking the point a bit further, it is doubtful that merely assuring children that their sex-linked characteristics are normal and good would have the same confidence-enhancing effects. Since the insecurity resulting from the withdrawal of parental affection and from the humiliation of being ridiculed as effeminate is presumably severe, common sense dictates that it would need a strong antidote. The idea is to convince children that they are special despite their parents' evident indifference, but being normal is not being special. Thus, de Beauvoir's mechanism of autonomy generation is not universalizable, and her own account of autonomy precludes the outcome of reciprocal alterity—women defining themselves as different from men; men defining themselves as different from women; neither sex regarding the other as inferior—that she posits as an ideal (1953:xvii). Nor, I would add, is it desirable to subject all children to the protocols of traditional masculine socialization, for compassion surely argues for seeking a less harsh mode of socializing young children.

A further objection to de Beauvoir's solution is that is would engender lopsided homogeneity. De Beauvoir herself acknowledges that feminine socialization brings about some valuable results—for example, women's introspective sensitivity—but these desiderata would be lost in the rush to instill self-assertiveness and independence in girls. Moreover, in my estimation, de Beauvoir is overly critical of femininity. For example, she maintains that feminine altruism, appearances to the contrary notwithstanding, invariably gets perverted into a sadomasochistic maternal game (de Beauvoir 1953:494). While I do not wish to deny that this can happen—indeed, there may be an element of jealousy and martyrdom in many mother-daughter relations—I would also stress that these relations are not usually devoid of loving care. If they were, most children's emotional development would be blatantly stunted (Chodorow 1978:33). In addition, I believe that de Beauvoir overlooks a dysfunctional feature of masculine socialization—its reinforcement of aggression. The emotional isolation central to masculine socialization obliges boys to become independent, but it also heightens their aggressive tendencies because it makes them feel insecure. In this regard, it is worth recalling Hobbes's pivotal insight: when people feel threatened, they defend themselves by violent means. Implanting a mentality of embattled self-sufficiency in all people could only accelerate and perpetuate the violence so tragically characteristic of many men. Concomitantly, it would eradicate the pacific virtues of femininity. Unisex child-rearing has undeniable advantages; however, it should not be modeled on the masculine stereotype.

Nancy Chodorow advocates a structural solution to the gap between women's and men's autonomy. She contends that, as long as women have exclusive responsibility for child-care, girls will grow up other-directed, and boys will grow up independent (1978:206–209; for a detailed account of Chodorow's theory, see part 3, sec. 2). Thus, for Chodorow, co-parenting is the solution (1978:215, 218). If girls and boys alike were raised equally by parents of both sexes, girls could gain autonomy without losing the capacity to sustain deep interpersonal bonds, and boys could gain a capacity for deep interpersonal bonds without sacrificing autonomy. Girls would not be hobbled by exclusive, primary emotional ties to a same sex parent and would be able to establish separate personal identities with greater ease. Likewise, boys would have primary emotional ties to their fathers as well as to their mothers and would not see such emotional ties as threats to their sexual identity. Also, deep emotional bonds with parents of both sexes would help sever the link between sex and social roles since children would find it natural to identify with the activities of both parents.

Although equalizing parental roles would undoubtedly have many beneficial effects (for parents as well as for children), it is not clear that this arrangement would suffice to secure autonomy for both sexes. If de Beauvoir and Chodorow are correct in holding that male autonomy is largely an accidental product of a nurturance vacuum at a critical childhood stage, shared parenting might reduce male autonomy without increasing female autonomy. As before, girls would not be deprived of motherly warmth, but now boys would have the solace of fatherly warmth. Yet, according to this account, if no one undergoes the trauma of separation from a primary caretaker, no one will become autonomous. On the assumption that women would take advantage of co-parenting to work outside the home, this unwanted effect might be offset somewhat by the availability of independent female role models. However, defiance of traditional gender roles does not guarantee personal autonomy, and it is doubtful that the competency of autonomy can be acquired through imitation of unconventional outward behavior.

Janet Racliffe Richards' view can be seen as complementing Chodorow's. Richards favors exposing all children to a wide variety of options in a nonprejudicial fashion through public education (1980:88; Joel Feinberg takes a similar view in Feinberg 1980a:139–40). This pluralistic approach to fostering autonomy is designed to prevent parents from so restricting their children's awareness of possibilities or from so biasing their children's perception of possibilities that they are effectively prevented from adopting them. Schools can counteract parental narrow-mindedness by supplying a broader range of influences.

Educational pluralism has undeniable merits. However, it seems to me that bombarding children with sundry options will only confuse them unless this policy dovetails with a method of nurturing the competency of autonomy. Autonomy certainly requires the availability of diverse possibilities (Meyers 1987c:24–27). However, it also requires the ability to select those that match one's authentic self. Although the availability of a variety of options provides an incentive to master autonomy skills, children cannot gain autonomy competency simply by being flooded with options. A more direct attack on the problem is needed. The competency of autonomy must be handled in the same way that other desirable competencies are. It must be deliberately taught.[1] Parents and teachers must encourage their charges to attend to their self-referential responses and must help them to find acceptable ways to act on these insights.

Here, the contrast between my conception of teaching autonomy and Rousseau's approach to this matter in *Emile* is noteworthy. Rousseau's basic strategy for cultivating autonomy is to place children in situations which are structured to induce them to draw correct object lessons. He enunciates three basic educational principles. First, lessons must be harnessed to the child's "immediate and palpable interests"; otherwise, the child will not be engaged by them, and they will not last (Rousseau 1979:108). Second, since children reason very well in regard to matters that interest them, they can be counted on to instruct themselves provided they are placed in the right sort of environment (Rousseau 1979:108). Third, punishments must never seem imposed by the teacher; they must seem to come "from the very order of things" (Rousseau 1979:102). As Rousseau sums up his method, "Let him [the student] always believe he is the master, and let it always be you who are" (Rousseau 1979:120).

Emile's lesson in property rights illustrates Rousseau's pedagogy. Rousseau observes that the desire to be active and to create is a basic human drive which Emile evidences in his desire to grow a garden. Thus, Emile's inclinations provide his tutor with the occasion to inculcate the doctrine of property rights. Rousseau teaches Emile that property rights are founded on the labor of the first occupant by letting him plant and tend a garden on someone else's land—land where the owner had previously planted melon seeds that had not yet sprouted. When the owner discovers Emile's bean plants and uproots them, Emile acutely feels the chagrin of having his produce destroyed. Therefore, Emile not only deduces that he has wronged the owner; he also emotionally grasps the injustice he has done the owner by unwittingly ruining what the owner had previously planted. Emile realizes that his work had given him a sense of entitlement but that his work was not sufficient to sustain a property right (Rousseau 1979:98–99). Thus, Emile's desires, emotions, and reason coalesce in this lesson—a lesson which is not merely memorized, but which is graven on Emile's heart.

Now, keeping in mind that the objective of Emile's education is to make him an autonomous man—a man capable of supporting himself and of thinking for himself—it is paradoxical that Emile always draws a preordained conclusion. From his religious convictions to his choice of a wife, Emile follows the course his mentor sets out for him. Like the behaviorist's rat receiving electrical prods to teach it to run a maze, Emile is subjected to an ingenious system of rewards and punishments designed to shape his personality and principles. (For a similar view of Rousseau's educational philosophy, see Martin 1985:46–53). In this connection, we can see how apt is Rousseau's preference for the title "governor" (Rousseau 1979:52).

Still, Rousseau denounces the results of conventional education: "Thus, in conflict and floating during the whole course of our life, we end it without having been able to put ourselves in harmony with ourselves and without having been good either for ourselves or for others" (Rousseau 1979:41). Yet, however harmonious an adult Rousseau's educational methods may produce, this harmony is by no means anchored in the individual's authentic self. Rousseau seems to think that by concealing his own authority and power over his pupil while nurturing the boy's rationality, Emile will become so unaccustomed to acquiescing to other people and so accustomed to deciding for himself that he will be autonomous. The trouble with this scheme is that it leaves out the true self. Rousseau makes allies of the child's interests, but these interests are the interests of all children (at any rate, as the teacher inventories them), not Emile's distinctive inclinations. The latter have no part in his upbringing. At best, then, Emile learns to reason independently on the basis of a set of prototypical interests—he discovers a morality of rights and adopts a life plan answering to his basic needs—but he is not sensitized to or capable of acting on his personal desires.

Whereas Rousseau advocates immersing his charge in a series of situations contrived to instill preconceived object lessons, I believe that education for autonomy necessitates taking advantage of serendipity in three respects. First, children should not be isolated from other children and kept under the tutelage of an adult. Second, real situations should be used as educational materials. Third, the child's idiosyncratic responses to these situations should be explored.

Jean Piaget emphasizes the role of peer interaction in the development of autonomy. Piaget observes that it is only when children escape from authority—that of their parents and also that of older children—that they start to regard the rules of the games they play as created by children and therefore as subject to modification by children (Piaget 1960:54). More specifically, he stresses that the reciprocity that grows from cooperative interaction among equals enables children to adopt a critical perspective on the rules they follow, yet to regard the rules as binding unless the other children agree to a change (Piaget 1960:62–63,89). Far from ensuring autonomy, the seclusion in which Rousseau proposes to raise Emile would obstruct the development of his autonomy competency. Not only does the autonomous person need to be able to think independently, but also this individual needs to be able to work with other people to achieve common aims and to enjoy shared goods. Childhood companionship is the prerequisite for both characteristics.

Piaget's research also suggests that the uses of idealized situations in education for autonomy are quite limited. He found that the nitty-gritty mechanics of keeping their games going inspired his subjects to reflect and innovate. Such everyday circumstances may exhibit paradigms which illustrate general principles. But, since real situations often bring general principles into conflict in ways that cannot be dispensed with through neat rankings, it is equally important that children learn to puzzle out these messier situations. (Carol Gilligan comments on the short-comings of understanding moral development exclusively through ideal dilemmas [1982:68–70].) A child who is adept at deriving the lesson from a fable is not necessarily equipped to handle many actual situations. In these contexts, children must learn to maintain equanimity under pressure and must learn to cope with a give-and-take process of deciding between alternatives that all have distinct advantages and disadvantages. While a caretaker can guide a child in recalling and applying relevant principles, this person must also help the child to decipher the special constellation of circumstances and desires that makes the situation perplexing.

Here, it is particularly important for a caretaker to emphasize attention to the child's feelings and desires. The cognitive psychologist, Augusto Blasi, claims that those of a child's desires that are contrary to the demands of recognized authorities play a crucial role in the genesis of moral autonomy. For it is in response to the tension between such desires and the desire to avoid punishment that children begin to see that obeying an authority can be wrong and that disobedience can be mandatory (Blasi 1985:10–14). Blasi's view can be extrapolated to the sphere of personal autonomy. In relation to personal autonomy, the tension would arise between a deviant occurrent desire and the desire to conform to social norms, and the resolution would take the form of compliance with the directives of the authentic self.[2] Thus, to foster personal autonomy, caretakers must encourage children to attend to those of their feelings and desires that do not mesh with social norms, to factor them into the deliberative process, and to chart a course that takes them into account.

On those occasions when a caretaker can safely leave a decision to a child, the caretaker should elicit the child's ideas and feelings, should join with the child to delicately probe them, and should assure the child that what is important is that he or she be satisfied with whatever course is chosen. Plainly, in a situation of this kind, the caretaker cannot presume to know the correct answer in advance; the caretaker can only discern the best course by sharing the process of self-discovery with the child. Since morality is not at issue, there can be no presumption of the advisability of the socially condoned course. Thus, caretakers must be prepared to accept non-conformist outcomes. Whatever good the exercise of self-reading may do would be neutralized if children were subsequently deterred from carrying out their own decisions or were made to feel foolish or ashamed after they behaved unconventionally. Of course, children will sometimes end up very unhappy with their decisions. But such disappointments can be turned to good use, for they can provide occasions for instruction in the techniques of self-correction and redirection, and they also provide opportunities to affirm the value of choosing for oneself despite the risk of mistakes.

Apart from cultivating autonomy competency, the pedagogical method I have described would have a number of desirable consequences. Compared to children raised in rigidly conformist or emotionally deprived environments, children raised in emotionally supportive environments in which differences are respected and enjoyed are more likely to be tolerant of others' beliefs and practices. In this regard, it is worth recalling that a major problem with traditional masculine socialization is the aggression it promotes. But, if personal autonomy were supportively taught as I have suggested, this competency could be enhanced without instigating unwanted collateral violence. In other words, self-assertiveness would be separated from aggression.

Furthermore, children who are accustomed to discussing their feelings and desires with others gain a capacity for intimacy that can itself contribute to autonomy, for people who are able to communicate their concerns to others can benefit from others' suggestions (part 3, sec, 4). Also, talking over one's views with people who may be adversely affected by one's actions creates an environment of frank and friendly disagreement, as opposed to one of concealed and hostile contention. By helping to defuse the antipathy that some of one's actions might provoke, the former sort of environment supports ongoing autonomy. Moreover, if the differences between the individuals are not too great to allow for mutual accommodation, such interaction may lead to autonomous cooperation. Broadly, my educational approach to autonomy development carries with it the implication that autonomy could shed its connotations of stridently competitive individualism and could be recognized as the foundation for social relations that both respect individuals and bind them to one another.

Finally, it is clear that educational practices of the sort I have recommended can be applied equally to children of both sexes by parents of both sexes. Accordingly, such childrearing practices explain why co-parenting, as opposed to exclusive mothering in a two-parent, heterosexual family, is desirable with respect to autonomy. Co-parenting cancels the gender associations of assertiveness and intimacy. Both the mother and the father supply the love the child needs and share the child's day-by-day concerns. In the child's mind, emotion and closeness become linked as much with masculinity as with femininity. But, since neither parent is devoted exclusively to the child, and since neither parent regularly dominates decisions pertaining to the child, self-realization, judgment, and compromise are perceived as equally appropriate for women and men. But most importantly, from the child's point of view, to be cared for by both parents is to experience independence reconciled with attachment. On the one hand, the parents supply a model of this reconciliation in their conduct of their relations with their child and also with one another in regard to their child. On the other hand, the child enjoys attachment to both parents as well as independence from each of them. In conjunction with a regimen of frequent practice in autonomy skills, this symmetrical backdrop makes autonomy as attainable for girls as for boys. Neither parent threatens to smother the girl's independence, and each parent gives her the emotional support necessary to gain self-assurance. Yet, this arrangement preserves the desirable results of traditional feminine socialization, since it eliminates the need for an abrupt separation from a primary caretaker that precipitates anxiety, insecurity, and aggression before engendering self-sufficiency.

If such nonsexist training were given at school as well as at home, it would show girls and boys alike that personal autonomy is an approved competency while fostering its development. Although this educational recommendation is hardly revolutionary, it is by no means universally accepted. In some quarters, this reluctance stems from distrust of the educational system as an avenue of liberation. Another source of resistance is a widespread failure to recognize socialization for minimal autonomy or, in other words, relative heteronomy as a type of wrongful subordination and hence as a type of oppression. The fourth part of this book addresses the connection between autonomy and justice; however, I shall close this part by considering the arguments of radical critics of the school system.

Samuel Bowles and Herbert Gintis have convincingly documented the failure of universal public education in the United States to ameliorate poverty and to guarantee equal opportunity, and I have no quarrel with their distrust of political theories relying on education as a panacea for endemic social ills. However, I believe that Bowles and Gintis' attack on the free school movement is not entirely warranted because they overlook the autonomy-enhancing potential of this approach to education while they underrate the benefits to be gained through widespread autonomy.

Free schools are ones in which students are encouraged to take an active part in formulating their curricula and in which programs are tailored to the needs of individual students. Now, it is undeniable that the focus on autonomy can be carried to counterproductive lengths. To the extent that the free school movement has insisted that children can only learn freedom of thought if they have choices about what is taught, a moderating corrective is needed, for learning autonomy skills does not presuppose the opportunity to exercise them regarding all aspects of the child's life, and in some areas the child's interests are best served by deference to adult expertise and authority. Thus, I grant that leaving some educational choices to children would be irresponsible. Still, dire projections of illiteracy and other forms of ignorance consequent upon children's ill-advised decisions to skip disliked subjects are not the basis of Bowles and Gintis' criticism of free schools. Rather, they object to the successes of the schools; that is, they complain that these schools teach autonomy skills when there is no outlet in the real world for these skills.

Setting aside the objection that this is a prohibitively expensive way to educate masses of children, Bowles and Gintis complain that it would produce "occupational misfits and a proliferation of the job blues" (1977:252). Since most jobs require docile, dependable employees, Bowles and Gintis affirm, such reforms would cruelly raise expectations that are bound to be dashed. But Bowles and Gintis also seem to hold that this possibility poses no danger because "the schools are destined to legitimate inequality, limit personal development to forms compatible with submission to arbitrary authority, and aid in the process whereby youth are resigned to their fate" (1977:266). Since a capitalist economy cannot sustain anti-capitalist schools, in their view, free schools will never proliferate to the point where the composition of the labor force would undermine capitalism.

Although there is not room in a capitalist economy for everyone to be educated in free schools, there is a place in a capitalist economy for some products of these institutions. However, Bowles and Gintis contemptuously dismiss young professionals who are graduates of pupil-centered schools and who rank work autonomy and lifestyle individualism among their most urgent personal values:

These ideals may be traced to the aspirations of the property-owning class in the epoch of petty capitalism. In the corporate era, they constitute an anachronism—granted an inspiring and evocative one—unless altered in ways compatible with the political needs for a radical transformation of the U.S. economic and social structure. (1977:253).

These people are outmoded dreamers, if not elitists, who refuse to recognize the underlying political nature of their personal objectives. Educated in free schools but having unconsciously internalized corporate norms, these people become innovative managers who serve the ends of capitalist domination (Bowles and Gintis 1977:254).

For Bowles and Gintis, the alternative is socialist education. Instead of teaching children to seek fulfillment through individual life plans which may or may not have a political component, socialist education is to teach children to struggle in cooperation with others against arbitrary authority (Bowles and Gintis 1977:270). Now, I readily grant that the ability to forge associations of like-minded cohorts can facilitate autonomy and that the ability to defy arbitrary authority is indispensable to autonomy. However, Bowles and Gintis seem to deny that the questions of what sort of affiliations are worth having and what sort of authorities should be resisted are matters of personal belief. Their view is reminiscent of de Beauvoir's requirement that autonomous people fight for progressive political causes (part 3, sec. 3). Thus, they merely design a system favoring one form of "self-development" over another—that is, socialist life plans over others—without regard for personal autonomy—that is, without regard for individual selves.

It seems to me that what is valuable in Bowles and Gintis' analysis is that it alerts us to structural as well as incidental social and economic obstacles to education for autonomy. For example, they point out that working-class parents tend to oppose free schools on the grounds that such institutions fail to prepare their children for the exigencies they will face in the work world (1977:133). A related form of conservatism has also been detected by social psychologists studying sex role socialization. Since working-class parents enforce traditional gender stereotypes more stringently than middle-class parents, girls growing up in this environment may be doubly fettered with respect to autonomy (Weitzman 1984:177). Plainly, schools cannot undo the socialization parents impose at home, but it is important to recognize that schools can mitigate the effects of excessively narrow role preparation. Moreover, though I do not share Bowles and Gintis' implacable pessimism about the possibility of major educational reform, I would stress that schools need not be altogether metamorphosed to do a better job of developing autonomy competency.

Schools already offer students a decent familiarity with foreign cultures and with different groups within their own society. Also, schools typically make information about educational opportunities and careers available to students. Such programs could be strengthened without revolutionizing the academic infrastructure. Furthermore, individual teachers can promote autonomy on a modest scale. Where the standard curriculum allows for flexibility—in the selection of library books, in the choice of play activities, and elsewhere—teachers can encourage students to reflect on and pursue their own preferences rather than foisting projects on them or giving them choices without providing any instruction in making choices of their own. Also, in keeping with Piaget's insights into the role of peer cooperation in the evolution of autonomy, educational theorists would recommend increased reliance on collaborative learning—peer tutoring, peer evaluation of individual projects, and work in small groups in the classroom (Bruffee 1984:636–637). For harassed teachers with too many students packed into their classes, collaborative learning offers a way of eliciting every student's participation as well as providing individual attention. Moreover, this egalitarian learning context fosters autonomy.

Still, Bowles and Gintis would not find such reforms congenial, for they would only awaken styles of thought and behavior that would later be crushed once the student left the protective classroom setting. I take this opposition to be theoretically misguided, since it undermines the humanistic objectives that Bowles and Gintis advocate.

Let us agree with Bowles and Gintis that the work world should be democratized and humanized—that hierarchy and subordination should be supplanted and that tedious and exhausting jobs should be divided up fairly. How is such change to come about? Is it to come about through action based on indoctrination or through action grounded in free conviction? Opposing paternalistic domination as they do, Bowles and Gintis would presumably prefer the impetus for change to come from people's considered beliefs. But, if this is to happen, people must be taught to assess the strengths and weaknesses of their society and to arrive at their own appraisal of it. They must learn to figure out what they really want and how their social setting must be transformed if it is to accommodate their autonomous desires. Although one can sympathize with Bowles and Gintis' worries that this may be an education for unhappiness, it is well-known that discontent, coupled with the revelation of the social origins of this discontent, provides the foundation for social change. Whether Bowles and Gintis' vision of the good society should be realized, I leave aside. I would emphasize only that any democratic ideal would profit from education that cultivates autonomy competency.

Still, it is important to remember that school is not the only place where education for autonomy should take place. In view of the tremendous influence of the home environment on early childhood development, it is clear that teachers' capacity to impart autonomy skills to children would be sharply limited without the cooperation of parents and other caretakers. Why justice obliges them to provide this cooperation will be considered in the next part.

# PART IV

# The Value of Personal Autonomy

Anyone who allows himself to be led and dictated to by the bad habits and opinions of his surroundings has no respect for himself. But without self-respect, there's no morality, no order, no continuity, no life-giving warmth.

Franz Kafka, quoted by Gustav Janouch in *Conversations with Kafka,* p. 174

# The Personal and the Political Value of Autonomy

PEOPLE DO not live entirely autonomously or entirely heteronomously. Autonomy is a matter of degree which depends on a person's proficiency with respect to the skills constituting autonomy competency and the extent to which this competency is exercised. Thus, fully autonomous people possess a complete repertory of well developed and well coordinated autonomy skills coupled with many and varied independent competencies. Social-psychological data indicate, however, that full autonomy is rare. At the other end of the spectrum, minimally autonomous people possess at least some disposition to consult their selves and at least some ability to act on their own beliefs, desires, and so forth; but they lack some of the other skills from the repertory of autonomy skills; the autonomy skills they possess are poorly developed and poorly coordinated; and they possess few independent competencies that could promote the exercise of available autonomy skills. In between are medially autonomous people. Although it is not possible to draw sharp lines between minimal and medial autonomy and between medial and full autonomy, studies of gender socialization suggest that women tend to cluster near the minimal autonomy pole, whereas men are apt to be medially autonomous and range in the direction of the full autonomy pole. (For detailed treatment of the social-psychological literature and its implications regarding gender and autonomy, see part 3, secs. 2–3.)

In experiential terms, the minimally autonomous individual can best be understood in contrast to the strictly heteronomous individual and the medially autonomous individual. Unlike strictly heteronomous people, ones who are minimally autonomous are sufficiently adept in the skills of autonomy to be able to take advantage of a conducive setting to identify a small selection of integral values, emotional bonds, personal interests, and the like. But because minimally autonomous people use the repertory of autonomy skills awkwardly, their self-probing is cruder than the medially autonomous individual's, and their commitment to their own desires and standards is shaky. Lacking facility in reasoning critically about practical issues and ingenuity in imagining workable options, minimally autonomous people are prone to recoil from seemingly abnormal priorities. Often enough, the result is that their conduct expresses their authentic selves only approximately. Moreover, since minimal autonomy typically operates episodically or within the confines of narrowly programmatic issues, minimally autonomous people do not have globally autonomous life plans (part 3, sec. 3). They are not in control of the overall direction of their lives.

Because minimally autonomous people commonly find self-reflection a plodding and unrewarding endeavor, they are loathe to initiate change. The upshot of this passivity may be an incomprehensibly tenacious loyalty to nonautonomous components of their life plans— for example, the persistently bored, housebound mother whose professed shock that anyone could hire a stranger to care for a baby or even that the baby's father could do the job is adamant, though reflexive. Nevertheless, when novel and powerful external forces are brought to bear upon minimally autonomous people, the result may be fickleness—for example, the traditional woman who held working women in contempt until her husband lost his well-remunerated job in heavy industry, but who now forcefully affirms her desire to keep her dreary part-time job regardless of whether she needs to work. The common theme in these apparently divergent behaviors is the tendency of minimally autonomous people to take refuge in salient models.

To be autonomous at all, people must have and use a selection of the skills of autonomy competency to guide some part of their lives, but, at the lowest levels of proficiency, autonomy is only a fragmentary phenomenon. Yet, since minimally autonomous people can live happy and useful lives, it may seem doubtful that there is anything wrong with socializing people to be minimally autonomous.

One argument against the claim that socialization for minimal autonomy as it is practiced in Western societies today is unjust maintains that this socialization process is too weakly coercive to qualify as oppressive. To this contention, it may be replied that the insidiousness of feminine socialization and its lack of overt brutality disguise its coerciveness. Because the formative pressures of childhood socialization are ubiquitous, and because no child is in a position to assess or to resist them—of course, this is as true of masculine socialization as it is of feminine socialization—this process is coercive. To the extent that socialization practices are changing or to the extent that a pluralistic social setting undercuts monolithically feminine socialization, women may be achieving greater autonomy. However, it is important to remember that identification with different roles and an expanded stock of behaviors need not signify augmented autonomy. Such changes may merely reflect modifications in the feminine stereotype as the ideal of the superwoman supplants that of the tender homebody. Yet, if women are in fact becoming more autonomous, it is not because socialization is not coercive that such advances are being made; rather, it is because girls are being subjected to a different sort of coercive socialization.

The question is not whether to have a coercive or a noncoercive form of childhood socialization. Since there is no such thing as noncoercive childhood socialization, but since socialization is an inescapable feature of civilization, some form of coercive socialization must be justifiable. Indeed, it is not the coerciveness of socialization that generally draws fire. It is when socialization harms people that the process itself falls under suspicion. In the case of girls, we have seen that traditional feminine socialization funnels them into a dependent mindset which curtails their control over their lives. Many feminists have condemned this result. The question we must ask, then, is whether this form of socialization should be replaced with one that promotes autonomy.

Against such a reform, it might be argued that even medial autonomy is not necessarily good since the value of autonomy itself is open to dispute. Alison Jaggar has dismissed autonomy as "characteristically masculine as well as characteristically capitalist" (1983:131). Moreover, Vinit Haksar has claimed that autonomy is a form of perfectionism—a standard of human excellence as opposed to a basic human interest—for some people may reasonably prefer the simplicity and ease of a predefined and conditioned life over the complexity and stress of autonomy (1979:187; for a related view, see Sher 1983:47–49). Anticipating these views, some philosophers have maintained that servility is immoral (Tormey 1973:221; T. Hill, Jr. 1973:142; Friedman 1985:147), while others have argued that lack of autonomy frustrates altruism as well as self-interest (Blum, et al. 1973:232, 237; Postow 1978:184; Grimshaw 1986:182–183), that a measure of autonomy is inextricable from our conception of agency (Grimshaw 1986:178), or that autonomy is necessary to account for the value of liberty and utility (Haworth 1986:136–182). I shall take a related, but different tack.

Whatever one's pre-philosophical views about autonomy may be, self-respect cannot be construed as a masculine or perfectionist value. Self-contempt or even a dearth of self-respect are cause for despair. Most self-contemptuous people suffer from their condition, and those who do not are vulnerable to disillusionment and pain. Accordingly, if minimal autonomy compromises self-respect, and if most people are capable of achieving medial autonomy, medial autonomy cannot be an androcentric or otherwise elitist value. I shall argue that this is so in the next section.

Still, that medial autonomy is an egalitarian value does not entail that anyone lacking it is a victim of injustice. Perhaps there is nothing that societies can do to ensure that people will become medially autonomous, and, even if societies are not altogether helpless in this regard, there may be goods that are more urgent for societies to secure. Though the disvalue of minimal autonomy pales in comparison with such disvalues as physical violence and chronic unemployment and destitution, the problem of minimal autonomy is by no means negligible. Assuming that under socialism as well as capitalism, justice requires equal opportunity—that is, the distribution of goods in accordance with morally relevant criteria—I shall urge in section 3 that opportunities to obtain desirable social positions cannot be equal unless all of the competitors are medially autonomous, for minimal autonomy too often prevents people from taking advantage of the opportunities afforded by legal equality. Thus, medial autonomy is an indispensable substantive foundation for the procedural good of equal opportunity, which is central to our concept of justice. Not only is medial autonomy a personal good insofar as it enhances individuals' self-respect, but it is also a political good since depriving people of it is unjust.

# Self-Respect and Autonomy

## A. A PORTRAIT OF SELF-RESPECT

ON A steamy July afternoon at a bus stop in downtown Manhattan, a homeless woman approached each person who came to wait for the bus. In her hand, she clutched a transfer which she offered to sell for fifty cents. Bus transfers are given out gratis as one boards New York City buses and pays the one dollar fare. They entitle passengers to a free ride on any bus on an adjoining, perpendicular line. To enable the bus drivers to quickly identify cheaters trying to pass transfers from distant or parallel routes, the transfers are coded. But no one except the drivers bothers to study the system of codes. So no one standing at the bus stop, losing patience in the summer heat, had any idea what transfer the drivers on the Sixth Avenue line would accept.

The woman who was trying to sell her transfer for fifty cents was offering her prospective customers a ride at half price. However, one person after another turned her down. Some of them said they doubted that the transfer was any good on the Sixth Avenue line. To these accusations, she replied, "It's good. I wouldn't be selling it if it wasn't good." But no one was persuaded until a young man dressed in a plaid shirt, well-worn jeans, and penny loafers appeared. When she offered him the transfer, he not only said he would buy it, but he also insisted on paying her the dollar it was worth to him. At first, she refused the additional money, but finally, she took it and left.

At that, a woman standing near the youth crowed, "She finally found a sucker!" Disingenuously, she added, "I hope it's good." "It doesn't matter," the youth quietly replied. Several more passengers gathered before the bus came. When at last we all boarded the bus, the youth handed his transfer to the driver and took a seat.

I have related this story because I think it illustrates the concept of self-respect in action. Both the homeless woman and the youth seem to me exemplars of self-respect, and I shall use them to explicate this concept in a preliminary fashion.

In different ways, the homeless woman and the youth displayed a fine sense of proportion in regard to their own desires and those of other people. When people declined to purchase her transfer, the homeless woman did not persist. She moved away and waited for another customer to arrive. She did not make a pest of herself. The youth, I am sure, preferred not to lose a dollar, but he balanced the urgency of the homeless woman's need against his desire and saw that her need was more pressing. Maybe he was taking a gamble on her good faith, but the fact that he refused to buy the transfer at the bargain rate she proposed suggests to me that he simply wanted her to have a little money. Self-respecting people are capable of putting other people ahead of themselves (Friedman 1983:144–46).

Self-respect by no means requires overbearing self-assertion, but neither are human doormats paragons of self-respect. The homeless woman and the youth would not stand for insults. She proclaimed her honesty, and he rejected the label "sucker." A number of philosophers have contended that the hallmark of self-respect is the self-respecting person's refusal to submit passively to victimization. People who sheepishly acquiesce in violations of their rights lack self-respect, as do people who do not resent others' gratuitous indifference to their concerns (Hill 1973:142; Thomas 1978:264; Sachs 1981:352).

But self-respect is not solely a defensive posture. The homeless woman had found a way to ease her poverty, and the work she had improvised for herself showed self-respect. She retained her dignity through an open and aboveboard enterprise that enabled her to give people something in return for their assistance. Likewise, the youth acted on his compassion and, despite the jeer of his neighbor, showed no sign of embarrassment. Indeed, his very lack of self-importance coupled with his undramatic, yet decisive conduct was a reproach to everyone who had thought him a fool. Needlessly secretive or dissimulating people are deficient in self-respect, for they conceal or betray themselves (Boxill 1976:69). Put positively, satisfying one's desires and pursuing one's plans evidence self-respect, for such conduct affords the individual's capacity for agency its rightful scope (Sachs 1983:122–123). Engaging in one's preferred activities furnishes an outlet for one's attributes and an affirmation of the worth of one's self.

Closely related to the self-respecting person's commitment to his or her projects is the link between maintaining personal standards and self-respect. In my story, both of the figures uphold moral values— honesty, on the part of the homeless woman; charity, on the part of the youth.[1] Although moral standards are central to self-respect, nonmoral standards are by no means peripheral. The homeless woman, though plainly destitute, was remarkably clean compared to most of the other homeless people one encounters on the streets of New York. What might seem to those of us who take baths for granted a small defiance of the street person's plight may well, in her eyes, have been essential to preserve her dignity. People may have settled convictions about what sorts of behavior are debasing to them as persons—for example, they might regard the titilation of pornography as beneath them (Hill 1983:132). Or they may identify with enterprises which in turn set standards for those associated with them—for example, a scholar might consider displaying her knowledge on a television quiz show a desecration (Massey 1983:249). These need not be moral standards. The people who embrace them may not think less of those who do not share their views; however, they would feel themselves diminished if they abrogated these strictures.

Adopting and upholding principles of this kind brings the complexity of human agency to prominence. Human agency is not merely a matter of choosing actions; it also comprises self-chosen constraints on choice. To make only first-order decisions to do this or that, then, is to neglect an important potentiality inherent in personhood, hence to show disrespect for the fact that one is a person. But, perhaps more importantly, the possibility of establishing and adhering to personal standards explains one way in which self-respect shields people from others' adverse opinions. Both the homeless woman and the youth had ready answers to others' taunts. Although the difficulty of retaining one's self-respect in the face of other people's manifest contempt is evident, one of the most compelling reasons to think self-respect good is that it can protect the individual from others' scorn— from derision as well as from icy avoidance. Though an unreasoned affirmative attitude toward oneself could conceivably stand one in good stead, a reflective commitment to a set of values or projects should prove more reliable. For such convictions enable one to justify oneself—alone in the mirror, as well as in the company of others.

I have described only the outward signs of self-respect, which I could observe as I watched the events at the bus stop unfold. Still, the sine qua non of self-respect is what is unobservable, the basic attitude one bears to oneself. It is tempting to characterize this attitude by negation. Self-respecting people are not dissatisfied with their self-images and disheartened by their inability to improve them; they do not have major qualms about their personalities, they do not constantly regret their conduct. All of this is true. Yet, self-respect is not simply the absence of self-contempt.

Self-respect is a standing favorable attitude toward oneself predicated upon a sense of one's own worth as a person. In linking self-respect to people's worth as persons, I follow Stephen Darwall's basic line of argument (1977–1978:42–43). Darwall maintains that self-respect is based on those characteristics that are constitutive of one's personhood or, in other words, one's character as a human agent; however, it is not clear how restrictive he takes this category to be.

For Darwall, the relevant characteristics are "dispositions to act for particular reasons or a higher level disposition to act for the best reasons" (1977–1978:45). Though he states that these are "aspects of a person relevant to moral praise and blame," it is evident that a characteristic can satisfy this criterion yet contribute to conduct that is personal rather than moral in nature (1983:152; for the distinction between the personal and the moral, see part 1). One can be resolute in one's charitable work, but one can also be resolute in one's dieting. Furthermore, Darwall has doubts about whether sensitivity, prudence, and discernment warrant respect, for these qualities apparently strike him as natural dispositions over which agents have no control

(1977–1978:42–43). This worry seems misguided, however, since these characteristics are no less open to cultivation than honesty or resoluteness, and they figure as importantly in our assessments of people's conduct as the virtues Darwall mentions. While I agree with Darwall that one's high soprano, one's hazel eyes, or one's knack for picking up foreign languages are not proper grounds for self-respect, I see no reason to exclude one's reliability, one's sympathy, or one's self-possession. Whereas lacking the former qualities in no way undermines one's agency, lacking the latter can be paralyzing.

There was nothing in the conduct of the homeless woman or the youth that would have led me to suspect that either of them lacked a favorable reflexive attitude nor that this attitude was anchored in anything other than their sense of their worth as agents. To some extent, this positive view of oneself seems to take the form of an emotional primitive—one simply feels this way about oneself, and, like a happy disposition, this feeling can override reasons to the contrary. But, in addition, self-respect is amenable to rationally grounded support and sabotage. One may consider one's failings more or less grievous, and one may consider oneself more or less deserving of respect. Still, self-respect is not so sensitive to the individual's reflexive approval or disapproval as to be like the barometric pressure, rising and falling with the weather. Since self-respect reflects a cumulative assessment of one's worth as a person, trivial pratfalls and exceptional misadventures are discounted. Thus, self-respect is stable (compare Darwall 1983:154). If the homeless woman were permanently reduced to begging or stealing, she might gradually lose her self-respect, but she could retain her self-respect, one would hope, if she occasionally had to resort to these practices.

Self-respecting people have due regard for their dignity as agents. Not obsequious, not imperious, they neither belittle nor overrate the importance of their own inclinations. They take their own desires to be worthy of consideration, but they give these desires only their proper weight in deliberation. Conscious of their powers of choice and of the significance of choosing well, self-respecting people adhere to personal as well as moral standards. Neither their own momentary impulses nor faddish social currents buffet them about. Though self-respecting people are not rigid, their sense of their own identity precludes chameleon-like change.

Self-respect is not volatile. For the most part, it endures. Yet, it is clear that self-respect can be strengthened or weakened. People can find themselves improving, stagnating, or degenerating; they can discover that they are better or worse than they had realized. Though steady, then, self-respect is not fixed.

This observation points to the question of how autonomy is related to fluctuations in self-respect. After providing a structural analysis of the concept of respect, I shall urge that autonomy is related to self-respect in two main ways. First, low proficiency in the skills of autonomy can attenuate self-respect. Though virtually all people have sufficient autonomy competency to form a base for self-respect, the self-respect of minimally autonomous people is compromised, and it is less intrinsically good than that of more autonomous individuals. Second, the exercise of autonomy competency stabilizes self-respect on a secure psychological foundation. But inasmuch as compromised self-respect is psychologically precarious, it is not as instrumentally good for the individual as uncompromised self-respect. Whereas nonautonomous people have trouble keeping serious disappointments in perspective, autonomous people are not prone to the self-recrimination and prolonged despair that unfavorable outcomes or other people's disapproval can precipitate. Since the remedy for compromised self-respect is proficiency in autonomy skills, socializing some people to be minimally autonomous inflicts a serious injury on them.

## B. COMPROMISED AND UNCOMPROMISED RESPECT

RECENT PHILOSOPHICAL discussions of self-respect divide into two competing camps—one advocating a moral view of self-respect, the other advocating a psychological view. The former approach construes self-respect as a moral duty to uphold one's dignity, a duty one owes to oneself in virtue of one's personhood. This duty is a complex one that requires people to resist affronts to their dignity or attacks on their rights and to adhere to moral standards in their own conduct. Thus focusing on the moral propriety of self-respect, this view denies that self-respect can be excessive, unjustified, or undesirable (Sachs 1981:350–357).[2] The alternative view treats self-respect as a psychological phenomenon that gains support from whatever behavior one engages in that one happens to deem worthy of oneself. Although this psychological variant of self-respect requires fulfilling one's plans and measuring up to one's ideals, one's plans and ideals are relative to individual beliefs and desires. In this view, self-respect has no special moral import, for it is compatible with patently immoral conduct (Massey 1983:249, 258–261). Furthermore, since one can be deluded about one's success, one can respect oneself more than one should.

Supporters of the moral view dismiss the alternative account by banishing anomalous forms of self-respect—those that violate moral imperatives—to the purportedly psychological category of self-esteem. What appears to be respect for vice is really misguided esteem (Darwall 1977–1978:48). Meanwhile, supporters of the psychological view explain away intuitions that support the moral view by denying that these intuitions stem from the internal logic of the concept. When we seem to question the self-respect of a vicious person, we are really questioning the goodness of this person's self-respect (Massey 1983:253).

Though the moral account and the psychological account conflict, neither of them is unattractive. Yet, since neither of them is compelling alone, I blended elements from both in my "portrait" of self-respect. On the one hand, the moral account captures our recognition that there can be something disturbing about some forms of self-respect, but it does so at the cost of denying that these degenerate forms of self-respect can correctly be called self-respect. The latter claim seems merely stipulative. In the hands of this theory, self-respect withers into a dry little knot of obstinate ethical fastidiousness. On the other hand, the psychological account excludes nothing that people ordinarily classify as self-respect, but, in so doing, it denies that self-respect is intrinsically desirable. The latter conclusion is counter-intuitive. Here, the healthy self-regard that is the juice of self-respect is scrutinized and found morally dubious. Each of these accounts seems rather artificial, for neither is faithful to the whole range of phenomena associated with self-respect.

In what follows, I shall present a unified account of self-respect. An advantage of the account that I shall offer is that it explains why neither the moral nor the psychological view of self-respect can be dismissed and also why neither of these accounts is altogether satisfying. I shall urge that respect is a triadic relation, but that there are forms of respect in which one component of the triad is defective. Proponents of the moral view of self-respect deny the latter claim, and proponents of the psychological view discount the significance of the defective component in the latter forms of self-respect.

In general, respect can be a mystifying phenomenon because it comprises a subjective component—an attitude—and two objective components—conduct and the object it is aimed at—and because these three components can be at odds. One's respectful attitude may fail to find expression in one's conduct; one may act respectfully despite an indifferent or disrespectful attitude; one's respectful conduct may be addressed to an object unworthy of respect. An unexpressed respectful attitude is *suppressed* respect. (Since it sheds little light on the relation between autonomy and self-respect, I shall not have much to say about this type of respect.) Respectful conduct that is not grounded in a respectful attitude is *insincere* respect. Respectful feelings and conduct that are aimed at an unworthy object is *unwar ranted* respect. Any one of these discrepancies, I shall argue, *qualifies* respect. Thus, a respectful attitude must converge with respecting conduct vis-à-vis a respectable object if a person is to respect so-and-so without qualification. Moreover, I shall urge that none of these qualified forms of respect is intrinsically good, but that unqualified respect is intrinsically good. To convey the thought that qualified respect is not intrinsically good, I shall say that qualified respect is *compromised*.

To clarify the triadic relation of respect, I shall begin by examining two contrasting diadic concepts. One, trust; requires the convergence of an appropriate attitude with appropriate conduct but can dispense with an appropriate object. The other, indebtedness, requires the convergence of appropriate conduct with an appropriate object but can dispense with an appropriate attitude.

Consider, first, the case of trust. If Alan believes in Denise's honesty, discretion, or benevolence, and proceeds to confide his interests to her care, Alan has trusted Denise regardless of whether she is in fact trustworthy. He can trust her because he is ignorant of her true character. Or he can trust her because he is a dauntlessly trusting person given to trusting anyone and everyone, or because he decides to take a chance on Denise though he knows she is not trustworthy. Though Alan's trust may be woefully misplaced, it is nonetheless correct to say in all of these cases that he has trusted Denise. Here and in affective states like hatred, tenderness, anger, and delight, subjectivity governs the logic of the concept. As long as Alan is not merely acting as if he trusted Denise—that is, as long as Alan's trust is sincere—his trust is unqualified. If an agent has certain beliefs or feelings and acts accordingly, the conduct fully instantiates the concept, regardless of how irrational the agent's beliefs and feelings may be and regardless of how ill-advised the agent's conduct may be.

Now consider the case of owing and paying a debt. Helen can believe she is indebted to Ken; she can feel indebted to him; and she can act in a manner designed to discharge the debt. But unless Helen does in fact owe Ken something, her conduct cannot be correctly described as paying a debt. Quite the contrary, under some circumstances her ostensible debt-paying behavior could have the effect of creating a debt. Although Helen's debt-paying behavior may well express her sense of indebtedness, going through the motions of paying a debt is not sufficient to bring about the intended result. To pay a debt, a debt must exist. The subjective state governing the action— Helen's sense of indebtedness—must mesh with an objective state of affairs—Ken must be a creditor who has not forgiven the debt—if the agent's conduct is to have the standard practical effect—Helen's discharging a debt. Objective circumstances control the logic of indebtedness, for one can pay back what one owes without being convinced that one is indebted and without feeling the least indebted. As with the concepts of reward and punishment, carrying out the appropriate action in the requisite circumstances suffices; one's subjective state is dispensable.

The category to which respect belongs is a class of concepts that apply unequivocally only when attitudes or feelings find expression in actions addressed to worthy objects. Unlike the cases of trust and indebtedness, respect is qualified unless all three components obtain. Two familiar members of this class are sympathy and resentment. Sympathetic conduct devoid of sympathetic feelings is not straightforwardly sympathizing, and commiseration backed by sympathetic feelings also raises questions if it is addressed to someone who acts gloriously happy and is in fact entirely care-free. Resentment works the same way. We are reluctant to say that an agent resents someone else when the agent harbors no complaint against the person but perversely treats that person resentfully. Likewise, we hesitate to say that someone resents an associate whose conduct is above reproach, despite the fact that the agent feels slighted and acts resentfully. Whatever the explanation of these peculiar behaviors, they fall short of standard cases of sympathizing and resenting.

Of course, it must be acknowledged that sympathetic or resentful conduct that is unhinged from sympathetic or resentful attitudes is, in a sense, sympathy or resentment. It is insincere sympathy or resentment. Also, it is evident that sincere, but misdirected sympathizing or resenting is, in a sense, sympathy or resentment. It is unwarranted sympathy or resentment. Still, where one of the elements—the appropriate attitude, the appropriate conduct, or an appropriate object—is missing, the concept pertains only in a qualified sense. That this is so is demonstrated by the fact that, where one of these elements is missing, one could in principle give a more perspicuous characterization of the conduct in question—a characterization that illuminates the state of mind behind the insincerity or the misdirection. For example, the agent may be fawning on the person with whom he or she sympathizes, or the agent may be overreacting to the person he or she resents. Still, since we often do not have the information needed to formulate a discerning and precise characterization, the theoretical availability of such a characterization does not rule out less perspicuous ones. Still, in verbal communication, the discrepancy between qualified forms of sympathy and resentment and standard forms often shows up in the speaker's inflection. An astonished or disbelieving tone of voice (sometimes played for its comedic possibilities) may signal the speaker's awareness that the concept applies only in a qualified sense.

Similarly, the logic of respect lies between that of trust and that of indebtedness. From the standpoint of the relation of the individual's subjective state to his or her conduct, respect resembles trust and differs from indebtedness. Millicent can listen attentively to her aging parents' advice and take care of their every need, but, if she secretly despises them and bridles at their demands, her filial respect is vitiated. Without feelings of respect or a respectful attitude, respectful behavior is insincere, if not calculating or hypocritical.

Still, respect differs from trust and resembles indebtedness since the assertion that one respects so-and-so is undermined if one's conduct expressive of a respectful state of mind is not directed at a worthy object. There is a spectrum of cases in which respectful attitudes and respectful conduct are misdirected. Consider a naive, but concerned citizen, Harry. Harry respects a political candidate who is a mere figurehead—a politician who has no principles or ideas of his own. Still, his admirable staff of researchers and writers instructs him to support sensible and fair positions; he appears knowledgable and candid in interviews thanks to professional coaching in the art of public appearances; and he has gained a reputation for effective management thanks to the ingenuity of his public relations firm's television spots. Though the candidate's emptiness is abundantly evident to more sophisticated voters, Harry shows his respect by contributing to the candidate's campaign and by voting for him. Now consider a star-struck teenager, Barbara. Barbara respects the svelte sensuality of a glamorous movie actress, and she expresses her feelings of respect for the actress by trying to emulate her and by bringing her films to the attention of friends. More sensitive film buffs regard the actress's physical charms as minor attractions and dismiss her movies as trite vehicles. Finally, consider a callow youth, Andrew, who respects a famous real estate developer for his ruthless greed. By purchasing the developer's best-selling autobiography and by justifying the developer's conduct in conversations with others, Andrew demonstrates his respect. Yet, more acute observers of the real estate scene are appalled by the developer's indifference to environmental and aesthetic considerations, not to mention the developer's preying on poor tenants whom he wants to evict to make way for profitable luxury condominiums.

Although Harry, Barbara, and Andrew feel respectful and act respectfully, I would urge that their respect is problematic. Less naive people and people who have more cultivated taste and higher standards do not share Harry's, Barbara's, and Andrew's views. One cannot deny that, in a sense, they respect the politician, the actress, and the developer. Yet, one is prompted to add that each of them has been taken in, and therefore that the respect of each is misplaced. They respect their idols only in a qualified sense. Their respect is unwarranted.

No doubt, it is generally desirable that one have good reasons for trust, anger, delight, and like states of mind, yet trusting, angry, and delighted behavior are fully intelligible in the absence of good reasons. Whereas people can be indiscriminately trusting, a person does not understand what respect is if that person is indiscriminately respectful. Thus, as in the case of indebtedness, one *needs* good reasons for respect, as well as for sympathy and resentment. As we have seen, one can believe that such reasons obtain; one can be wholeheartedly moved by these ostensible reasons; and one can take action to express one's attitude. Still, if there are in fact no good reasons, something is amiss.

The assymmetry between trust and respect is brought into relief by the following considerations. A person can provisionally trust a stranger—that is, one can act as if one feels trust while reserving judgment; or a person can fully trust a stranger—that is, one can "take a chance on" that individual. In either case, the stranger will prove worthy or unworthy of one's trust, and one's trust will be vindicated or not. Such trust does not necessarily impugn the agent's character or judgment. Not only is there something inherently wrong with inveterate mistrustfulness, but also there is nothing inherently wrong with trusting people who are not trustworthy—even those who are known to be untrustworthy. When someone lavishes trust on strangers, then, we worry, if we worry at all, about the bad consequences the trusting individual might incur. We do not doubt the individual's decency or the propriety of the individual's trusting conduct.

In contrast, one cannot fully respect a person who has not earned one's respect—except, of course, insofar as one respects all people simply in virtue of their personhood. One can, for example, act as if one feels respect for a stranger's reliability. If one's provisional respect proves well-founded, a respectful attitude will take root; if one's provisional respect proves ill-founded, a wary, if not contemptuous, attitude will result. Thus, provisional respect can evolve into unqualified respect or contempt. Alternatively, one can feel respect for a stranger's reliability and act respectfully, but such commitment would be both premature and inappropriate. In contrast to the case of trust, we suspect the character and judgment of an individual who bestows respect prematurely. Respect is not properly given in the hope that it will be vindicated; respect is properly given when it is deserved. Although there is something wrong with being disrespectful in the absence of proven merit, there is also something wrong with dispensing respect in the absence of due circumspection.

In this connection, it is useful to reflect on the elemental respect that persons are owed as persons—consideration for their feelings and desires, compliance with their rights, and so forth. Here, it might seem that no circumspection is needed; however, I think it is accidental that this seems to be the case. As it happens, we can generally rely on the easily ascertainable fact that someone is an adult human being to establish that that individual deserves such basic respect. A glance suffices. However, if there were a large population of mindless humanoids among us—humanoids who were hard to distinguish from people—a glance would not suffice. Moreover, notice that controversies occasionally erupt regarding the respect owed to human youths. At what age should they be allowed to drink alcoholic beverages?

This is a question about the age at which individuals become mature adults who deserve full respect. Likewise, controversies have recently arisen about the status of some animals. Are dolphins sufficiently sensitive and intelligent to warrant our respect? This is a question about whether the agency of other species is such as to deserve our respect. Although this elemental form of respect is not earned, questions like these suggest that we apply a standard of due circumspection in according anyone even this measure of respect.

Saying that someone respects the base, the ridiculous, or the inconsequential begs for qualification and calls for explanation. One may feel respect, and one may make appropriate gestures of respect. But, as in the case of indebtedness, if one is under the mistaken impression that one is in the presence of something worthy of respect, one's conduct is otiose. One's subjective respectfulness has failed to make contact with a respectable reality, and, when this happens, one's respectful behavior is unwarranted.

Millicent's, Harry's, Barbara's and Andrew's respect share a common defect. None expresses a correspondence between the individual's subjective state and an instantiation of value. Insincere respect is missing an appropriate subjective state, and unwarranted respect is missing an instantiation of value. But it is the unity of one's subjective state with an instantiation of value, I submit, that makes respect intrinsically good. Needless to say, respectful behavior typically brings about good consequences. But it need not always do so, and it might on balance bring about detrimental results. Still, there would remain something good about the respect itself provided that it was heartfelt and provided that it was directed at a worthy object. If it were unwarranted, it would seem lame or worse. If it were insincere, this falsity would contaminate it. Neither form of qualified respect could counterbalance harmful consequences of any weight. But unqualified respect would remain valuable—though not necessarily of paramount value—regardless of whether it contributed to bad consequences. Only the desideratum of conforming one's subjective state and one's behavior to an instantiation of value can account for this residual, intrinsic goodness.

Here, it is worth noting that this unity is presupposed by the further claims that respect is due regard for some object and that respect is stable. If one's subjective state inflates or deflates something's value, one's respect is disproportionate, and one is apt to be disillusioned or enlightened about the real value of the object. Undue respect is liable to abrupt change. (For discussion of the psychological hazards of qualified self-respect, see part 4, sec. 2D.) Thus, it can only be unqualified respect—the intrinsically good congruence between the self and value—that people have in mind when they affirm the fittingness and the persistence of respect.

Contrariwise, respecting things that are unworthy of respect is intrinsically bad when a unity of one's self with disvalue is effected. Likewise, respecting things that are unworthy of respect is intrinsically bad when the agent sees value in what is negligible, though obviously this sort of misplaced respect is not as intrinsically bad as respect for what is evil or base. Not only is the agent deluded about the true value of what he or she respects, but also, as a result, the self is more attached to this object than it should be. In either case, respect is compromised.

Still, it is important to appreciate that respect can be unwarranted for different kinds of reasons. Harry, Barbara, and Andrew fasten their respect on inappropriate objects. The difference between Barbara and Andrew, on the one hand, and Harry, on the other, is that Barbara and Andrew falsely believe that certain types of things deserve respect and accurately aim their respect at targets their beliefs prescribe, whereas Harry knows what deserves respect but mistakenly directs his respect at a target his beliefs exclude. Harry's unwarranted respect for the empty politician is innocent, albeit unfortunate. If he were disabused of his illusions about the candidate, his respect would presumably dissolve. In contrast, Barbara's respect for the starlet is misguided, and Andrew's respect for the real estate tycoon is corrupt. (For discussion of the relation between autonomy, on the one hand, and corrupt, misguided, and innocent respect, on the other hand, see part 4, sec. 2C.) Since their respect is based on deficient values, it is intrinsically more pernicious, and it is harder to dislodge. Nonetheless, unlike Andrew's respect for the real estate developer, Barbara's respect for the movie actress is unwarranted, but not indecent.

Perhaps, proponents of the moral conception of self-respect focus on respect that is both indecent and unwarranted while overlooking respect that is unwarranted, but innocent or misguided. As a result, they suppose that all unwarranted respect is reprehensible and conclude that reprehensible respect is not respect at all. It is undeniable that odious respect compounds the error of unwarranted respect. Yet, once one realizes that unwarranted respect can be morally innocuous, it becomes implausible to maintain that only morally mandated respect can count as respect. That someone feels respect for something and acts accordingly does not make it worthy of respect. But the unworthiness of the object need not extinguish the feelings or halt the behavior, and it may not justify moral condemnation.

Those who defend an independent psychological account of self-respect also neglect the complexity of the logic of respect. Consequently, they affirm that unwarranted self-respect is a second kind of unqualified self-respect. But once the three different ways in which respect can be qualified have been laid out, it becomes clear that psychological self-respect differs from moral self-respect in quality, not in kind. Sometimes psychological respect is not intrinsically good, for it may not evidence the requisite correspondence between one's subjective state and an instantiation of value. But psychological respect is not a discrete phenomenon. Moreover, to deny that some forms of self-respect that are certified by the psychological account, but not by the moral account, can be intrinsically good is to affirm that moral worth is the sole type of value that people instantiate. However, I shall argue below that this view is unduly restrictive.

## C. UNCOMPROMISED SELF RESPECT AND AUTONOMY

THE SECOND point of contention between the moral account of self-respect and the psychological account concerns the sort of self that can be the object of self-respect. Whereas the moral view insists that only the morally autonomous self and its good qualities can be respected, the psychological theory counters that any self together with its traits can be respected. For the purposes of this discussion, I shall asume, with Kant and his followers, that the morally autonomous self is a worthy object of self-respect, though I shall depart from this view by acknowledging that people can respect themselves in a compromised way for immoral conduct. The question I wish to raise is whether the personally autonomous self is also a proper object of respect and whether failure to exercise autonomy competency in personal decisions compromises self-respect.

I shall urge that the moral account of self-respect is too narrowly discriminating—that is, it should not exclude the personally autonomous self as an object of respect; but I shall also urge that the psychological account is too indiscriminate—that is, it should exclude the nonautonomous self. A further advantage of my unified account of self-respect, then, is that it exposes the relation between self-respect and both moral and personal autonomy. Kant furnished a persuasive account of the link between moral autonomy and self-respect, but he simultaneously obscured the link between personal autonomy and self-respect. In order to appreciate the importance of the contribution the psychological view makes to our understanding of self-respect, it is necessary to recover the role of personal autonomy in self-respect.

Since self-respect requires a worthy object, it seems natural to suppose that there are standards that any self-respecting person must meet along with failings that are sure to engender self-contempt. The most obvious candidates to serve as objective standards for self-respect are moral requirements. A common strategy used to persuade people not to behave immorally is to appeal to their self-respect: "Have you *no* self-respect?" or "No self-respecting person could do *that!*" However, these very same exclamations can be used to enforce societal norms that have assumed a quasi-moral status under the sway of nearly unanimous opinion. Strict, yet nonmoral imperatives continue to govern sexuality in many cultural groups, and it is not uncommon for people to aver that they could not respect themselves if they violated these norms. When female chastity was enforced and publicly revered in the United States and Europe, many women considered promiscuity a reason for self-contempt.[3] As I shall argue, failure to fulfill one's moral duties does compromise self-respect. Nevertheless, it is important to see, on the one hand, how people can violate core moral requirements and give every appearance of unimpaired self-respect and, on the other hand, how people can abrogate immoral and nonmoral social norms and maintain their self-respect.

Since people readily embrace prevalent standards, social tradition can protect the self-respect of people who engage in immoral behavior. A prime example of self-respect shielded in this way from moral scrutiny is the unregenerate macho male. Expected to exert absolute power over his wife and, in some groups, expected to beat her once in awhile to remind her of her place, the macho male respects himself for categorically immoral conduct. Imbued from childhood with the masculine stereotype and egged on by his pals, this individual undoubtedly believes that he could not forgo his prerogatives—which, of course, he does not deem immoral—without losing face and self-respect. Thus, the good of self-respect can help to conceal the evil of entrenched social conventions.

When customary social practices conflict with morality, the former typically take precedence in people's assessments of their self-worth, since all too often people lack the intellectual and emotional independence necessary to embrace unconventional views (Coopersmith 1981:140). To the extent that self-respect is widely founded on morally defective conventions, then, autonomy competency not only provides the only hope of relief for the victims of these conventions until social practices finally change for the better, but also it provides the only hope of establishing a worthy object of self-respect. (For discussion of moral autonomy as a form of autonomy competency, see Meyers 1987b:147–152.) Thus, the moral view of self-respect denies that the proper object of reflexive respect is merely the socially condoned self, for the socially condoned self too often proves to be morally wanting.

But the moral account has a further reason for resting self-respect on the autonomous self. In this connection, Stephen Darwall has observed that respect for an ant's ability to heft enormous loads relative to its body weight is suspect, though amazement at this capacity is not (1977–1978:42). Since the ant's feats result from the natural capabilities its species has gained over the course of evolution, they are not suitable objects of respect. Whoever warrants respect does so in virtue of his or her dignity as an agent or, in other words, in virtue of capacities to choose reflectively and to cultivate desirable dispositions to choose as opposed to natural endowments (Darwall 1977–1978:47). Thus, taking precautions to avoid stepping on the ants parading around one's kitchen because they are carrying gigantic crumbs seems a misplaced expression of respect.

Similarly, absorbing and following a socially enforced code manifests a natural capacity comparable to the ant's ability to transport heavy loads. When self-respect is based on this sort of adaptability rather than on a capacity for reflection and choice, self-respect is directed at a natural capability rather than at one's distinctive capacities as an agent. Thus, this respect is unwarranted, and uncompromised self-respect requires the exercise of the complete range of one's moral faculties.

Moreover, if people realize that they are observing immoral conventions and understand that they should be doing otherwise, their self-respect is compromised in two additional ways. Not only is this respect insincere inasmuch as these people do not feel respect for themselves for acting in these ways, but also their respectful feelings are suppressed inasmuch as they refrain from acting in a manner for which they do feel respect. Thus, conformity to morally deficient norms can tarnish people's self-respect, despite other people's admiration for them. Not all conduct that looks self-respecting is. Conversely, defying such norms in the name of a higher law, thereby eschewing standards that had been the bulwark of one's self-respect and also losing the respect of one's peers, need not undermine one's self-respect. Not all conduct that looks self-contemptuous is.

There is some truth, then, in the doctrine that immorality is incompatible with self-respect. The macho male I mentioned above stakes his self-respect on a nonautonomously adopted and immoral role. Thus, his self-respect is doubly misdirected. Social expectations have so shaped his mentality that he is blind to the cruelty of his behavior. Thus, he aims his respect at a social fabrication, not at a self-governing agent. In addition, by unconsciously guarding himself against recognizing the error of his ways, he obviates the possibility of discerning any antagonism between his true self and his violence against women. Still, the immorality of people's lives cannot be counted on to erode their favorable opinions of themselves, and it is futile to maintain that people cannot feel good about themselves, however contemptible their conduct may be. What is wrong with these people's self-respect is that it lacks a worthy object. To the extent that their self-respect is based on conduct that no morally autonomous agent could adopt, it is compromised.

Now, it is important to notice that people's everyday attributions of self-respect and self-contempt extend to nonmoral norms, too. To see this, let us turn to the macho male's opposite number—the henpecked husband. Many people would accept the latter as a humble, retiring, figure of fun—a paradigm of self-contempt. If he testified that he could not respect himself if he ever spent an evening playing poker with the boys, most people would scoff. Why does the self-respect of the henpecked husband provoke such skepticism? First, he violates conventions of masculinity—he does not dominate his wife. Since he must realize that he is not a "real man," he must be contemptuous of himself. Second, simply because he is a man, he is assumed to be capable of resisting his wife's demands. If he does not do so, it must be because he has no respect for his dignity. He must not care if he looks pathetic and ridiculous. Not only does the henpecked husband fail to meet relevant standards, he is not properly chagrined by his inadequacy. Though no one would accuse the henpecked husband of immorality—at most, he might be snidely accused of betraying his sex—he is seen as lacking self-respect.

We have already established that not being henpecked does not guarantee unqualified self-respect. Though by no means henpecked, the macho male's self-respect is unwarranted since he lacks moral autonomy. Can the henpecked husband be self-respecting?

If there is anything that would convince us that the henpecked husband has not sacrificed his self-respect on the altar of his marriage, it would be evidence that he really considers poker a waste of time, really believes that men should share domestic chores, really loves and admires his wife, and so forth—that is, evidence that this man is not playing the patsy to his wife; evidence that he himself spurns certain prevalent masculine modalities. If the man whom others laughingly call "henpecked" describes himself in terms of autonomously adopted desiderata that belie the subservience implicit in the popular epithet, there is no reason to doubt his self-respect. Just as a morally autonomous, reformed macho male can be self-respecting despite others' scorn, a personally autonomous violator of gender norms can be self-respecting. Indeed, once a man has become disenchanted with these norms, he will need to violate them in order to preserve his self-respect. Under these circumstances, autonomy skills are indispensable, for they not only assure individuals that they are not giving up others' respect in vain, but they also give individuals the strength to withstand others' ridicule. An unorthodox life plan can support self-respect, provided that it is a projection of the individual's authentic self.

There are four salient parallels between moral and personal autonomy. First, both involve the deployment of the complete repertory of the person's faculties of reflective choice. The difference is that moral autonomy turns these skills outward while personal autonomy turns them inward. Second, people gain knowledge of their authentic selves through both forms of autonomy. Both moral autonomy and personal autonomy ensure that people do what they, as individuals, really want to do. Third, moral autonomy enables the individual to benefit other people and to contribute to society. Similarly, personal autonomy gives individuals the satisfaction of acting on their own beliefs, feelings, desires, and the like. Fourth, moral autonomy protects other people from wrongful harm, and personal autonomy protects the individual from needless frustration.

These parallels militate in favor of accepting the everyday assumption that, like moral autonomy, personal autonomy supports self-respect. Thus, they call into question the narrow construal of the grounds for self-respect that the moral account of self-respect stipulates, and they buttress the psychological account's less restrictive view of the possible grounds for self-respect. However, I did not merely argue that moral autonomy supports self-respect; I maintained that moral autonomy is necessary to uncompromised self-respect. Yet, people do not usually think that someone who heteronomously complies with prevailing nonmoral social norms lacks self-respect, and the psychological account concurs with this inclusive assessment. Thus, it is necessary to inquire whether this view of nonautonomous, conventional people mistakes compromised self-respect for uncompromised self-respect—that is, whether personal autonomy is also necessary for uncompromised self-respect.

It is easy to understand why conventional people are presumed to have their self-respect intact. Since they have been socialized to assume their roles, they slide smoothly into these assigned positions. They do not grudgingly go through the motions of conformity. Nor do they report ambivalence or self-betrayal. In addition, conventional people may have a meta-rationale for striving to perform their roles well. If they believe in the value of the social order, conventional people can be satisfied that they are acting in a worthwhile way insofar as living up to the standards implicit in their roles helps to maintain the social order. Though society molds nonautonomous conventional people, they see themselves as mature, upstanding members of the community. Moreover, they give every appearance of caring about their dignity because they act in ways that others regard as commendable.

Only when we have evidence that someone conforms to customary practices unwillingly are we moved to deny that conventionality invariably supports self-respect. As I remarked earlier, some behavior that looks self-respecting is not, and one way to live a lie is to carry off a conventional life plan superbly while inwardly deploring it. To bow to convention against one's better judgment is not to show due regard for oneself. Still, there is no reason to believe that autonomous conventionality is incompatible with self-respect. In this case, the individual and society concur about what befits the dignity of human agents. Furthermore, nonautonomous, but willing conformity to nonmoral norms seems sufficient for self-respect, too.

Still, self-respect founded on nonautonomous, though willing conventionality is troublesome. When a person has a life plan that is not that person's own life plan, a gap opens between the person's fulfilling the life plan and the person's authentic self. Since the life plan is alien to the person, however estimable the plan may be and however impressively it may be carried out, undertaking it does not seem to evidence *self*-respect. Just as a person who nonautonomously pursues typical human interests may not be promoting what is distinctively in his or her own self-interest, a person who carries out a conventional life plan may not be demonstrating self-respect. (For discussion of autonomous and nonautonomous self-interest, see part 2, sec. 5.) From this vantage, personal autonomy seems more crucial to self-respect than it otherwise might.

Defense mechanisms and cognitive filters represent the most treacherous and pervasive threat to the self-respect of nonautonomous individuals. The extensive reach of these protective devices is familiar. In the film version of E. M. Forster's *A Room with a View* (directed by James Ivory), when Lucy justly accuses her Aunt Charlotte of betraying a confidence, Charlotte melodramatically announces that she will never forgive herself. But her trenchant niece answers that, these protestations notwithstanding, Charlotte always manages to forgive herself in the end. Even the most cold-blooded hit-man in John Houston's *Prizzi's Honor* can take refuge in his love for his mother or in his loyalty to his crime family and thus preserve some semblance of decency in his own eyes.

Although social psychologists have found that nearly everyone uses the same socially approved standards to assess their worth, these investigators have also discovered that this common fund of standards does not commit people to objectivity in appraising themselves (Coopersmith 1981:140; also see part 3, sec. 4). People limit their aspirations to levels they can sensibly expect to achieve, and they unconsciously exaggerate their own success on seemingly inflexible scales (Coopersmith 1981:141, 245–246). Moreover, since they measure themselves within the framework set by their immedaite social environment, and since they have some control over which environments they enter, the puny swimmers in small ponds often class themselves as big fish (Coopersmith 1981:243). Though people seldom adopt idiosyncratic standards to preserve their self-worth, they are by no means at the mercy of a stern, incontrovertible metric.

People may regard themselves as inferior in many ways and mediocre in many others; they may be afflicted by grave doubts about their merits; but, if worst comes to worst, virtually everyone has a system of defense mechanisms and cognitive filters that ensures at least a modicum of positive self-regard in the face of damaging experience (Coopersmith 1981:42–43). Indeed, most people would find a life altogether bereft of the salve of these protective devices unendurable (*New York Times* November 26, 1987:B12). Among other benefits, defense mechanisms and cognitive filters ensure that people have enough positive self-regard to sustain a respectful attitude toward themselves when they occasionally behave abominably or when they suffer a grave set-back. Defense mechanisms and cognitive filters function as a tonic against self-contempt.[4]

But when these devices conceal serious and remediable faults from agents, or when they grossly mislead agents about the nature of their projects or the degree of their success, they interfere with self-respect. For, when people are mistaken about their attributes, they are open to charges that they are misdirecting their respect. They respect themselves for good qualities they do not have or for projects they do not realize are undesirable, and their self-respect is reinforced by their obliviousness to unpleasant truths about their shortcomings. Of course, on the assumption that these people are sane and therefore are not totally deluded about themselves, their self-respect is not entirely compromised. Yet, the social psychological evidence suggests that many people's self-portraits bear scant resemblance to their actual personalities and achievements and that their self-respect is extensively compromised.

Not only do defense mechanisms and cognitive filters compromise self-respect by blinding people to the realities of their lives, but they also compromise self-respect by preempting self-definition. Promiscuously self-affirming people are not self-respecting. To be self-respecting, one may have to reform oneself by disavowing discredited beliefs, harmful habits, demeaning associations, trivial goals, and so on. Self-respect may require change, but defense mechanisms and cognitive filters often prevent minimally autonomous people from noticing that change is called for. Moreover, change that is imposed from without or unconsciously insinuated from within may again defeat self-respect.

Harry Frankfurt has termed the nonautonomous person a wanton (1971:11). Wantons do what they want, but they have no autonomously accepted personal standards with which they identify and which curb their impulses. They epitomize self-indulgence. This does not prevent them from taking the initiative on many projects, nor from being very exasperated when they are opposed. As a result, they may seem self-respecting, and it is altogether possible that some of them would not describe themselves as indifferent to themselves, let alone self-contemptuous. But since nothing is beneath them, however moving and appealing they sometimes appear to be, they cannot be said to respect themselves without qualification. Accordingly, the need for autonomy as an underpinning for self-respect seems inescapable.

At this point, it might be countered that people who have not autonomously chosen the overall direction of their lives can respect themselves for performing the duties incumbent on them well or for exercising autonomy competency in the performance of these duties. While I do not deny that people can obtain a measure of self-respect in these ways, I would note that these bases for self-respect do not guarantee that a person's self-respect is uncompromised.

People who measure up to standards or fulfill plans that they do not autonomously embrace are less wanton than thoroughly self-indulgent people, but only slightly so. Though the former individuals discipline themselves to play delegated roles, and though they may respect themselves for the willpower they exert in order to comply with these strictures, nothing precludes the standards being inferior, if not contemptible. If they are, living up to them may demonstrate respect for the established social order or for some authority figure, but it hardly demonstrates unalloyed self-respect. Similarly, exercising autonomy competency to handle some situations—that is, episodic autonomy—or to set some policies—that is, narrowly programmatic autonomy—while fulfilling a pre-ordained role gives the individual some control over the values his or her life expresses. (For discussion of these forms of autonomy, see part 2, sec. 2 and part 3, sec. 3.) Nonetheless, the general life plan that subsumes these activities may be inferior, if not contemptible. If it is, fulfilling it does not evidence unqualified self-respect.

Still, it might seem that socialization could bypass autonomy by inserting people into benign social roles. As basic human interests constitute a default conception of self-interest in the absence of autonomous choice, so conventional life plans may constitute a default basis for self-respect in the absence of autonomous choice. Yet, however redoubtable one's cultural heritage may be, no one could confidently assume that it only endows people with incontrovertible beliefs, justifiable practices, and elevated goals. Moreover, it is well-known that cultures often fail to assign people roles that are calibrated to their abilities and inclinations. Caste systems notoriously oblige the so-called lower orders to limit themselves to menial enterprises and to cede social responsibility to their purported superiors. Just as no self-respecting person would cling desperately to a position that was beyond his or her capacities, so self-respecting people do not repress potentialities that they regard as good and that they want to fulfill. Suppressed respect, it must be remembered, is another form of qualified respect (part 4, sec. 2B). Although nonautonomous conventionality can immunize people against feelings of self-contempt, such people may nonetheless be behaving in a self-contemptuous way, and their self-respect may be compromised.

Though developed autonomy skills are not infallible, they do enable people to generate more accurate self-portraits, to alter undesirable characteristics, and to pursue plans that comport with their authentic selves (part 2, sec. 4). People who exercise these skills can correct their misconceptions about themselves and can change as needed. Also, whether by fitting into the existing social system or by working to change it, they can devise ways to join in social life without betraying their own desires, values, and the like. Accordingly, autonomy enables people to confront themselves honestly without undue risk of collapsing into despair and self-contempt, and autonomy provides the remedy for self-respect that defense mechanisms and cognitive filters compromise.

There is no assurance that self-respect is intrinsically good, as the proponents of the moral account maintain it is, unless it is grounded in autonomy. However, personal autonomy is as necessary to self-respect as moral autonomy. Moral autonomy ensures that people's moral decisions are as wise as is humanly possible. Personal autonomy ensures that people's personal ideals and life plans befit their individual strengths and needs and that their lives match their personal ideals and life plans. Moreover, both modes of autonomy exhibit respect for human agency by utilizing the full range of people's deliberative and volitional capabilities.

However, self-respect can be compromised. Self-respect that is unwarranted because people have execrable traits and plans which they regard as splendid is intrinsically bad, for these agents are doubly bonded to evil. (For discussion of the intrinsic goodness of uncompromised self-respect and the intrinsic badness of compromised self-respect, see part 4, sec. 2B.) They are bad, and they respect that very badness. Such self-respect is corrupt, and, when people's autonomy competency is well developed, corrupt self-respect is morally blameworthy. (For explication of corrupt, misguided, and innocent respect, see part 4, sec. 2B.) People endowed with autonomy competency have no excuse for endorsing such defective values. But neither is self-respect that is predicated on jejune or trivial values intrinsically good. In this case, self-respect is disproportionate, for these agents are over-invested in their traits and plans. Such self-respect is misguided, and, if people have well-developed autonomy skills, they deserve to be criticized for adopting such deficient values. Although these people do not embrace wicked traits or plans, they should realize that the traits or plans they do embrace are not meritorious. Misguided self-respect is not immoral, but neither is there any reason to applaud it. Still, it is important to recognize that unwarranted self-respect can be innocent. If the agent's autonomy skills are weak, the agent is at the mercy of defense mechanisms and cognitive filters. Such people's values are in order. Nevertheless, they have vile or mediocre traits and plans which they do not notice at all or which they take for admirable ones, or they have good traits which they perceive as wonderful. Such people can hardly be held accountable for the compromised nature of their self-respect, yet their self-respect is not intrinsically good. Whereas corrupt and misguided self-respect are deplorable (though, of course, not equally so), innocent, yet compromised self-respect is pitiable.

Since personal autonomy together with moral autonomy brings into play the individual's complete repertory of powers as an agent, human dignity is most fully realized in the autonomous self. Thus, it is not surprising that, the moral account of self-respect notwithstanding, the proper object of self-respect proves to be the personally and morally autonomous self—the authentic self as it emerges through the exercise of autonomy competency. Still, I have argued that people possess self-respect in varying degrees and that their respect for themselves can be more or less well-grounded. Lack of autonomy compromises self-respect by depriving self-respecting attitudes and conduct of a worthy object. The trouble with the psychological view is that it neglects the possibility that self-respect can be unwarranted; that is, it refuses to acknowledge that anything is amiss when respect is aimed at an unworthy object. In specifying what sort of self is worthy of self-respect, the moral account of self-respect is under-inclusive, but the psychological account is over-inclusive.

Now, it is important to recognize that, since few people live completely heteronomous lives, hardly anyone's self-respect is altogether compromised. Elsewhere I have stressed that virtually all people have some proficiency in the repertory of autonomy skills and sometimes successfully use these skills (part 3, sec. 3). Accordingly, to maintain that autonomy is necessary for uncompromised self-respect is not to deny that most people have self-respect. It is only to contend that the self-respect of many people is to a significant degree compromised. Insofar as their self-respect is compromised, it is not intrinsically good. Still, it could be objected that warranted self-respect may be no better than unwarranted self-respect from an instrumental standpoint. In people's psychological economy, that is, unwarranted self-respect may feel just as ennobling and may motivate dignified conduct just as assuredly as warranted self-respect. In the discussion to follow, I shall focus on the fragility of this sort of compromised self-respect and the psychological problems it poses.

## D. THE PSYCHOLOGICAL LIABILITIES OF COMPROMISED SELF-RESPECT

I HAVE argued that uncompromised respect is intrinsically good in virtue of the congruence it establishes between respectfulness and an instantiation of value, but that, lacking this relation, compromised respect is not intrinsically good. I have also noted in passing that there are other-regarding instrumental reasons for thinking uncompromised self-respect good and compromised self-respect bad. Respect for worthy objects generally supports humane behavior, whereas respect for unworthy objects may instigate harmful behavior. As mentioned above, the macho male's respect for deficient values leads him to degrade his wife, and, in the absence of cultural regeneration, only autonomy could convert him to respect for more decent values that would in turn bring surcease to his wife. I shall now focus on the self-regarding instrumental reasons for considering compromised self-respect undesirable. Specifically, I shall urge that uncompromised self-respect shields self-respecting people from suffering by protecting them from the self-condemnation that disillusionment and disappointment with oneself can bring.

By calling upon the full range of one's capacities as an agent, autonomy secures uncompromised self-respect. Still, we have seen that people who are far from maximally autonomous often feel perfectly respectful and behave respectfully towards themselves. In light of this fact, the claim that minimally autonomous people do not show unqualified respect for themselves seems dubious. To still this doubt, it is necessary to probe the psychological burden compromised self-respect imposes. Preliminary to doing so, I shall suggest that there is no reason to accept the appearance of unqualified self-respect as the reality. Since self-respect is part of an integrated psychological system, independent psychological factors can bolster compromised self-respect and can prevent it from being exposed. Thus, people may not feel as much respect for themselves as they suppose they do. Then I shall describe the traps that compromised self-respect sets. Though people whose self-respect is compromised are often unaware of it, their psychological equilibrium is needlessly imperiled.

As I noted earlier, people can behave respectfully yet have no respect. That people object to dismissive or demeaning treatment while routinely pursuing their interests and proceeding with their plans does not entail that they respect themselves. Instead, they may act assertively because they are obstinate, proud, domineering, irascible, compulsive, or insensitive to others. They may even produce a simulacrum of self-respect because they are eager to please someone who is known to place a high value on personal dignity. (David Sachs draws a related distinction between respect for others and behavior stemming from sundry passions that resembles respect [1983; 115].) Likewise, people's subjective experience can mimic self-respect. They can feel offended by dismissive or demeaning treatment, and they can care about their interests and their plans without respecting themselves. Among the less noble explanations of these responses, apart from self-respect, are importunity, rapacity, and conceitedness, but notice that excessively self-effacing dedication to a wholly admirable cause could foster these same responses. Furthermore, since people often worry that they will be excluded from social groups or shunned by particular individuals unless they make themselves interesting and attractive, a normal desire for affiliation probably contributes to many people's feelings of self-concern.

Many of the motives I have mentioned can coexist with self-respect. Self-respect does not exist in isolation from other psychological forces; it is one factor in a complex psychological economy. But extraneous motives can mask deficient self-respect. Though some of these motives are liable to mushroom into bloated regard for oneself while others are liable to devolve into slavish obsequiousness, in a wide range of circumstances they subjectively and behaviorally resemble self-respect. For this reason, I would question the credibility of testimony from minimally autonomous people affirming that their self-respect is unqualified. Especially when people's self-reading skills are weak, this putative evidence does not inspire confidence.

Now, the considerations I have adduced might be dismissed as experientially vacuous and practically trivial. Since people whose self-respect is only partially warranted are not aware that other psychological forces are camouflaging their compromised self-respect, compromised self-respect does not bother them. They do not suffer from dejection and despair. Quite the contrary, they are often happy. Since they feel good about themselves, it may seem presumptuous and counterproductive to pronounce their self-respect compromised.

Of course, self-respect normally blends with other attitudes and motives in the human psyche. Since few situations isolate self-respect and put it to the test, it is rarely possible to dissect the sources of an action or of a self-referential response with any precision. Nevertheless, it does not follow that the question of compromised self-respect can be safely ignored. When self-respect is compromised, I shall urge, people are needlessly exposed to the withdrawal of others' approval and other reversals. Thus, it seems to me that there are two reasons why it would be cynical not to take the problem of compromised self-respect seriously. First, this cavalier view of the matter is indifferent to the relative fragility of many people's positive feelings about themselves and therefore to the potential for misery they conceal. Second, it justifies refusing to implement the social reforms necessary to promote autonomy and uncompromised self-respect. I shall close this section by considering the first of these rejoinders, but I shall reserve the question of justice for section 3.

The trouble with compromised self-respect is that people can take pride in their self-control or in the quality of their performances, and they can go about some of their tasks independently; yet they can, at the same time, have compelling reasons to dislike, if not to despise, themselves for lending their talents to the broader enterprise in question. The most casual acquaintance with human history amply demonstrates that no one can justifiably assume that conventional life plans are necessarily unobjectionable. Moreover, that a life plan is not wicked does not entail that there is no compelling reason to reject it. An individual's personal standards and preferences may rule out life plans that are morally unexceptionable.

Let us consider the predicament of a person whose self-respect is compromised. There are three main sources of compromised self-respect: illusions about the goodness of one's attributes, compliance with standards of which one would disapprove if one were to scrutinize them, adherence to a life plan that does not comport with one's authentic self. In each case, the object of self-respect is unworthy of the individual, and, plainly, the respectful person would cease to feel respect if only this individual realized how wrongheaded his or her beliefs or actions were. Since compromised self-respect is susceptible to reversal in this way, it is tenuous. Though it is undeniable that supportive social arrangements or powerful psychological defenses can shelter people from disillusionment, compromised self-respect is perilous.

When compromised self-respect rests on fairly unimportant misconceptions about one's self or one's conduct, the exposure of these misconceptions is ordinarily not terribly discomfiting. Indeed, Shelley Taylor and Jonathan Brown argue that social and cognitive filters typically render most negative information about one's self as benign as possible (1988:201). People with positive self-concepts tend to dismiss negative feedback as inaccurate (Taylor and Brown 1988:202). Moreover, if they accept the accuracy of such feedback, their self-concepts are temporarily adjusted to compass it but soon drift back in a positive direction (Taylor and Brown 1988:202). One might feel foolish for one's lack of discernment or irritated with oneself for missing some opportunity, but one is hardly plunged into despair.

Nevertheless, people's discovery that their self-respect is compromised can precipitate reactions much more serious than embarrassment or annoyance. When compromised self-respect rests on momentous choices or on abiding features of one's personality—as all too often it does when people's autonomy skills are poorly developed—the revelation of the fatuousness or the odiousness of one's decisions or one's attributes can be deeply disturbing.

Peter Lewinsohn, Walter Mischel, William Chaplin, and Russell Barton have studied the relations between the adequacy of people's social skills, the accuracy of their self-perceptions, and depression. Contrary to expectations, they found that depressed people had fewer desirable interpersonal characteristics and less ability to interact with others and that they perceived their failings accurately, while nondepressed people had more desirable interpersonal characteristics and more ability to interact with others but that they exaggerated their strengths (Lewinsohn et al. 1980:208). This study points to two factors that figure in the genesis of depression: a deficit of desirable traits combined with an undistorted awareness of this deficiency. In other words, perspicacious self-reading skills coupled with weak self-definition and self-direction skills are characteristic of depression. Depression is consistently associated with low self-regard (Rosenberg 1979:55). Thus, when people acknowledge their failings, but poorly developed autonomy skills prevent them from taking corrective measures, they are vulnerable to depression and reduced self-respect.

More dramatically, the Stanford prison study conducted by Phillip Zimbardo and his associates confronted some of the participants in the experiment with their altogether unexpected and alarming tendencies to infirmity and the rest with their equally unexpected and alarming sadistic propensities. College males whose psychological normality and stability had been tested were recruited to participate in a role playing experiment in which some of the subjects were assigned the role of prisoners and others were assigned the role of prison guards. The physical environment of a prison was convincingly evoked, and the local police helped to achieve verisimilitude by carrying out mock arrests and station house processing. In the course of the experiment, the guard-subjects became verbally and physically aggressive and arbitrarily abused the prisoner-subjects (Zimbardo 1973:245). Meanwhile, the prisoner-subjects responded to their condition by developing symptoms of learned helplessness syndrome (Zimbardo 1973:245). Although the experiment was planned to run two weeks, the investigators were obliged to curtail it because most of the prisoners collapsed into pathetic submissiveness and most of the guards began to take pleasure in being cruelly despotic.

In this study, the subjects were compelled to acknowledge that situations could elicit from them "reactions they believed to be ego-alien" (Zimbardo 1973:249). Realizing the seriousness of the psychological damage their inquiry could have caused, the research team provided poststudy monitoring and counseling services. Though the subjects were traumatized in the immediate aftermath of the experiment, Zimbardo reports no persistent negative reactions to the prison experience (1973:249). Rather, the subjects put their experience to constructive use in the long run. Some volunteered their time to work in prisons, and most became advocates of prison reform (Zimbardo 1973:249). Although Zimbardo and his colleagues assumed that people would need professional help to cope effectively with such appalling revelations about themselves and intervened accordingly, they ascertained that people are capable of assimilating such information and redirecting themselves in light of their discoveries. In the Stanford prison study, potentially crippling, yet realistic alterations in the subjects' self-concepts were offset by therapeutically enhanced self-definition and self-direction. Thus, despite the blow to their self-respect inflicted by the revelation of the prisoner-subjects' pliant submissiveness or by the revelation of the guard-subjects' enjoyment of authoritarian power, the subjects' self-respect was restored.

The plight of women whose automatic submission to the role of housewife-mother has recently been called into question provides a broad-based test case for my claims regarding the fragility of compromised self-respect. What traditional women had regarded as a natural and inevitable division of labor—wife as domestic caretaker and husband as provider—feminists and, to a large extent, federal and state law have declared an option. Thus, a possible rejoinder to my account of the harm minimal autonomy can do to self-respect stems from the popular belief that housewife-mothers have lost self-respect as alternative roles have become available to them. The anecdotal evidence for this view is certainly worrisome. For if the prognosis for self-respect is improved by a social climate hospitable to autonomy, the shift over the last two decades away from compulsory marriage, motherhood, and homemaking should have been accompanied by commensurate advances in self-respect among women. Yet, it seems that creating a social environment more conducive to autonomy need not augment self-respect, indeed, that the reverse has occurred.

The traditional woman's battle for self-respect manifests a number of the principles I have developed in my discussion of compromised self-respect. Larry Blum, Marcia Homiak, Judy Housman, and Naomi Scheman have persuasively argued that the traditional woman's dependency and lack of individual identity undermine her altruism, that is, her "feminine virtue." For example, the traditional woman is inclined to conflate providing emotional support, which is beneficial to her husband, with providing uncritical emotional support, which is potentially harmful to him (Blum et al. 1973–1974:234; for a similar view, see Friedman 1985:147–148). Thus, the traditional woman's self-respect rests on an inflated conception of the help she is giving her family and a correspondingly suspect self-image.

In addition, as I have urged, people who are not programmatically autonomous can to some degree compensate for this lack by setting standards for themselves within their assigned roles. Ann Oakley has found that the housewife's main strategy for obtaining satisfaction from her work is to invent stiff criteria of hygiene and efficiency that she can commend herself for satisfying (1981:174). Confirming their devotion to their families in this way, these women demonstrate to themselves that they are "good women," women who deserve respect.

Yet, these tactics are not altogether successful. A recent study contends that one third of the women in an urban population were borderline depressives, if they were not clinically depressed (Oakley 1981:80). Further, it was found that four factors were positively correlated with the onset of depression: having three or more children under fourteen years old; lacking an intimate relationship with a spouse or other adult; the death of one's mother before the age of eleven; not having paid employment outside the home (Oakley 1981:80). It is obvious that the first three of these factors are sources of emotional strain; however, the fourth directly contradicts the position of those who maintain that sequestering women in the home is natural and beneficial. Since depression is associated with self-denigration, it is evident that whatever self-respect women obtain from their domestic wizardry is commonly offset by the contempt they feel for themselves as homemakers.

Still, it is important to recognize that the self-contemptuous homemaker is by no means the norm. In a study of university educated women ranging in age from their twenties to their forties, Douglas Hall and Francine Gordon found that married women who prefer to work full time and who do work full time are most satisfied with their lives, married women who prefer to work part time and who do work part time are least satisfied with their lives, and married women who prefer to be housewives and who are housewives rank between these other two groups in life satisfaction (1973:44). Though there is evidence that women's identification with traditionally masculine roles promotes self-respect and that their identification with traditionally feminine roles undermines self-respect (Stericker and Johnson 1977:25), the alleged reduction of generations of housewife-mothers to self-loathing and despair is a myth.

In this connection, it is important to keep in mind that few women have gone so far as to wholly reject the traditional feminine role. A major result of recent changes in attitudes toward gender has been a bifurcation and differential valuation of housewifery and motherhood. While most women continue to see motherhood as a gratifying occupation—one that is worthy of them—many of them report disdain for their activities as housewives (Oakley 1981:175; Harrison et al. 1981:1185). Yet women are by no means unanimous in their hostility to housewifery. The least educated women in America were as satisfied with housework in 1976 as they were in 1956, and the numbers of these women who acknowledged that they once wanted a career declined during this period. It was housewives who attended high school or college who became disenchanted with domestic labor and swelled the workforce between 1962 and the present (Mansbridge 1986:106). In other words, the more possible it was for a woman to shed her traditional role, the more likely it was that she would perceive her own dissatisfaction and lose self-respect if she did nothing about it.

Still, many educated housewives have remained at home and kept their self-respect. Moreover, Sarah Usher and Mort Fels have determined that support for feminist ideas is positively correlated with self-respect among both working and nonworking, university educated, middle-aged, married mothers (1985:51). That is, educated housewife-mothers who have come to grips with the recent undermining of assumptions about women's proper role and who have remained committed to the traditional feminine role have retained their self-respect. Educated housewife-mothers who cannot accept the greater freedom and equality that feminists advocate for women have been less able to preserve their self-respect.

Although housewife-mothers taken as a group have not lost as much self-respect as is commonly thought, recent social and economic developments have created a new category of women—the part-time workers—who do seem to be in turmoil. Hall and Gordon's data show that the latter women are least satisfied with their lives. In view of the fact that part-time jobs are rarely challenging or prestigious, it is not surprising that these women find life less rewarding than others. What is surprising is that, despite their greater dissatisfaction, part-time working women are less willing to change roles than any other group (Hall and Gordon 1973:44). Hall and Gordon suggest that these women have struck a compromise between traditional femininity and contemporary careerism, but that their dissatisfaction indicates incomplete identity resolution (1973:47). Part-time employment may be the refuge of many of the least autonomous women. They have been raised to be housewife-mothers, but new social forces are pressuring them to work outside the home.

Pulled in opposing directions but unable to choose between them, these women undertake to do both and suffer from this attempt to straddle two roles. That their unhappiness with this arrangement fails to subvert their allegiance to it points to an underlying problem with poorly developed autonomy skills.

Jane Mansbridge holds that women who are oriented to traditional feminine values and functions and who have recently lost self-respect have suffered in this way because high status women have entered the world of paid employment (1986:105). Yet, it is unlikely that these women have simply internalized other people's newly critical attitudes towards their occupation and thereby lost self-respect. Since public opinion remains divided on the question of women's proper role, there are no unambiguous social norms that can account for these women's downcast feelings about themselves. Moreover, social-psychological studies do not confirm the oft-repeated claim that self-respect and self-contempt merely mirror the respect or contempt in which other people hold a person. Though there is some correlation between people's self-referential attitudes and their beliefs about others' attitudes toward them, there is little correlation between these beliefs and their associates' actual attitudes (Shrauger and Schoenman 1979:558). Since people communicate ambiguous information about their views of their fellows, individuals must interpret the cues they receive, and their interpretations rarely supply accurate pictures of the way others see them (Shrauger and Schoenman 1979:565). The process of self-scrutiny that leads to self-respect or self-contempt does not take place in a social vacuum, but self-respect and self-contempt are not reducible to the internalization of others' favorable or unfavorable attitudes.

Though some traditional women may have come to believe that many people no longer hold housewifery in the same esteem they once did, and though this belief may figure in some of these women's diminished self-respect, the question remains as to why these women are so adversely affected by shifting social mores. Why do they not dismiss women who have embraced careers as dupes of a misguided fad? Why do they not remind themselves of the gratification they obtain from their own work, instead of taking on tedious part-time jobs? If economic need obliges them to work, why do they profess an unassailable loyalty to their dual role, instead of acknowledging that they would prefer not to work at all?

I would contend that the best explanation of the drop in their self-respect is that socioeconomic developments have brought the compromised nature of these women's self-respect to the surface. As their commitment to the feminine role was never anchored in their true selves, so their self-respect was never founded on an autonomous life plan. Since they are most probably minimally autonomous, they lack the skills to assimilate their transformed self-perception, as well as the skills to generate an alternative course of action (part 3, sec. 3). Having relied on compromised self-respect, many women were vulnerable to feminist criticism of gender stereotypes, and they are now condemned to self-contempt. Once people relinquish the assumption that they have no choice about some matter, their self-respect comes to hinge in part on making wise choices. In the face of expanding opportunities, some women sank into depression or adopted conflict-ridden stopgap measures; however, many others took the opportunity to renew their previous commitments or to reorient their lives.

Women who were receptive to the feminist challenge despite long-standing traditional marriages often discovered that their major life choices had been made unreflectively and acquiescently. Some of these women then went on to accuse themselves of self-betrayal and cowardice while others became convinced that they had settled upon satisfying and worthwhile life plans. Though it appears that many housewives lost self-respect, I would maintain that they never really had the self-respect they thought they had. Without their realizing it, their self-respect was compromised; social and economic changes merely opened their eyes to this compromise and, in many cases, spurred them to take steps to put their self-respect on a solid basis. Whatever the outcome, these individuals moved from viewing self-respect as a superficial question about how well one does a predetermined task to viewing it also as a profound question about whether one's life is worthy of and congruent with one's self.

These observations highlight the integral relationship between autonomy and uncompromised self-respect. Autonomous people have a realistic understanding of their capacities as well as the limits of their ability to control their circumstances, and self-respecting people are not disposed to degrading self-flagellation. Thus, autonomy and uncompromised self-respect together provide a bulwark against adverse circumstances and against others' disdain. Yet, autonomy and uncompromised self-respect both entail accepting responsibility for one's conduct. Autonomy prevents people both from evading responsibility and from inflating their responsibility and thus sustains self-respect, while uncompromised self-respect preserves people's sense of their worthiness as agents and thus prevents people from confounding their capacity for self-governance by giving in to social pressure or undesirable impulses. Thus, autonomy and uncompromised self-respect reciprocally reinforce one another.

But people whose self-respect is compromised respect themselves for good characteristics they do not have but believe they have; they respect themselves despite bad characteristics they have but do not acknowledge; or they respect themselves for carrying out life plans they believe to be their own but that are socially imposed. Since minimal autonomy is widespread, compromised self-respect that depends on nonautonomous, yet major elements of people's self-portraits or that depends on nonautonomous, yet major life choices is all too common. But the disclosure of such distorted self-concepts can lead to devastating condemnation of one's own character or the overall course of one's life. Thus, compromised self-respect threatens people's emotional stability.

It is clear, then, that whatever self-respect people obtain from disciplining themselves to fulfill standards implicit in social roles that have been imposed on them or from making episodically autonomous choices once in awhile is comparatively precarious. When people's self-regard is confined to their level of achievement or occasional self-expression within an assigned activity and does not penetrate to the overall shape of their lives, they are vulnerable to the most profound form of self-contempt. Reflecting on his own misspent life, F. Scott Fitzgerald lamented his lack of autonomy and his deflated self-respect:

> So there was not an "I" anymore—not a basis on which I could organize my self-respect—save my limitless capacity for toil that it seemed I possessed no more. It was strange to have no self—to be like a little boy left alone in a big house, who knew that now he could do anything he wanted to do, but found that there was nothing that he wanted to do. ("Pasting it Together," *The Crack-Up*, p. 79)

Of course, luck, social approbation, or self-deception can save minimally autonomous people from this fate. However, such cosseting does not so much ensure self-respect as it obviates the need for self-respect, thereby allowing individuals to rest content with compromised self-respect.[5]

To be self-respecting, people must chart their own courses. Discovering a mismatch between one's self and one's life plan which one is powerless to remedy detracts from self-respect. But, as we have seen, uncompromised self-respect is both intrinsically and instrumentally valuable. It should not be disdained as a relic of patriarchy. Accordingly, insofar as official social policy and entrenched cultural norms subject people to a contracted sense of self-worth, society owes these individuals a reappraisal of the options it countenances. Of course, nothing I have said entails that societies are obligated to ensure that everyone's dreams can come true. Mature people modulate their aspirations and expectations in accordance with a realistic assessment of what should be possible. However, if socially enforced deficiencies in autonomy competency leave some people minimally autonomous and ill-equipped to respect themselves, there is a powerful reason to condemn those practices that constrain people to minimal autonomy and to implement reforms designed to enhance autonomy. Likewise, if obdurate prejudice forces some individuals to classify reasonable projects as idle fantasies, the society sponsoring these restrictions wrongs some of its members. It compels them either to distort their personalities or to become pariahs. Both options put self-respect in jeopardy. Though this risk may be supportable for people who have a high degree of autonomy but who have less than full autonomy, it can be tragic for marginally autonomous people.

# SECTION 3

# Justice and Autonomy

I HAVE argued that, to have due regard for one's dignity, one must conduct one's life autonomously. While this requirement does not entail that every self-respecting person's life plan must be astonishingly idiosyncratic, it does entail that no self-respecting person can follow convention simply because it is what is socially expected. Lack of autonomy compromises self-respect, and self-respect is a highly desirable personal good. Still, it does not follow that suppressing autonomy is unjust, let alone that justice requires fostering autonomy. As a personal good, autonomy may be a desideratum that is best left to individuals to pursue or not to pursue depending on their temperament. I believe, however, that the issue of autonomy cannot be confined to the private sphere. For autonomy bears a reciprocal relation to equal opportunity, and, as a result of this relation, autonomy must be counted among the cardinal political values.[1] Without equal opportunity, autonomy is severely constrained, but, without autonomy, equal opportunity is a sham.


## A. GENDER ROLE ENFORCEMENT

WE HAVE seen how feminine socialization impairs the development of autonomy competency and how minimal autonomy compromises self-respect (part 3, sec. 3; part 4, sec. 2). Though there is no need to recapitulate these arguments here, it is worth observing that neither minimal autonomy nor compromised self-respect prepares women to contend effectively with the lynchpin of feminine socialization, namely, gender role enforcement. Gender role enforcement compounds the limiting effects of minimal autonomy by guiding the individual into a specified life plan. (For related discussion of the influence of conventionality on self-knowledge and self-direction, see part 3, sec. 4.) Whereas minimal autonomy stunts the individual's ability to discover and act on her own values, needs, and desires, gender role enforcement preempts whatever halting attempts at global self-governance she might make by assigning her a place in society. Role enforcement thereby cements her minimal autonomy. Before addressing a selection of abstract issues concerning the interplay between equal opportunity and autonomy, I would like to give these issues a human face by considering the ways in which gender role enforcement limits the life prospects of traditional women.

Gender role enforcement can be aptly characterized as a modern vestige of social ascription. With respect to gender, biological sex at birth is often the chief criterion determining how a child should be raised and what role he or she will eventually fill. On the basis of this determination, children are imbued with norms appropriate to their sex, and, later on, social sanctions keep adults from shedding their gender identities.[2] This type of role enforcement presents a particularly vexing problem since it is largely accomplished through customary practices, ingrained attitudes, and standardized expectations. Though it is easy enough for right-minded governments to rescind discriminatory laws in such areas as matrimony and divorce, education and employment, and property ownership and inheritance, it is difficult to convince individuals that they are free to avail themselves of these officially expanded possibilities. For the informal sanctions associated with these socially dictated roles—including mockery, ostracism, self-doubt, and shame—continue to ensure compliance where official sanctions have been nullified.

Yet, strict gender role enforcement might be defended on the grounds that it confers a desirable role on women. Despite the disadvantages of its inferior social status, the role of wife, mother, and homemaker can reasonably be portrayed as an advantageous one. The wife whose husband is legally obligated to support her is relieved of the strain of financial responsibility; the mother makes a valuable social contribution and performs demanding and rewarding services for her children; the homemaker manages her own domain. What is curious about traditional marital norms, then, is that they arguably confer privileges upon women, and yet feminists have rightly objected to them.

To address this paradox, it is first necessary to survey the historical record. Although the role of housewife and mother has been imposed on virtually all women, only a small percentage of women have enjoyed the benefits this role is supposed to confer (Berg 1978; Rubin 1976). It was not until recently, it must be remembered, that unionization enabled many male workers to provide adequately for their families. If the family is impoverished, it is no benefit for the wife to be barred from ameliorating this condition by working outside the home. Nor is it a benefit, if she is forced to enter the labor market, to be segregated into stereotypically feminine jobs which are underpaid because they are done by women. In addition, circumstances have often deprived women of the satisfaction of caring for their children. Before child labor was prohibited, economic necessity commonly took children out of the home and prematurely halted maternal nurture. But even after legislation ended the exploitation of children, women who lacked birth control and who could not afford nursemaids often found that they had so many children that they could hardly care for any of them. Finally, it is important to recognize that without a comfortable income, domestic sovereignty reduces to a desperate and incessant struggle to feed and clothe the family and to keep marginal housing as habitable as possible. Plainly, the feminine role cannot be counted a privilege—it is a Sisyphean duty—in the absence of considerable economic means.

Still, whether advantaged women suffer any injustice as a result of strict enforcement of the feminine role remains to be considered. Here, it seems advisable to leave aside such ancillary burdens as sexual subordination and vulnerability to domestic violence. Though these liabilities are serious and not unrelated to women's dependency in the traditional marriage, they could in principle be corrected without freeing women from their conventional role. The trouble with this role is not limited to the price exacted for the benefits it grants. To see why enforced housewifery and motherhood would remain objectionable, even supposing their hidden disadvantages were removed, attention must be focused on role enforcement and its deleterious effects on autonomy. John Stuart Mill crystallized the problem as follows: "In the case of women, each member of the subject class is in a chronic state of bribery and intimidation combined" (1971:26). Both the inducements and the threats function to sever the tie between the woman's life plan and her authentic self.

By threatening people with penalties for refusing to comply with social expectations, role enforcement makes it harder for people to discover their own beliefs and desires, that is, to gain self-knowledge. Role enforcement complicates the problem of separating what one really wants from what is merely prudent to want by prodding people to conclude that they really want to do what is prudent. Early socialization that limits people to minimal autonomy, as traditional feminine socialization does, redoubles the effects of role enforcement. Plainly, the less proficient one's autonomy competency is, the less credible one's identification of one's true self with enforced conventions will be. Where there is no apparent tension between people's life plans and their fulfillment of an enforced social role, the coercive character of the role circumvents personal initiative, thus driving a wedge between individuals' conduct and their authentic selves. Though obeying the law or following entrenched custom may be unobjectionable, few people are so attuned to themselves and so indifferent to sanctions that they can convincingly claim (except when a law or a social norm is known to be unenforceable or unenforced) that their obedience is not prompted by fear of punishment or by habitual social conformity.

It is undeniable, however, that people who have been socialized to be minimally autonomous sometimes attempt to break out of the roles for which society destines them. Using Kate Chopin's novel, *The Awakening,* Kathryn Pyne Addelson recounts a fictional, but verisimilar tale of a woman's rebellion against the strictures and indignities of the feminine role as it was defined by polite society in New Orleans toward the end of the nineteenth century. Addelson's treatment of this story is fascinating for its subtle explication of the gradual, tentative process through which Edna Pontellier discovers herself and seeks to liberate herself from the confines of the feminine role. However, what I want to emphasize here is Addelson's conclusion regarding Edna's undoing, because this conclusion is instructive with respect to the ways in which gender role enforcement can counteract individual choice.

In the end, Edna drowns herself in despair over the conflict between her own aspirations and her ties to her children (Addelson 1983:592–593). Defending Edna against charges that her suicide was selfish and self-indulgent, Addelson explains Edna's situation as follows:

> Her society did not allow to her an integration of the facts of life that needed integrating. . . . It wasn't lack of imagination. It was lack of means. Edna says the children are trying to possess her. But it is the social organization of her world that she ran aground on. (1983:594).

Addelson maintains that the structure of the society in which Edna lived, along with the kinds of explanations current in that society, made Edna seem immature and made it impossible for her to portray her conduct as a moral revolt (1983:593). Edna could not regard herself as a person ahead of her time and standing up for her rights. Left with the alternative of seeing herself as a childish rebel who could not accept the way things should be, Edna could not preserve her dignity, no matter what she did. Either she could refuse to capitulate to the norms, or she could abandon her own desires. There was no socially tenable way to do the former, and there was no personally tenable way to do the latter.

Addelson's remarks about the cultural availability of explanations that certify the dignity of agents and the legitimacy of their choices imply that women often lack a conceptual framework capable of rendering their frustrations and yearnings intelligible to themselves. In my terminology, it is the lifelong enforcement of gender roles that leads to this impasse. Two components of this enforcement encroach on the process of self-discovery: a regimented social environment and the individual's psychological adaptation to it. Where gender roles are rigorously enforced, there is a social consensus regarding the meaning of womanhood and manhood along with a consensus regarding the manner in which those meanings are to be enacted (de

Beauvoir 1953:xiv–xvi, 402; Rousseau 1979:357–409; Hunter College 1983:174–175). Fulfillment of these norms is equated with self-realization, and other ostensible modes of self-realization are dismissed as pathological. Having internalized norms of feminine or masculine behavior in such a way that their identity becomes linked to observing these constraints, women and men cannot spurn their respective gender roles without calling into question their own respectability, if not their very sanity (Friedan 1964:11). As Addelson puts it, the problem is not an inability to imagine living otherwise. Rather, it is the impossibility of detaching alternative ways of life from their stigmatizing connotations of contemptible failure or sordid perversity and thus the impossibility of perceiving the alternatives as viable ones.

Yet, gender role enforcement seems to provide people with one unequivocal good, and consequently it may seem that this practice is not necessarily inimical to autonomy. Indeed, it may seem to provide the best possible solution to the very problem Addelson notices. One might maintain that role enforcement ministers to an easily overlooked precondition for autonomy, namely, self-confidence. Without self-confidence, people would have little reason to take their own ideas and inclinations seriously and would lack the audacity to express themselves through unconventional life plans. Since individuals lacking confidence typically seek to mold themselves to fit the image of an exemplary figure or to fit into a social milieu, they skirt the issue of autonomy. Whereas quashed dedication to an unorthodox life plan is rare, the argument continues, insecurity is sadly common and deserves surcease. A firm infrastructure of enforced roles seems a promising antidote to anxious imitation. By putting a social stamp of approval on selected life orientations and assigning one to each individual, these positions assure compliant individuals that they are launched on acceptable courses. Once endowed with this cushioning base of security, persons will presumably have sufficient confidence in themselves to act on their own beliefs and desires.

The assignment of social and economic positions through legally or customarily enforced roles may seem mildly attractive because this arrangement gives every individual a place where he or she belongs. For those who mesh well with the operative system, crises of identity never erupt, and crises of confidence cannot penetrate to the individual's basic plan of life. No doubt, it is a blessing to be spared these alarms. However, for those whose temperament and abilities lead them to scorn their designated roles, gender role enforcement is a form of oppression that poisons the individual's entire life. Accordingly, to advocate gender role enforcement on the grounds that it nurtures self-confidence and thereby promotes autonomy is to disregard the potential victims of social calcification whose development would be blocked and whose autonomy would be sacrificed.

Fortunately, there are means other than role enforcement through which self-assurance can be imparted to people and through which people can be discouraged from conflating difference with pathology. Child-rearing methods emphasizing tolerance and delight in diversity, familiarity with a common heritage, and emotional openness in a supportive atmosphere foster self-confidence and take the sting out of the charge of abnormality. (For further discussion of autonomy-augmenting child-rearing, see part 3, sec. 5.) Moreover, associations of adults whose talents and interests overlap help to sustain this sense of personal competence and worthiness (Rawls 1971:440–442). With respect to gender, in the last two decades we have witnessed a proliferation of women's professional organizations, caucuses, and support groups of all sorts (Hunter College 1983:515–517). Whereas role enforcement nurtures the self-confidence of some at the expense of the autonomy of others, educational and associational supports for self-confidence do not have damaging secondary effects on autonomy. Quite the contrary, they support autonomy.

In conjunction with strict role enforcement, minimal autonomy can blind individuals to wrongs inflicted upon them. If they discern a conflict between themselves and social expectations, or if they feel frustrated because certain avenues of self-realization are closed to them, they do not even consider blaming their society. Castigating themselves for being failures, they overlook the possibility of injustice (Friedan 1964:14–15). The most poignant evil of socialization that produces minimally autonomous individuals, then, is that it helps to secure its victims' collaboration with the injustices they may suffer.

## B. EQUAL OPPORTUNITY AND AUTONOMY

THE RIGHT to equal opportunity comes into play in education preparatory to work, in the search for employment, and in consideration for promotion and raises. At each of these stages, this right guarantees that no one's opportunities will be limited by discrimination on grounds irrelevant to performance. In this way, it shields people from arbitrary and humiliating rejections which could cumulatively injure self-respect. Moreover, by offering people the chance to work at occupations of their own choosing, if not of their own design, this right helps to release people from tradition-bound assumptions about which social niches they belong in. Though it is evident that the right to equal opportunity—even if vigorously enforced—cannot overturn profound socialization, legally guaranteeing the possibility of self-expression in a person's choice of an occupation remains a notable and valuable function of this right. Thus, equal opportunity is plainly crucial to autonomy and conducive to self-respect.

Setting aside the question of how inegalitarian a just society can be, but allowing that some inequalities can be justified, let us grant that unequal rewards for work, including income, power, and prestige, are unjustified unless equal opportunity is enforced. Whatever one thinks society ought to do to alleviate the various obstacles to individual advancement, it seems clear that society cannot rightly confer advantages on an elect if it preempts the possibility that others will compete for these advantages. As is well known, the primary purpose of equal opportunity is to give people from all ranks of society a fair chance to obtain society's rewards.

Traditionally, ascription—the assignment of individuals to social roles according to their birth—and discrimination—the dismissal of applicants' credentials on grounds irrelevant to performance—have counted as violations of equal opportunity. However, it has become apparent that these are not the only ways in which equal opportunity can be abrogated. Social institutions can deprive people of ambition or education, and these deficiencies can destroy a person's prospects in life as effectively as ascription or discrimination can (Rawls 1971:74). Careers open to talents, we have come to realize, does not suffice for equal opportunity. Equal opportunity is not achieved unless individuals with similar natural endowments and similar willingness to work are able to attain similar positions (Rawls 1971:73). Equal opportunity requires a fair chance to develop one's talents and to conceive commensurate aspirations. Although it is beyond the scope of this book to provide an exhaustive account of equal opportunity, it is important to appreciate the way in which personal autonomy figures in this widely accepted doctrine. My contention is that differential allotments of wealth, power, and prestige are unjust unless the prospective recipients are at least medially autonomous or unless the allotments serve rectificatory ends. (For an account of medial autonomy, see part 3, sec. 3.) Setting aside issues of historical injustice, this means that equal opportunity will not be realized in our present social environment until steps are taken to ensure the medial autonomy of the pool of competitors.

Prime among the ways in which a society can limit individuals' aspirations are socialization practices that secure minimal autonomy but that impede progress toward medial autonomy. Although minimal autonomy does not guarantee that a person will pursue a conventional or unchallenging life plan, it needlessly limits the range of options an individual is likely to contemplate seriously. To the extent that this constraint is socially imposed—that is, to the extent that a society's institutions and public policies condone or reinforce the suppression of some individuals' potential for autonomy—the legitimacy of the penalties drawn by minimally autonomous people and, correlatively, the legitimacy of the rewards collected by medially and fully autonomous people are questionable. Just as liberal democratic states have assumed responsibility for providing free education partly in order to give people a fair chance to acquire marketable skills, these states ought to make sure that pedagogical practices and curricula in these schools evenhandedly develop the autonomy of all pupils. What I am suggesting is that medial autonomy gives individuals sufficient control over their lives to render them, rather than their social environment, accountable for the directions their lives take. Thus, a societal commitment to cultivating at least this level of autonomy is necessary for the society to be at liberty to compensate its members differentially.

Vinit Haksar has anticipated a major objection that could be lodged against my position. Discussing John Rawls' fair equality of opportunity principle, Haksar contends that from the standpoint of the original position—that is, taking into account whether a policy could be justified to the worst-off members of society—conditioning people to fill tedious, ennervating, and unhealthy jobs which are nonetheless economically essential would be preferable to developing these people's autonomy only to consign them to these roles despite their enhanced capacities.[3] As Haksar puts it, "Assume that society requires that some 'inferior' jobs, such as coal-mining, have to be done; is it not better from the contractarian standpoint that those who fill these jobs are doing things they want to do, rather than doing them in a discontented spirit, wishing they were doing something else?" (1979:177).

In taking up this question, the parties to the original position might concede that intensive socialization could relieve the dissatisfaction people experience as a result of being stuck in undesirable occupations. But then it would be necessary to decide how workers would be chosen for adaptive socialization. The only fair procedure would be a lottery. Even if the participants in the original position thought it would be advantageous to be socialized out of their discontent in the event that they ended up among the least advantaged, they would never volunteer for this position, nor would they agree to permanently relegate their descendants to oblivious acceptance of the lowest social rank. Enlisting themselves or their descendants in this program would violate the assumptions that these individuals are motivated to maximize their allotments of primary social goods and that they care about the prospects of the next generation (Rawls 1971:128, 142, 144). Accordingly, for such a socialization policy to be adopted, those who have the most ability and ambition must be willing to risk being selected and having their children selected to be conditioned into distasteful and dangerous occupations.

Not only would this scheme be an inefficient waste of talent, but also it is hard to believe that even mildly risk averse people would agree to it. Wouldn't people rather know that they can try to attain their economic goals through ability and effort than know that, if they end up at the bottom, they will still be pleased with their lot? If they are unlucky in the lottery, the latter arrangement would rob them of control over the overall direction of their lives, for people cannot be conditioned into mindless delight with their work and yet retain their autonomy with respect to their avocations, families, and friendships. Since job satisfaction is only one source of happiness, this loss of control seems an absurd sacrifice to prevent occupational discontent. Furthermore, under a system of equal opportunity, people who start out in menial jobs sometimes advance to better ones. But enforced satisfaction with one's job, one's work environment, and one's salary would eliminate this possibility. By removing the main reason people have for seeking promotion or for changing jobs, namely, dissatisfaction with their present situation, it would lock the least advantaged into their status once and for all. In short, if the parties to the original position would accept this plan, they might as well institute a system of conditioned slavery in which the jollified, but vacant slaves are picked by lot. After all, slavery is bound to be cheaper than wage labor.

But I believe that Haksar's point, and therefore this whole line of argument, is based on a misconstrual of the original position. A major assumption of the original position is that, although the participants do not know the details of their life plans, they do know that they have some life plan or other (Rawls 1971:142). Thus, their assignment is to figure out which principles of social cooperation would be most conducive to their carrying out these plans whatever they turn out to be. To think that political and economic systems should be constructed so as to facilitate the fulfillment of diverse life plans is to think that these life plans are morally inextricable from people. If, on the contrary, one holds that life plans are extraneous to people, the charge to the parties in the original position would be to produce a scheme for manipulating life plans so as to oil the social machine, not to find a system of fair principles to distribute social goods and to adjudicate conflicting claims.

I trust that no one would endorse a conception of the original position in which people are treated as mere cogs in a wheel.[4] If I am right, it matters how desires arise because people and their life plans cease to form an integral unit insofar as their life plans are nonautonomous, and the integrity of this unit is a necessary assumption for the issue of justice among persons to make sense.

Now, it might be countered that there are bases other than autonomy for the moral inseparability of individuals and their life plans. Obstructing people's life plans tends to make them unhappy; it reduces their probable contribution to social progress; it provokes dissent and rebellion. Accordingly, if morality mandates promoting individual happiness, social progress, or social harmony, it must respect the unity of individuals and their life plans, regardless of whether these plans are autonomous.

Though cogent, this line of thought is beside the point. The contention that morality dictates a policy of permitting people to pursue their life plans is not equivalent to the contention that the moral inextricability of people and their life plans is a necesssary presupposition of our understanding of moral relations. Happiness, social progress, and social harmony may commend such a policy, but whether they do or not depends on whether any other policy would better serve these ends. And, evidently, a program to condition some people into acceptance of socially ordained plans might prove optimific. But to affirm the moral integrity of people and their life plans as a presupposition of moral relations is to deny that a policy of manipulating people's choices could be morally admissible.

Still, it is not obvious why such a strong tie between people and their plans should be acknowledged. Since no one believes that all creatures that have desires are morally inextricable from their desires—no one thinks there is anything wrong with training dogs not to nab steaks from the dinner table, and no one thinks there is anything wrong with training children not to defecate in public—the question arises as to why human adults and their life plans should be sacrosanct.

One explanation might be that these latter individuals are self-conscious. Since they are self-conscious, they know when they are being manipulated, and this knowledge itself causes them distress. While it is clear that people sometimes suffer from the realization that they are being manipulated more than they suffer from being deprived of what they want, it is also clear that people are often happy to abdicate responsibility and let others decide what they should want and what they will get. Thus, awareness of being manipulated is not necessarily associated with anxiety, resentment, or frustration. Moreover, despite their self-consciousness, people commonly fail to realize that they are being manipulated. When this is the case, any frustration they may feel can only stem from not getting something that they want; it cannot stem from their awareness of being toyed with. Since self-consciousness guarantees neither awareness of being manipulated nor distress when one is aware of being manipulated, self-consciousness cannot account for the moral inextricability of people and their life plans. Indeed, it could be seen as a reason to manipulate people subliminally rather than as a reason to assume the integrity of persons and their life plans.

The capacity for autonomous choice can account for this moral unity. The difference between the desires of animals and children, on the one hand, and those of normal human adults, on the other, is that the latter are capable of exercising autonomy competency. Since their exercising this competency is good (part 4, sec. 2), and since exercising this competency has the effect of constituting the individual's authentic self and binding the individual's life plan to that self (part 2, sec. 2), no tenable conception of justice can institute a policy of sundering people from their life plans. Admittedly, many people's life plans are largely heteronomous. To this extent, their plans are no less accidental than those of instinctual animals and impulsive children. Nevertheless, almost everyone's plans contain autonomous elements (part 3, sec. 3). Yet, most of the time it is not feasible for the public institutions that implement principles of distributive justice to distinguish the autonomous from the nonautonomous components of these plans. Though it may be possible for hospitals to determine whether or not individual patients have autonomously consented to the withdrawal of respirators and other life-prolonging technologies, it is not possible for the Internal Revenue Service to allocate bigger refunds to persons who would use this largesse for autonomously chosen projects. Thus, distributive justice must rest on the presumption that people's life plans are expressions of their true selves or, in other words, the assumption of the moral inextricability of people and their life plans.

Haksar's suggestion that socializing people to be happy in inferior social and economic positions might appeal to the parties to the original position fails at two levels. First, it is implausible that reasonably self-interested and risk averse people would gamble on being selected for this conditioning, and it is still more implausible that they would opt to deprive themselves of the chance to escape their fate. Thus, despite the risk of dissatisfaction, they would prefer to keep the possibility of autonomous choice open. Second, it would be inappropriate to choose principles of justice from the standpoint of a Rawlsian original position were it not for the moral unity of individuals and their life plans. Since it is the exercise of autonomy competency that secures this unity, the parties to the original position cannot consistently decide to suppress autonomy.

But why would they agree to foster autonomy as part of a policy of equal opportunity? Their recognition that their capacity for autonomous activity is what makes them recipients of justice provides a general reason for them to undertake to develop autonomy competency.[5] More specifically, they would choose to buttress their commitment to equal opportunity with programs to support autonomy because such programs would enhance everyone's ability to take advantage of extant educational and employment opportunities. Just as the parties to the original position would regard a society that provides inferior public education to its least advantaged children as a society that abrogates equal opportunity, they would regard a society that socializes some of its children to eschew formally available opportunities as a society that denies equal opportunity. Since medial autonomy gives individuals the capacity to assess their options openmindedly and to base their choices on their own needs and desires, and since minimal autonomy impairs individuals' capacities to adopt unconventional courses of action, medial autonomy cannot be excluded from the prerequisites for equal opportunity.

Still, it is obvious that societies cannot simply bestow autonomy on their members in the same way that they can bestow voting rights or medical care. At most, they can vigorously endorse and indirectly support the autonomy of individuals. In this capacity, the state can fund research on autonomy competency and its development, and it can underwrite the costs of implementing autonomy-enhancing pedagogical practices in public schools. (For further discussion of autonomy-enhancing socialization, see part 3, sec. 5.)

Such programs would provide incentives for parents to cultivate their children's autonomy competency. If pupils proficient in autonomy skills are rewarded at school, many parents will want to help their children succeed by providing complementary instruction and practice at home. However, some parents might choose to resist these inducements, and societies cannot be held responsible for autonomy-stifling influences originating in children's homes. Insofar as the state could only effectively counteract parental hostility to autonomy in outrageously invasive ways that would wreck many family bonds, the state should not undertake such far-reaching measures. Its policies and its responsibility for encouraging children's autonomy must be confined to the schools and the political and economic climate that surrounds them. Nevertheless, on an optimistic reading, parents who have been educated in the skills of autonomy will gladly cooperate with a similar education for their children. Thus, imaginative and humane education—both in the schools and through the media—can help to quell opposition to autonomy and can directly promote the achievement of medial autonomy for most members of society.

At this point, it might seem incongruous that I have not maintained that people must be fully autonomous before equal opportunity can justify differential rewards. Why should medially autonomous people not be considered unfairly disadvantaged relative to fully autonomous people? And why does the fact that many men are only medially autonomous not serve to delegitimate the advantages fully autonomous men have obtained? Here, the argument shifts to some extent from questions of principle to empirical matters.

While it is reasonable to suppose, in view of the accessibility of the skills involved in the competency of autonomy, that nearly everyone is capable of becoming medially autonomous, it is not equally clear that everyone is capable of becoming fully autonomous. (For an inventory of the repertory of skills constitutive of autonomy competency, see part 2, sec. 4.) No amount of training will equalize everyone's imaginative powers and reasoning capacities at maximum levels of proficiency. Also, there will always be some people who are more attentive to their feelings and more adept at grasping their import than others. Thus, to demand universal full autonomy as a precondition for equal opportunity would be to rule out realizing equal opportunity in practice.

An analogous problem arises in connection with educational support for equal opportunity. Though some individuals are capable of going on to college and professional school, high school graduation has been established as an educational baseline—a level of achievement that virtually everyone is capable of attaining, that no one should be prevented from attaining, and that the state is obliged to finance. While public funding of postsecondary education for the academically talented should also be available, equal opportunity is not undermined if some people who lack academic aptitude never attend college. Likewise, I am suggesting that medial autonomy constitutes a baseline in regard to self-governance. Virtually all people are capable of becoming medially autonomous, and there is much that societies can do to support the development and exercise of autonomy competency. Thus, societies that take steps to secure medial autonomy for all their members cannot be accused of excluding some people from joining in the competition for advantageous positions. Again, to demand more would be to deny the possibility of equal opportunity, but to demand less would be to countenance burdening some individuals with remediable handicaps in the vocational competition.

Philosophers have often observed that equal opportunity must be seen as a compromise between the marked differences among individuals, the proper limits of institutional interference in individuals' lives, and the justice of equalizing the prospects of individuals who have similar potentialities (Rawls 1971:74; Williams 1971:133–135; O'Neill 1977:184–187). For the same reasons that such draconian measures as genetic engineering and yanking children out of their parents' homes cannot be justified in the name of educational equality, full autonomy cannot be accepted as a baseline for equal opportunity. Supposing that equalizing autonomy competency at the highest level were to prove practicable, the moral costs of doing so would remain intolerable. Since medial autonomy can be achieved by acceptable means, it must serve as the baseline for equal opportunity.

While medial autonomy is too personal a good to hold societies strictly accountable for their members' failure to achieve it, the sensitivity of autonomy to all kinds of regimentation makes it too vulnerable to societal restrictions to be ignored by the political process. Concretely, autonomy is properly viewed as a political issue because apparently innocent legal stipulations and customary patterns can be injurious to it without inflicting conspicuous deprivations. Thus, a society that couples enforced social roles with socialization aimed at minimal autonomy to disguise an illicitly repressive social order is particularly insidious, for these practices are especially resistant to criticism and reform. Moreover, because conversion to educational practices that cultivate autonomy competency and respect for human diversity, vigilant enforcement of laws prohibiting discrimination, and, where significant inequalities exist, enactment of suitable entitlement programs facilitate autonomy, social institutions cannot elude responsibility in this area.

We have seen that minimally autonomous agents can attain at best a compromised form of self-respect and cannot join in the competition for social advantages on a par with medially autonomous individuals. Accordingly, a society that socializes one group of its members to be medially, if not fully, autonomous and another to be relatively heteronomous perpetrates two kinds of injustice. First, since self-respect is a universal desideratum, it is unjust that some members of society should be arbitrarily singled out for diminished self-respect. Second, since the medial autonomy of competitors is a necessary condition for equal opportunity, and since equal opportunity is a necessary condition for justice, no society that arbitrarily limits some of its members to minimal autonomy can be just. Though socialization that limits people to minimal autonomy is not as devastating a form of oppression as physical coercion or abuse, it must be taken seriously both because it is harmful in itself and because it can sabotage equal opportunity. It may not always be feasible for a society to give priority to the problem of autonomy. But societies that persistently subordinate personal autonomy to other objectives deprive their members of their dignity as human agents.

There is a great difference between societies that merely observe just forms and societies that achieve justice in the fullest sense. Societies of the latter kind seek justice not only to avoid charges of illegitimacy, but also to attract the allegiance of unbowed individuals—people who are jealous of their own visions of the good life and who demand that social arrangements enable them to fulfill these visions. To satisfy such exacting individuals, societies must harness respect for basic rights and liberties to the pursuit of personal autonomy.

# ENDNOTES

## PART II. A PROCEDURAL ACCOUNT

### SECTION 1. RECENT ACCOUNTS OF AUTONOMY

1. It is possible, of course, that Benn would insist that any rationally constructed, coherent personality could be given expression on the grounds that no rational individual would embrace feelings, desires, and so forth that were sure to be frustrated. But this seems implausible. Surely, one might believe in the value of fidelity to one's feelings and desires, and upholding this value might sometimes override the disvalue of frustration of this sort. In short, we would need an extremely powerful account of rationality to exclude the rationality of coherent, but unfulfilled personalities.

2. George Sher has pointed out to me that it is not clear whether we regard people who vacillate as nonautonomous because their identification with their desires does not persist or because they have conflicting desires. Anticipating this concern, Frankfurt stresses that autonomous people seek to identify with a coherent configuration of first-order desires (Frankfurt 1976:248–250). Plainly, coherence would neutralize one source of vacillation.

Still, this concession would not entail that persistence of identification does not matter to autonomy. Much of the appeal of Frankfurt's identification criterion is that meeting it means that an individual has a self-chosen and well-defined identity. Since a person who has a coherent set of desires may regard many of these desires as alien, Frankfurt sees the need to introduce the relation of identification, and, since a person who has a coherent set of desires may not identify steadily with any of them, Frankfurt sees the further need to insist on decisive identification. For to have a well-defined identity is not to have a different identity every other day. Whatever the cause of transitory identification, a theory of autonomy must exclude it. The trouble with Frankfurt's theory of autonomy is that the device he fixes on to stabilize identification—namely, decisions—will not do the job.

3. In fairness to Watson's differences with Frankfurt and Dworkin, it should be noted that Watson rejects the hierarchy of desires that is central to these other philosophers' theories (Watson 1982:109). Specifically, Watson denies that rationally certified desires are desires that are desired in a special way. Nevertheless, Watson can be grouped with these other thinkers because he regards valuation as the way in which people make desires their own or, in other words, as the way in which people come to identify with certain of their desires.

4. Gerald Dworkin's attitudinal version of the identification account could incorporate a conception of implicit identification more easily than Frankfurt's theory can. One might have an attitude that has never been directed toward a certain desire but that could be so directed and would be favorable if it were. Unlike decisions, which must have a definite content, attitudes can be indeterminate and can become attached to new objects as occasions arise. Someone who has a contemptuous attitude toward unfamiliar cultures might be described as implicitly having an unfavorable attitude toward a particular culture that he or she had never encountered. Still, though Dworkin's theory seems better equipped to handle the problem of implicit identification, it is in no better position to account for the persistence of identification or to establish a resting place for identification.

5. It is worth noting that a recent social-psychological study of the personalities of identical twins, some of whom were brought up together and others of whom were raised in different environments, lends support to Feinberg's contention that personality has a genetic component. This study maintains that such traits as social potency, traditionalism, vulnerability to stress, and alienation are strongly influenced by genetic factors ("Major Personality Study Finds that Traits Are Mostly Inherited," Daniel Goleman, the *New York Times* December 2, 1986:C1–2). However, the study does not conclude that nurture has no impact on genetically based traits. Rather, it emphasizes that parental practices need to be tailored to the individual child in order to minimize the effects of undesirable dispositions. While the study is controversial, its findings will not allow us to rule out Feinberg's suggestion that children are born with a basic temperament.

## SECTION 2. AN ALTERNATIVE ACCOUNT OF AUTONOMY

1. Here, it should be noted that programmatic autonomy is a matter of degree. People who have autonomous comprehensive life plans have global programmatic autonomy. However, people who fall far short of having global programmatic autonomy can nonetheless make plans for themselves or set policies to which they will adhere regarding specific questions. Someone whose overall plan of life is heteronomous could be an autonomous vegetarian. When people make autonomous decisions of this kind, they have narrow programmatic autonomy with respect to these matters.

In addition, it should be noted that whether some decisions should be classified as examples of episodic or programmatic autonomy depends in part on how the decision makers regard the scope of their decisions. A person who autonomously decides to eat vegetarian tonight has episodic autonomy, whereas a person who autonomously decides to give up meat starting tonight has narrow programmatic autonomy. The former decision is confined to one occasion; the latter sets a policy. Of course, many decisions span these two categories. For instance, an autonomous episodic choice that an individual makes with the explicit proviso that it can be continued if it works out may turn into a programmatic decision if, in the event, it does work out. (For detailed consideration of these distinctions, see part 3, sec. 3.)

2. Lawrence Haworth, who has advocated a procedural view of autonomy, sees autonomy as competence—that is, developed abilities to cope and to perform specific tasks—supplemented by critical competence—that is, the ability to think through one's purposes and to find reasons for pursuing them (Haworth 1986:46). My view coincides with Haworth's in many respects; however, my account places greater emphasis on understanding one's emotional life and on self-definition skills.

3. For this example, I have chosen a quality—leadership ability—that is ordinarily viewed in a favorable light. However, it is important to keep in mind that many people become reconciled to, and adapt their lives to accommodate, straightforwardly undesirable qualities, such as irrational fears. Therefore, it should be emphasized that the process of self-discovery and self-definition that I am describing applies equally well to the transformation of unfortunate attributes.

4. Eva Kittay has pointed out that breathing and walking must be seen as highly complex activities. The biology of respiration is hardly simple, and robotics reveals how difficult it is to move about without bumping into things. Still, however complex these processes may be, their complexities are not for the most part subject to our conscious control. Since they are natural activities, we are not normally able to apply ourselves to improving our performance of them. The exceptions, of course, are deficiencies resulting from accidents or diseases that require therapeutic exercise.

SECTION 3. SELF-DIRECTION AND PERSONAL INTEGRATION

1. Lawrence Haworth has disparagingly labeled theories of autonomy that involve self-definition along with self-discovery and self-direction "romantic" (Haworth 1986:63–65). While I agree with Haworth that people are not as malleable as they often wish they were and that a "realistic" theory of autonomy must take this fact into account, I would maintain that people are capable of changing themselves in some respects and that failure to do so can damage autonomy. Since Haworth cites Benjamin Franklin's self-improvement program as an example of autonomy, I am inclined to believe that our difference is more terminological than substantive (Haworth 1986:65). (For further discussion of the role of self-definition in autonomy and the limits of self-definition, see part 2, sec. 2 and part 3, sec. 4.)

2. Conversations with Eva Kittay and Lewis Meyers have helped me to develop this line of argument.

3. This proposal for an autonomous personality comprising a number of compartmentalized true selves may bring to mind the controversy in psychology between personality theorists who analyze personality and explain behavior in terms of stable dispositional traits and social learning theorists who analyze personality and explain behavior in terms of the capacity to discern and deliver what situations require of people (Mischel, 1973:252–283). However, the question of the nature of the autonomous personality is independent of this empirical debate.

The major point of contention between personality theorists and social learning theorists is which model is a better predictor of behavior. The social learning theorists maintain that more can be anticipated about human behavior by examining the environment in which it will occur than by projecting the consequences of a list of traits. However, even supposing this claim to be vindicated, it would not be relevant to autonomy. It may be true that, once people have entered a restaurant, virtually all of them will observe the routines of being seated at a table, perusing the menu, ordering from the waiter, eating the meal, and paying the bill. But, from the standpoint of autonomy, the important questions concern the minutiae of people's conduct in this situation, for example, how the diners interact with one another—what they talk about and how they converse. Once the decision to eat at a restaurant has been autonomously made, it is hardly news and certainly no violation of autonomy that people do not stage a wrestling match there. As I have stressed, autonomous programmatic decisions confer autonomy on the particular actions involved in carrying them out (part 2, sec. 2).

In this connection, however, it is important to remember that social learning theory, in its more sophisticated forms, does not hold that people's behavior is simply a product of immediate circumstances. Rather, it recognizes that situations are always colored by the expectations and modes of interpretation people bring with them quite apart from the particulars of circumstances and also that situations may be too weak to control the behavior of participants (Mischel 1973:259–260, 269–270, and 276). Thus, the insights into the role of cognition in shaping conduct that social learning theory has yielded need not lead to the dismaying conclusion that compartmentalization is inevitable or adaptive.

I am grateful to Jonathan Adler for bringing these matters to my attention.

4. Steve McGrade has suggested to me that there are virtues that are conducive to personal autonomy. For example, patience, fortitude, and calmness would often promote autonomous conduct. While many virtues do contribute to autonomy and it is doubtful that anyone could be autonomous without some of them, I am reluctant to maintain that all autonomous people must share a determinate set of virtuous characterological strands. Establishing a mandatory set of personal virtues would impinge upon the uniqueness of autonomous individuals, and it would prescribe the nature of autonomous conduct. Neither seems desirable in a theory of personal autonomy.

SECTION 5. INTERESTS, SELF-INTEREST, AND AUTONOMY

1. To the extent that it seems rational for Ann to act on an extremely powerful, nonautonomous desire to shorten her life for the sake of her work, I suspect it is because, in supposing that Ann is not being coerced and that her faculties are unimpaired, one is smuggling in the assumption that Ann's desire is not altogether heteronomous. In that case, one's assessment of whether Ann can rationally act on this desire will depend on one's assessment of its autonomy, which is the point I am trying to bring out.

2. This line of argument assumes that autonomy is good. Since I shall address the question of the value of autonomy at length in part 4, I shall not digress here to defend this assumption.

3. Closely related to the question of whether it is rational for a person to secure basic interests at the sacrifice of other personal values is the question of the person's attitude toward risk. I shall consider individual variations in regard to risk tolerance and risk aversion in part 2, section 6.

4. As George Sher has pointed out, other interpretations of Kay's desires are possible. For example, she may really want to have written poetry or to enjoy the acclaim that successful poets receive. But, since it is important to recognize, as I shall argue, that the autonomy of second-order desires does not necessarily transfer to their first-order realizations. I shall focus on the interpretation of Kay's desires offered above.

SECTION 6. RESPONSIBILITY FOR SELF

1. It goes without saying that other people may have excellent reason to oppose Martha's and Scott's courses of action on grounds other than imprudence. For example, religious people could reasonably try to dissuade Martha from joining forces with an intolerant political movement on the grounds that this movement fails to respect their beliefs and their rights to hold these beliefs. However, such arguments are altogether independent of the principle of responsibility to self.

2. I am grateful to George Sher for pointing this out to me.

3. Elsewhere Parfit denies that desires are different from wishes on the grounds that they are subjectively identical (Parfit 1984:171). However, our ability to wish extends the scope of our concern beyond the scope of our agency, while our capacity to desire is confined to the scope of our agency. Surely concern divorced from any possibility of action is subjectively distinguishable from concern coupled with the possibility of action.

# PART III. OBSTACLES TO PERSONAL AUTONOMY

## SECTION 1. THEORIES OF SOCIALIZATION

1. Nancy Chodorow's work on mothering is an important exception to this generalization (Chodorow 1978). I shall make use of her research in part 3, section 2.

SECTION 3.  AUTONOMY AND FEMININE SOCIALIZATION

1. I set aside the possibilities that no cogent plan is implicit in the set of episodically autonomous acts and that more than one cogent plan is implicit in the set of episodically autonomous acts.

2. It is worth noting in connection with these definitions that I have included the disposition to consult the self and the ability to act on the conclusions of one's autonomous reflection among the skills constitutive of autonomy competency (part 2, sec. 4). Consequently, although it is necessary to make explicit mention of these skills in the definition of minimal autonomy in order to ensure that the other skills will not languish unused, it is not necessary to include clauses exacting the exercise of self-reading skills and the implementation of integral attributes in the definition of full autonomy.

3. Since Lawrence Haworth has used a similar terminology in his analysis of autonomy, it is important to distinguish his conception from mine. For Haworth, minimal autonomy is the infant's prereflective striving for competence; normal autonomy is the average adult's modestly reflective conduct; and full autonomy is full rationality combined with full competence (Haworth 1986:17, 39, 64). In my view, though minimal, medial, and full autonomy are attained through a developmental process, all of these forms of autonomy are exhibited by normal human adults. Whereas Haworth is primarily concerned to demonstrate that virtually all mature people are autonomous, I am primarily concerned to differentiate degrees of autonomy attained by different classes of individuals.

SECTION 4.  FULL AUTONOMY—AN ATTAINABLE IDEAL

1. I am grateful to Eva Kittay for bringing Wilson's work along with several additional articles in Mike W. Martin's volume, *Self-Deception and Self-Understanding*, to my attention.

2. For a provocative view of the way in which emotions can be obscured by ideological theories, see Ronald B. De Sousa 1978.

3. For a penetrating discussion of the dangers attendant upon labeling traits or activities "natural," see J. Richards 1980:32–62.

4. Using the plight of a person whom he calls Jane, Robert Audi has shown how self-deception can help people gain control over their lives (Audi 1985:181–182). Though public speaking is unavoidable in Jane's work—let us assume that she chose her occupation autonomously and that she is generally successful in it—she is afraid of appearing before an audience. Realizing that the thought of her fear makes her lose her composure and begin to stammer, Jane deceives herself into thinking that public speaking holds no fear for her with the result that her presentations improve. From the standpoint of autonomy, it would be better if Jane could overcome her fear; that way she would not be vulnerable to the snares of over-confidence. Still, her self-deception could be an initial step in the direction of sensible self-confidence. Meanwhile, it is clear that the trick Jane plays on herself helps

her to realize her autonomous objectives. As such, it is compatible with programmatic autonomy.

## SECTION 5.  AUTONOMY-ENHANCING SOCIALIZATION

1. Against this proposal, Lawrence Haworth has maintained that, since autonomy naturally develops as children mature, autonomy skills need not be taught (Haworth 1986:54–62). While I agree with Haworth that normal socialization instills second-order desires that govern first-order desires— that is, virtually everyone has a conscience—I am not persuaded that people naturally develop the critical thinking skills Haworth considers necessary for these second-order desires to become autonomous. If people are genetically programmed to master these skills (provided only that their development was not suppressed), either there is an appalling amount of suppression going on in American families and elementary schools, or the need for critical thinking courses in American colleges has been wildly exaggerated. Since I think it doubtful that parents and educators are systematically crushing children's intellectual powers, but since I am convinced that many college students badly need instruction in critical thinking, I conclude that critical thinking skills must be taught. At the same time (and here I differ with Haworth), I would stress that critical thinking skills are not the only skills necessary for autonomy competency—introspective, communicative, imaginative, and volitional skills are also needed. Though some facility in these skills typically emerges without special education, proficiency usually requires education geared to the cultivation of these skills.

2. It is important to emphasize at this point that satisfying deviant desires is not necessarily equivalent to acting on the desires of the authentic self. In the course of deliberation, the individual may find that other desires or values militate against immediate satisfaction of the deviant desire or that other desires or values provide a basis for modifying the deviant desire. In either case, the authentic self would dictate restraint. Nevertheless, it is also possible that autonomous reflection would lead to the conclusion that the deviant desire was the desire of the authentic self. In that case, satisfying the deviant desire would be identical to satisfying the authentic self's desire.

# PART IV.  THE VALUE OF PERSONAL AUTONOMY

## SECTION 2.  SELF-RESPECT AND AUTONOMY

1. Jonathan Adler has pointed out that the homeless woman's morality is questionable. She is dishonest since selling transfers is illegal, and she is undermining social welfare since the policy of giving out free transfers would be rescinded if reselling them became widespread. I think, however, that these accusations are overblown. Her violation of the law is no more serious than most parking violations, and no one considers someone who lets the time run out on a parking meter immoral. Moreover, there is no need to

worry that transfer recycling will join other lucrative underground vocations because, as my story shows, New Yorkers are too cynical and suspicious to take advantage of such a service.

2. Stephen Darwall complicates this picture by distinguishing recognition self-respect from appraisal self-respect (1977–1978:38–39). However, in view of my present purposes, I shall ignore this distinction.

3. Eva Kittay has stressed to me the way in which societal norms can serve as criteria of self-respecting behavior.

4. At this point, it might be tempting to conclude that building effective defense mechanisms provides the prime remedy for self-contempt. However, this suggestion runs afoul of two insuperable problems. First, since defense mechanisms operate unconsciously, it is not possible to instruct self-contemptuous people in the subtleties of denying their failings. Second, even if it were possible to instill effective defense mechanisms in the self-contemptuous, they would not necessarily be better off from the standpoint of self-respect, for their respect would be misdirected and therefore compromised. Though the salubrious effects of defense mechanisms are undeniable, autonomy is the only reliable remedy for self-contempt.

5. In this connection, it is worth adding that people's economic circumstances can compromise self-respect by severely restricting their autonomy. Recalling my tale of the homeless woman and the youth in section 2A, it is evident that the homeless woman's hold on her self-respect is tenuous because her material circumstances are extremely uncertain and largely beyond her control. In telling her story, I mentioned that her self-respect would probably suffer if she were forced to turn to begging or stealing. A person's circumstances may become intractable; that is, no matter how ingenious and determined they are, severe deprivation can prevent them from pursuing life plans that are minimally acceptable to them. When this happens, self-respect is undermined, if not converted into self-contempt.

## SECTION 3. JUSTICE AND AUTONOMY

1. Some philosophers directly locate autonomy among the political values by asserting a right to autonomy, i.e., a right to make certain decisions for oneself without undue interference from others (Hill 1987:133–134). While I agree that there is a close link between rights and autonomy, I do not find the idea of a right to autonomy particularly illuminating. In many respects, it seems to duplicate the familiar Lockean right to liberty. Also, it seems to compass various Constitutional rights, such as the right to freedom of religious worship, the right to free speech, and the right to freedom of association. In view of these coincidences, I find it more perspicuous to say that our various rights support autonomy in different ways and that no one right constitutes a right to autonomy. Another approach to the issue of autonomy and justice could be made through the concept of self-respect. Since Rawls counts self-respect among the primary social goods, and since I have argued that autonomy is necessary to self-respect, it might be argued that compromising people's self-respect by depriving them of autonomy is unjust (Meyers 1986:83–93).

2. Since some may object that hardly anyone believes in gender role enforcement anymore and that no one advocates legal stipulations enforcing gender roles, it may be worth citing Phyllis Schlafly's influential views. While paying lip service to personal liberty, Schlafly endorses perpetuation of the feminine role through protective legislation in her tract, "The Right to Be a Woman." 1972. *The Phyllis Schlafly Report*, vol. 6 (no. 4).

3. The similarity between Haksar's view of autonomy and that of Bowles and Gintis (see part 3, sec. 5) is noteworthy. Both condemn education for autonomy on the grounds that it prepares people to be dissatisfied with their lot. The difference between them is that Haksar sees conditioned acquiescence to prevailing economic arrangements as the solution, whereas Bowles and Gintis defend conditioned rebellion against capitalism as the solution.

4. It should be noted that, despite their focus on aggregate social welfare, Utilitarians do not usually see people as mere social ciphers. Both the claim that every individual's happiness and suffering must count equally and the claim that the principle of utility commends respect for individual rights show that the proponents of this theory do not presume that persons are morally separable from their life plans.

5. Rawls emphasizes that the capacity for just conduct or, more broadly, the capacity for moral autonomy qualifies individuals to receive justice (Rawls 1971:505). As I have mentioned elsewhere, Rawls is too traditional a Kantian to recognize the possibility of personal autonomy (part 2, sec. 4). However, I would note that the capacity for moral autonomy and the capacity for personal autonomy are undoubtedly coextensive. Moreover, though I would not deny the appropriateness of using the capacity for moral autonomy as a criterion for identifying the rightful recipients of justice, I would add that, since justice is centrally concerned with establishing a social context in which individuals can flourish by pursuing their life plans, it is hard to believe that the capacity for personal autonomy is not equally germane.

# BIBLIOGRAPHY

Abramson, Lyn Y. and Lauren B. Alloy. 1981. "Depression, Non-Depression, and Cognitive Illusions: Reply to Schwartz." *Journal of Experimental Psychology: General* 110:436–447.
Addelson, Kathryn Pyne. 1983. "Awakening." *Women's Studies International Forum* 6:583–595.
Adler, Jonathan. 1984. "Abstraction Is Uncooperative." *Journal for the Theory of Social Behavior* 14:165–181.
Aiken, William. "On Harming Children's Futures." Unpublished essay.
Andre, Rae. 1981. *Homemakers.* Chicago: University of Chicago Press.
Aristotle. *Politics.* Ernest Barker, trans. 1946. Oxford: Oxford University Press.
Audi, Robert. 1985. "Self-deception and rationality." In Mike W. Martin, ed., *Self-Deception and Self-Understanding,* pp. 169–194. Lawrence: University of Kansas Press.
Benn, S. I. 1975–76. "Freedom, Autonomy, and the Concept of a Person." *Aristotelian Society Proceedings* 76:109–130.
Berg, Barbara J. 1978. *The Remembered Gate: Origins of American Feminism.* New York: Oxford University Press.
Bernstein, Mark. 1983. "Socialization and Autonomy." *Mind* 92:120–123.
Blasi, Augusto. "Autonomy in Obedience: The Development of Distancing in Socialized Action." Unpublished paper.
Blum, Larry et al. 1973–74. "Altruism and Women's Oppression." *The Philosophical Forum* 5:222–247.
Bonnett, Michael. 1978. "Authenticity and Education." *Journal of Philosophy of Education* 12:51–61.
Bowles, Samuel and Herbert Gintis. 1977. *Schooling in Capitalist America.* New York: Basic Books.
Boxill, Bernard. 1980. "Self-Respect and Protest." *Philosophy and Public Affairs* 6:58–69.
Bruffee, Kenneth A. 1984. "Collaborative Learning and the 'Conversation of

Mankind.'" *College English* 46:635–652.

Bunch, Charlotte. 1981. *Building Feminist Theory*. New York: Longman.

Chanowitz, Benzion and Ellen J. Langer. 1985. "Self-Protection and Self-Inception." In Mike W. Martin, ed., *Self-Deception and Self-Understanding*, pp. 117–135. Lawrence: University of Kansas Press.

Cherniak, Christopher. 1981. "Minimal Rationality." *Mind* 90:161–183.

Chodorow, Nancy. 1978. *The Reproduction of Mothering*. Berkeley: University of California Press, 1978.

Coopersmith, Stanley, 1981. *Antecedents of Self-Esteem*. New York: Consulting Psychologists Press.

de Beauvoir, Simone. *The Second Sex*. H. M. Parshley, trans. 1968. New York: Bantam Books.

De Sousa, Ronald B. 1978. "Self-Deceptive Emotions." *The Journal of Philosophy* 75:684–697.

Darwall, Stephen L. 1983. *Impartial Reason*. Ithaca, N.Y.: Cornell University Press.

—— 1977–78. "Two Kinds of Respect." *Ethics* 88:36–39.

Dennett, Daniel. 1984. *Elbow Room*. Cambridge: MIT Press.

Dworkin, Gerald. 1970. "Acting Freely." *Nous* 4:367–383.

—— 1976. "Autonomy and Behavior Control." *Hastings Center Reports* 6:23–28.

—— 1982. "Is More Choice Better Than Less?" *Midwest Studies in Philosophy* 7:47–61.

Dworkin, Ronald. 1977. *Taking Rights Seriously*. Cambridge: Harvard University Press.

Elkin, Frederick and Gerald Handel. 1978. *The Child and Society*. New York: Random House.

Elshtain, Jean Bethke. 1981. *Public Man, Private Woman*. Princeton: Princeton University Press.

Elster, Jon. 1983. *Sour Grapes: Studies in the Subversion of Rationality*. Cambridge: Cambridge University Press.

Emmet, Dorothy. 1966. *Rules, Roles, and Relations*. New York: St. Martin's Press.

Feather, N. T. 1985. "Masculinity, Feminity, Self-Esteem, and Subclinical Depression." *Sex Roles* 12:491–500.

Feinberg, Joel. 1970. "The Nature and Value of Rights." *The Journal of Value Inquiry* 4:243–257.

—— 1980a. "The Child's Right to an Open Future." In William Aiken and Hugh La Follette, eds., *Whose Child?* Totowa, N.J.: Littlefield Adams.

—— 1980b. "The Idea of a Free Man." In Joel Feinberg, *Rights, Justice, and the Bounds of Liberty*. Princeton: Princeton University Press.

Frankfurt, Harry G. 1971. "Freedom of the Will and the Concept of a Person." *The Journal of Philosophy* 68:5–20.

—— 1976. "Identification and Externality." In Amelie Oksenberg Rorty, ed., *The Identities of Persons*, pp. 239–251. Berkeley: University of California Press.

Fried, Charles. 1970. *An Anatomy of Values*. Cambridge: Harvard University Press.

Friedan, Betty. 1963. *The Feminine Mystique.* New York: Norton.
Friedman, Marilyn. 1986. "Autonomy, Critical Reflection, and Principles of One's 'Own.'" *Southern Journal of Philosophy* 24:19–35.
—— 1985. "Moral Integrity and the Deferential Wife." *Philosophical Studies* 47:141–150.
—— "Self-Rule in Social Context: Autonomy from a Feminist Perspective." Unpublished essay.
Frieze, Irene H. et al. 1978. *Women and Sex Roles.* New York: W. W. Norton.
Gauthier, David. 1963. *Practical Reasoning.* London: Oxford University Press.
Gerson, Kathleen. 1985. *Hard Choices.* Berkeley: University of California Press.
Gibbs, Benjamin. 1979. "Autonomy and Authority in Education." *Journal of Philosophy of Education* 13:119–132.
Gibson, Mary. 1985. "Consent and Autonomy." In Mary Gibson, ed., *To Breathe Freely: Risk, Consent, and Air,* pp. 141–168. Totowa, N.J.: Rowman and Allanheld.
Gilbert, Daniel T. and Joel Cooper. 1985. "Social Psychological Strategies of Self-Deception." In Mike W. Martin, ed., *Self-Deception and Self-Understanding,* pp. 75–94. Lawrence: University of Kansas Press.
Gilligan, Carol. 1982. *In a Different Voice.* Cambridge: Harvard University Press.
—— March 22, 1985. Keynote address. The conference on Women and Moral Theory, SUNY at Stony Brook.
—— 1987. "Moral Orientation and Moral Development." In Eva Feder Kittay and Diana T. Meyers, eds., *Women and Moral Theory,* pp. 19–33. Totowa, N.J.: Rowman and Littlefield.
Grimshaw, Jean. 1986. *Philosophy and Feminist Thinking.* Minneapolis: University of Minnesota Press.
Haksar, Vinit. 1979. *Equality, Liberty, and Perfectionism.* Oxford: Oxford University Press.
Hall, Douglas T. and Francine E. Gordon. 1973. "Career Choices of Married Women: Effects on Conflict, Role Behavior, and Satisfaction." *Journal of Applied Psychology* 58:42–48.
Harman, Gilbert. 1983. *Change in View.* Cambridge: MIT Press.
Harrison, Betty G., Rebecca F. Guy, and Shirley Lupfer. 1981. "Locus of Control and Self-Esteem as Correlates of Role Orientation in Traditional and Nontraditional Women." *Sex Roles* 7:1175–1187.
Haworth, Lawrence. 1986. *Autonomy.* New Haven: Yale University Press.
—— 1984. "Autonomy and Utility." *Ethics* 95:5–19.
Held, Virginia. 1972. "Coercion and Coercive Offers." *NOMOS* 14:49–62.
—— 1973. "Reasonable Progress and Self-respect." *Monist* 57:12–27.
Hill, Sharon Bishop. "Self-Determination and Autonomy." In Richard Wasserstrom, ed., *Today's Moral Problems,* pp. 118–133. New York: Macmillan.
Hill, Thomas E., Jr. 1987. "The Importance of Autonomy." In Eva Feder Kittay and Diana T. Meyers, eds., *Women and Moral Theory,* pp. 124–138. Totowa, N.J.: Rowman and Littlefield.

—— 1983. "Self-Respect Reconsidered." *Tulane Studies in Philosophy* 31:129–137.

—— 1973. "Servility and Self-Respect." *The Monist* 57:87–104.

Hunter College Women's Studies Collective. 1983. *Women's Realities, Women's Choices.* New York: Oxford University Press.

Hyde, Janet Shibley. 1985. *Half the Human Experience: The Psychology of Women.* Lexington, Mass.: D.C. Heath.

Jaggar, Alison M. 1983. *Feminist Politics and Human Nature.* Totowa, N.J.: Rowman and Allanheld.

—— 1974. "On Sexual Equality." *Ethics* 84:275–291.

Janis, Irving L. 1983. *Groupthink.* Boston: Houghton Mifflin.

Kant, Immanuel. *Foundations of the Metaphysics of Morals.* Lewis White Beck, trans. 1959. Indianapolis: Bobbs-Merrill.

Kohlberg, Lawrence. 1966. "A Cognitive Development Analysis of Sex-Role Concepts and Attitudes." In E. Maccoby, ed., *The Development of Sex Differences,* pp. 82–173. Stanford: Stanford University Press.

—— 1982. "A Reply to Owen Flanagan and Some Comments on the Puka-Goodpaster Exchange." *Ethics* 92:513–528.

—— 1981. *The Philosophy of Moral Development.* San Francisco: Harper and Row.

Kraut, Richard. 1979. "Two Conceptions of Happiness." *The Philosophical Review* 88:167–197.

Kuflick, Arthur. 1984. "The Inalienability of Autonomy." *Philosophy and Public Affairs* 13:271–298.

Kupperman, Joel. 1984–85. "Character and Self-Knowledge." *Proceedings of the Aristotelian Society* 85: 219–238.

Lerner, Gerda. 1979. *The Majority Finds its Past.* New York: Oxford University Press.

Lewinsohn, Peter M. et al. 1980. "Social Competence and Depression: The Role of Illusory Self-perceptions." *Journal of Abnormal Psychology* 89:203–212.

Lipman, Blumen Jean. 1984. *Gender Roles and Power.* Englewood Cliffs, N.J.: Prentice Hall.

MacIntosh, Jack. 1972. "Roles and Role Playing." *Second Order* 1:53–73.

MacIntyre, Alasdair. 1984. *After Virtue,* 2nd ed. Notre Dame: University of Notre Dame Press.

Mansbridge, Jane. 1980. *Beyond Adversary Democracy.* New York: Basic Books.

—— 1986. *Why We Lost the ERA.* Chicago: University of Chicago Press.

Markus, Hazel. 1977. "Self-Schemata and Processing Information about the Self." *Journal of Personality and Social Psychology* 35:63–78.

Martin, Jane Roland. 1985. *Reclaiming a Conversation: The Ideal of the Educated Woman.* New Haven: Yale University Press.

Massey, Stephen J. 1983. "Is Self-Respect a Moral or a Psychological Concept?" *Ethics* 93:246–261.

Meyers, Diana T. 1985. *Inalienable Rights: A Defense.* New York: Columbia University Press.

—— 1987a. "Personal Autonomy and the Paradox of Feminine Socialization." *Journal of Philosophy* 84:619–628.

—— 1986. "The Politics of Self-Respect: A Feminist Perspective." *Hypatia* 1:83–100.

—— 1987b. "The Socialized Individual and Individual Autonomy: An Intersection between Philosophy and Psychology." In Eva Feder Kittay and Diana T. Meyers, eds., *Women and Moral Theory*, pp. 139–153. Totowa, N.J.: Rowman and Littlefield.

—— 1987c. "Work and Self-Respect." In Gertrude Ezorsky, ed., *Moral Rights in the Workplace*, pp. 18–27. Albany: SUNY Press.

Mill, John Stuart. 1971. *On the Subjection of Women*. Greenwich Conn.: Fawcett.

Millham, Jill and Richard W. Kellogg. 1980. "Need for Social Approval: Impression Management or Self-Deception?" *Journal of Research in Personality* 14:445–457.

Mischel, Walter. 1973. "Toward a Cognitive Social Learning Reconceptualization of Personality." *Psychological Review* 80:252–283.

Mitchell, Juliet. 1974. *Psychoanalysis and Feminism*. New York: Pantheon Books.

Myron, Nancy. 1974. "Class Beginnings." In Charlotte Bunch and Nancy Myron, eds., *Class and Feminism*. Baltimore: Diana Press.

Nisbett, Richard and Lee Ross. 1980. *Human Inference: Strategies and Shortcomings of Social Judgment*. Englewood Cliffs, N.J.: Prentice-Hall.

Norton, David. 1976. *Personal Destinies*. Princeton: Princeton University Press.

Nozick, Robert. 1974. *Anarchy, State and Utopia*. New York: Basic Books.

Oakley, Ann. 1981. *Subject Women*. New York: Pantheon Books.

—— 1974. *Women's Work*. New York: Pantheon Books.

O'Neill, Onora. 1981. "How Do We Know When Opportunities Are Equal?" In Mary Vetterling-Braggin et al., eds., *Feminism and Philosophy*, pp. 177–189. Totowa, N.J.: Littlefield, Adams.

Parfit, Derek. 1984. *Reasons and Persons*. Oxford: Oxford University Press.

Piaget, Jean. *The Moral Judgment of the Child*. Marjorie Gabain, trans. 1960. Glencoe, Il.: The Free Press.

Postow, B. C. 1978–79. "Economic Dependence and Self-Respect." *The Philosophical Forum* 10:181–205.

Puglisi, J. Thomas and Dorothy W. Jackson. 1980–81. "Sex-Role Identity and Self-Esteem in Adulthood." *International Journal of Aging and Human Development* 12:129–138.

Rawls, John. 1971. *A Theory and Justice*. Cambridge: Harvard University Press.

—— 1980. "Kantian Constructivism in Moral Theory." *The Journal of Philosophy* 77:515–572.

Richards, David A. J. 1971. *A Theory of Reasons for Action*. Oxford: Oxford University Press.

Richards, Janet Radcliffe. 1980. *The Skeptical Feminist*. Boston: Routledge and Kegan Paul.

Rosenberg, Morris. 1979. *Conceiving the Self*. New York: Basic Books.

Rousseau, Jean-Jacques. *Emile*. Allan Bloom, trans. 1979. New York: Basic Books.

Rubin, Lillian Breslow. 1976. *Worlds of Pain: Life in the Working Class Family*. New York: Basic Books.

Sachs, David. 1981. "How to Distinguish Self-Respect from Self-Esteem." *Philosophy and Public Affairs* 10:346–360.

—— 1983. "Self-Respect and Respect for Others." *Tulane Studies in Philosophy* 31:109–128.

Sandel, Michael J. 1982. *Liberalism and the Limits of Justice*. Cambridge: Cambridge University Press.

Scheffler, Israel. 1985. *Of Human Potential: An Essay in the Philosophy of Education*. Boston: Routledge and Kegan Paul.

Shatz, David. 1986. "Free Will and the Structure of Motivation." In Peter French et al., eds., *Midwest Studies in Philosophy*. Minneapolis: University of Minnesota Press.

Sher, George. 1987. "Other Voices; Other Rooms?" In Eva Feder Kittay and Diana T. Meyers, eds., *Women and Moral Theory*, pp. 178–189. Totowa, N.J.: Rowman and Littlefield.

—— 1983. "Our Preferences, Ourselves." *Philosophy and Public Affairs* 12:34–50.

Sher, George and William J. Bennett. 1982. "Moral Education and Moral Indoctrination." *The Journal of Philosophy* 79:665–677.

Schwartz, Adina. 1981. "Against Universality." *The Journal of Philosophy* 78:127–143.

Shrauger, J. Sidney and Thomas J. Schoenman. 1979. "Symbolic Interactionist View of Self-Concept: Through the Looking Glass Darkly." *Psychological Bulletin* 86:549–565.

Stericker, Anne B. and James E. Johnson. 1977. "Sex-Role Identification and Self-Esteem in College Students: Do Men and Women Differ?" *Sex Roles* 3:19–26.

Strube, Michael J. and Laurie A. Roemmele. 1985. "Self-Enhancement, Self-Assessment, and Self-Evaluative Task Choice." *Journal of Personality and Social Psychology* 49:981–993.

Tangri, Sandra Schwartz. 1972. "Determinants of Occupational Role Innovation among College Women." *Journal of Social Issues* 28:177–199.

Taylor, Charles. 1976. "Responsibility for Self." In Amelie Oksenberg Rorty, ed., *The Identities of Persons*, pp. 281–299. Berkeley: University of California Press.

Taylor, Shelley E. and Jonathan D. Brown. 1988. "Illusion and Well-Being: A Social Psychological Perspective on Mental Health." *Psychological Bulletin* 103:193–210.

Thalberg, Irving. 1978. "Socialization and Autonomous Behavior." *Tulane Studies in Philosophy* 28:21–37.

Thomas, Larry. 1978. "Morality and Our Self-Concept." *Journal of Value Inquiry* 12:258–268.

Tormey, Judith Farr. 1973–74. "Exploitation, Oppression, and Self-Sacrifice." *The Philosophical Forum* 5:206–221.

Trebilcot, Joyce. 1982. "Two Forms of Androgynism." In Mary Vetterling-Braggin, ed., *"Femininity," "Masculinity,"* and *"Androgyny,"* pp. 161–169. Totowa, N.J.: Littlefield, Adams.

Tversky, Amos and Daniel Kahneman. 1982. "Judgment Under Uncertainty: Heuristics and Biases." In Daniel Kahneman et al., eds., *Judgement Under Uncertainty*, pp. 3–20. Cambridge: Cambridge University Press.

Usher, Sarah and Mort Fels. 1985. "The Challenge of Feminism and Career for the Middle-Aged Woman." *International Journal of Women's Studies* 8:47–57.

Wasserstrom, Richard. 1979. "On Racism and Sexism." In Richard Wasserstrom, ed., *Today's Moral Problems*, pp. 75–105. New York: Macmillan.

Watson, Gary. 1982. *Free Will*. London: Oxford University Press.

Weinstein, Michael A. 1972. "Coercion, Space, and the Modes of Human Domination." *NOMOS* 14:63–80.

Weitzman, Lenore J. 1975. "Sex-Role Socialization." In Jo Freeman, ed., *Women: A Feminist Perspective*. Palo Alto: Mayfield Publishing.

Williams, Bernard. 1971. "The Idea of Equality." In Hugo A. Bedau, ed., *Justice and Equality*, pp. 116–137. Englewood Cliffs, N.J.: Prentice-Hall.

—— 1981. *Moral Luck*. Cambridge: Cambridge University Press.

—— 1976. "Persons, Character, and Morality." In Amelie Oksenberg Rorty, ed., *The Identities of Persons*, pp. 197–216. Berkeley: University of California Press.

Wilson, Timothy D. "Self-Deception Without Repression." In Mike W. Martin, ed., *Self-Deception and Self-Understanding*, pp. 75–94. Lawrence: University of Kansas Press.

Wolf, Susan. 1982. "Moral Saints." *The Journal of Philosophy* 79:419–439.

Wollheim, Richard. 1984. *The Thread of Life*. Cambridge: Harvard University Press.

Young, Robert. 1980. "Autonomy and Socialization." *Mind* 89:565–576.

—— 1979. "Compatibilism and Conditioning." *Nous* 13:361–378.

Zimbardo, Philip G. 1973. "On the Ethics of Intervention in Human Psychological Research: With Special Reference to the Stanford Prison Experiment." *Cognition* 2:243–256.

# Index